Praise from Job Seekers for the
Knock 'em Dead Books

"I got the position! I was interviewed by three people and the third person asked me all the questions in *Knock 'em Dead*. I had all the right answers!"
— **D.J., Scottsdale, Arizona**

"I just finished writing the letter I have dreamed of writing for three years: my letter of resignation from the Company from Hell. Thanks to you and the book, *Knock 'em Dead*, I have been offered and have accepted an excellent position with a major international service corporation."
— **C.C., Atlanta, Georgia**

"My previous employer asked me to resign. Your book got me through my depression, and in only four weeks, got me four job offers. This is the first time in my career I have this many options to choose from."
— **D.H., North Canton, Ohio**

"After college graduation, I searched and searched for a job, and ended up taking a few low-paying ones I was overqualified for. Finally, I read your book and have been offered *every* job I have applied for since."
— **L.E. (no address given)**

"I followed the advice in *Knock 'em Dead* religiously and got more money, less hours, a better hospital plan, and negotiated to keep my three weeks vacation. I start my new job immediately!"
— **A.B., St. Louis, Missouri**

"I found your book to be absolutely invaluable during my recent job search. Since then I have had a chance to speak with my interviewer, who informed me that it was my strong interview that landed me my job offer. He went on to outline what had turned him off about other candidates, and it was some of the very same mistakes I used to make before reading your book!"
— **D.D., Houlton, Maine**

"Every time I've used your book, I've gotten an offer! This book is incredible. Thanks for publishing such a great tool."
— **W.Z., Columbia, Maryland**

"Just a quick note to let you know how much your book has helped me. I was chosen for my job out of over one hundred applicants! I later loaned the book to a friend and circled the things that had helped me. She interviewed on a Thursday, and she was offered the position that Thursday night! Thanks for writing such a helpful book."
— **S.G., Sacramento, California**

"Your book is simply fantastic. This one book improved my yearly income by several thousand dollars, and my future income by untold amounts. Your work has made my family and myself very happy."
— **M.Z., St. Clair Shores, Michigan**

"Thank you for all the wonderfully helpful information you provided in your book. I lost my job almost one year ago. I spent almost eight months looking for a comparable position. Then I had the good sense to buy your book. Two months later, I accepted a new position. You helped me turn one of the worst experiences of my life into a blessing in disguise."
— **L.G., Watervliet, New York**

"I was out of work for four months—within five weeks of reading your book, I had four job offers."
— **S.K., Dallas, Texas**

"Yesterday I received two job offers in the space of fifteen minutes. I am now using the 'Negotiating the Offer' chapter to evaluate these positions."
— **W.B., Thornhill, Ontario**

"I read every page in the book and, after a two-month search, got ten interviews with top-performing companies and six offers (five of which I declined)."
— **M.V., Millington, Tennessee**

"I was sending out hordes of resumes and hardly getting a nibble—and I have top-notch skills and experience in my field. I wasn't prepared for this tough job market. When I read your book, however, I immediately began applying some of your techniques. My few nibbles increased to so many job interviews I could hardly keep up with them!"
— **C.S., Chicago, Illinois**

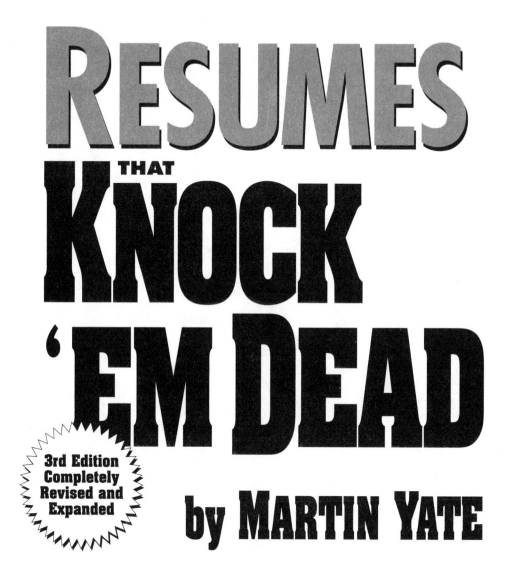

RESUMES
THAT
KNOCK
'EM DEAD

3rd Edition Completely Revised and Expanded

by MARTIN YATE

Adams Media Corporation
Holbrook, Massachusetts

Visit our Web Site: www.careercity.com

A leading job and career hub on the world wide web, CareerCity offers: free resume posting, tens of thousands of current job openings, links to 27,000 major US employers, and a comprehensive career center.

Acknowledgments

It is only fair to say that any book is teamwork, and this is one more than most.
I would like to thank five people especially: Donna Carnavale; my editors over the years, Eric Blume, Brandon Toropov, and Ed Walters; and Jeff Hunter, a man with a superior talent, and the president of First Impressions, a truly top-notch resume-writing firm.

Published by Adams Media Corporation
260 Center Street, Holbrook, MA 02343

ISBN: 1-55850-817-1

Printed in the United States of America

C   D   E   F   G   H   I   J

Library of Congress Cataloging-in-Publication Data
Yate, Martin John.
Resumes that knock 'em dead / Martin Yate. — Rev. and expanded ed.
     p.   cm.
ISBN 1-55850-817-1
1. Resumes (Employment) I. Title.
HF5383.Y38   1997
808'.06665—dc21   97-41514
                                               CIP

This publication is designed to provide accurate and authoritative information with regard to the subject matter covered. It is sold with the understanding that the publisher is not engaged in rendering legal, accounting, or other professional advice. If legal advice or other expert assistance is required, the services of a qualified professional person should be sought.
—From a *Declaration of Principles* jointly adopted by a Committee of the American Bar Association and a Committee of Publishers and Associations.

Rear Cover Photo: NICK BASILLION

This book is available at quantity discounts for bulk purchases.
For information, call 1-800-872-5627 (in Massachusetts 781-767-8100).

Visit our home page at http://www.careercity.com
Resumes may be posted for free at CareerCity and will be seen by hundreds of leading employers in all fields.

Table of Contents

Chapter 10: The Resumes **101**

Based on real resumes that got real jobs for real people. Which jobs? In alphabetical order:

Appendix **235**

Resumes for Special Situations; Off The Beaten Track; Resources; Sample Questionnaire

Introduction

Most of the books on writing resumes haven't changed to accommodate today's dynamic work environment. That is the reason for this book: To help "now" people get the very best jobs!

Look at the other resume books on the market; they are full of resume examples with dates going back to what seems, to most job seekers, like the Bronze Age. They use job titles that no longer exist and techniques that no longer work—techniques that in many instances can be downright damaging to your job hunt.

This book is unique in two very important ways.

First, you'll get to read real resumes from real people. Each of the resumes in this book is based on a "genuine article" that worked wonders for its writer. Included are resumes for today's and tomorrow's in-demand jobs, as defined by the Bureau of Labor Statistics and confirmed by the professionals on the front lines: Corporate recruiters and other employment industry professionals across the country. The odds are that you are already working in one of these jobs, or wishing you were.

Also included in the "real-life" section of this book is a selection of resumes from people with special challenges. These reflect the pressures and needs of a modern, profession-oriented society struggling into the information age. Like the resume that got a six-dollar-an-hour factory worker a $70,000-a-year job; or the one that helped a recovering alcoholic and drug-abuser get back on her feet again. There are winning resumes of people recovering from serious emotional challenges and mental problems, of people reentering society after jail, starting over after the divorce, and changing careers. There is even one for a teenage trick cyclist looking for advertising, film, and endorsement work. And what's more, these examples have proved themselves effective in every corner of the nation; their writers landed both interviews and jobs.

Second, I explain the ins and outs of putting a resume together as painlessly as possible. I'll show you the three best ways to look at your background and present your resume. Then I'll show you all the available options for inclusion. Why certain things should be in your resume and how they should look, and why other things should never appear. Wherever industry experts disagree, I'll give you both sides of the argument, and my reasoned solution to the dispute. That way you can make a prudent decision about your unique background, based on possession of all the facts and the best advice going. In addition, you will see the infinite variety of styles and approaches that can be used within my guidelines to help you create a truly individual resume.

These two unique concepts, the numerous resume examples, and the nuts-and-bolts sections about resume production and distribution give you everything needed to create a distinctive, professional resume: one that will Knock 'em Dead!

1 | The Marks of a Great Resume

Who needs a resume? Everyone. Certainly you do, unless you are so well known that your reputation is already common knowledge to all potential employers. If that were the case you probably wouldn't be reading this book in the first place.

Anyone, in any job, can be viewed more favorably than his or her competition—if he or she is better organized and prepared, which is what a good resume demonstrates. It's a staunch friend who only speaks well of you and can gain you entrance into undreamed-of opportunities.

Now, no resume ever gets carefully read unless a manager is trying to solve a problem. That problem may be finding a quicker way to manufacture silicon chips. It may be getting the telephone calls answered, now that the receptionist has left. As disparate as these examples might seem, both are still concerned with problem solving. And invariably, the problem that needs a solution is the same: Productivity. The simple question is, "How on earth are we going to get things done quicker/cheaper/more efficiently without a _____?"

Resumes that get acted upon are those that demonstrate the writer's potential as a problem solver.

Your resume must speak loudly and clearly of your value as a potential employee. And the value must be spoken in a few brief seconds, because, in the business world, that's all the attention a resume will get. The resume takes you only the first few paces toward that new job. It gets your foot in the door, and because you can't be there to answer questions, it has to stand on its own.

A resume's emphasis is on what has happened in your business life, what actions you took to make those things happen, and what supportive personal characteristics you brought to the job. It is about how you contributed to solving a business' problems. It has nothing to do with generalizations or personal opinions.

The resume itself came about as a solution to a problem: How does a manager avoid interviewing every applicant who applies for a job? Can you imagine what would happen to a business if everyone who applied for a job was given even a cursory ten-minute interview? The company would simply grind to a halt, then topple into bankruptcy. The solution: Come up with a way to get a glimpse of applicants' potentials before having to meet them face-to-face. The resume appeared and evolved into an important screening and time-saving tool.

While that solved one problem for the employer, it created another for the job applicant: "Considering that my background isn't perfect, how do I write a resume that shows off my best potential?" The first attempt to answer that question is how the gentle art of resume writing came into being.

In the world of recreational reading, resumes are pretty far down on the list. They are usually deadly dull and offer little competition to murder mysteries, tales of international intrigue, and love stories.

Nevertheless, resumes are a required part of every manager's daily reading, and, exactly because they are usually deadly dull, are generally avoided. To combat this deep-seated avoidance, there is a general rule that will help your resume get read and acted upon in the quickest possible time: It needs to be short and long. Short on words, but long on facts and an energy that reflects the real you.

Good resume writing focuses attention on your strengths and shows you as a potential powerhouse of an employee. At the same time, it draws attention away from those areas that lack definition or vigor. You can do this even if you are changing your entire career direction, or starting your life over for other reasons, and I'll show you how.

There is a hidden benefit, too, in the resume-writing process: It focuses your attention and helps you prepare for job interviews. In a very real sense, putting a resume together is the foundation for succeeding at the job interview. Preparation for one is preparation for the other.

For example, the interviewer's command to "tell me about yourself" is one of those tough interview demands that almost all of us have difficulty answering satisfactorily. Were you totally satisfied with your response the last time it came up? I doubt it. You can only answer it well if you have taken the time to analyze and package all your strengths and weaknesses in an organized fashion. It is the only way you will ever learn to speak fluidly about your background and skills in a fashion guaranteed to impress the interviewer. So, why not kill two birds with one stone—prepare for the interview by preparing a resume that will open all the right doors for you.

Interestingly enough, the majority of interviewers accept the contents of a resume as fact. Additionally, a good number of interviewers base all their questions on the resume content: This means that in a very real way you can plan and guide the course of the majority of your interviews by preparing an effective resume.

Those without resumes are forced to reveal their history on a job application form, which does not always allow the perfect representation of skills, and which gives the interviewer no flattering starting point from which to base the interview questions.

In addition to helping you get your foot in the door and easing the course of the interview, your resume will be your last and most powerful advocate. After all the interviewing of all the candidates is done, how do you think the interviewers review and evaluate all the contenders? They go over their notes, application forms, and the resumes supplied by the job candidates. You will want to make yours something powerful and positive.

Finally, the preparation of a good resume has the broad, intangible benefit of personal discovery. You may find, as you answer some of the questions in chapter 4, that your experience is deeper than you imagined, that your contributions to previous employers were more important than you thought. You may look on your career direction in a new light. And you may see your value as a solid employee increase. You will gain confidence that will be important not only for a good performance at the interview; but for your attitude toward the rest of your career.

No sane person will tell you that resume writing is fun, but I will show you the tricks of the trade, developed over the years by executive recruiters and professional resume writers, that make the process easier.

What makes this book truly different is that the resume examples in it are all real resumes from real people, resumes that recently landed them real jobs in "in-demand" professions. They were all sent to me by employment specialists from around the nation. For example, the health care examples were screened initially by professional health care recruiters, and those in the data processing by computer recruiters. These are the pros on the firing line, who know what works and what doesn't in today's business marketplace.

You will find everything you need to make resume writing fast, effective, and painless. Just follow my instructions, and in a few hours you'll have a knock-out resume and never have to read another word about the damn things as long as you live. With that in mind, do it once and do it right—you'll generate a top-flight resume without knocking yourself out!

So now, for your delight and edification, we'll review the marks of a great resume: What type of resume is right for you, what goes in (and why), and what always stays out (and why), and what might go in depending on your special circumstances. This is followed by countless resume examples and a "painting-by-numbers" guide that makes resume writing easy for anyone!

With the changing times and circumstances, there are few rigid rules for every situation. So in those instances where there are exceptions, I'll explain them and your choices. The judgment call will be yours. And when you are finished, you will have one of the very best resumes, one that will be sure to knock 'em dead.

2 | Three Ways to Sum Yourself Up

"Give me a moment of your busy day! Listen to me, I've got something to say!"

That's what your resume must scream—in a suitably professional manner, of course. Not in the manner of the would-be retail clothing executive who had his resume "hand-delivered"…attached to the hand and arm of a store window mannequin.

As it happened, that was only the first surprise in store for the personnel director who received the delivery: The envelope was hand-decorated in gothic script; the cover letter inside was equally decorative (and illegible); the resume writer had glued the four-page resume to fabric, and stitched the whole mess together like a child's book. The crowning glory, however, was yet to come: All the punctuation marks—commas, colons, periods, and the like—were small rhinestone settings. Yes, it got noticed, but its success had to depend entirely on the recipient's sense of humor—which in this case was most noticeable for its absence.

Here's the point: trying to do something out of the ordinary with any aspect of your resume is risky business indeed. For every interview door it opens, at least two more may be slammed shut.

The best (and most businesslike) bet is to present a logically displayed, eye-appealing resume that will get *read*. That means grabbing the reader right away—on that first page. And that's one big reason for short, power-packed resumes.

We all have different backgrounds. Some of us have worked for one company only, some of us have worked for eleven companies in as many years. Some of us have changed careers once or twice, some of us have maintained a predictable career path. For some, diversity broadens our potential, and for some concentration deepens it. We each require different vehicles to put our work history in the most exciting light. The goals, though, are constant:

- To show off achievements, attributes, and cumulation of expertise to the best advantage;
- to minimize any possible weaknesses.

Resume experts acknowledge just three essential styles for presenting your credentials to a potential employer: Chronological, Functional, and Combination (Chrono-Functional). Your particular circumstances will determine the right format for you. Just three styles, you say? You will see resume books with up to fifteen varieties of resume style. Such volumes are, alas, merely filling up space; in the final analysis, each additional style such books mention is a tiny variation on the above three.

The Chronological Resume

This is the most common and readily accepted form of presentation. It's what most of us think of when we think of resumes—a chronological listing of job titles and responsibilities. It starts with the current or most recent employment, then works backward to your first job (or ten years into the past—whichever comes first).

This format is good for demonstrating your growth in a single profession. It is suitable for anyone with practical work experience who hasn't suffered too many job changes or prolonged periods of unemployment. It is not suitable if you are just out of school or if you are changing careers. The format would then draw attention to your weaknesses (i.e., your lack of specific experience in a field) rather than your strengths.

The exact content of every resume naturally varies depending on individual circumstances. A chronological resume usually incorporates six basic components.

- *Contact Information*
- *A Job Objective*
- *A Career Objective*
- *A Career Summary*
- *Education*
- *A Description of Work History*

This last item is the distinguishing characteristic of the chronological resume, because it ties your job responsibilities and achievements to specific employers, job titles, and dates.

There are also some optional categories determined by the space available to you and the unique aspect of your background. These will be discussed in chapter 3.

The Functional Resume

This format focuses on the professional skills you have developed over the years, rather than on when, where, or how you acquired them. It de-emphasizes dates, sometimes to the point of exclusion. By the same token, job titles and employers play a minor part with this type of resume. The attention is always focused on the skill rather than the context or time of its acquisition.

In many ways, the content of the functional resume is similar to the chronological type. Only the approach is different. It is a case not so much of what you say, but of how you say it.

This functional format is suited to a number of different personal circumstances, specifically those of:

- Mature professionals with a storehouse of expertise and jobs
- Entry-level types whose track records do not justify a chronological resume
- Career changers who want to focus on skills rather than credentials
- People whose careers have been stagnant or in ebb, who want to give focus to the skills that can get a career under way again, rather than on the history in which it was becalmed in the first place
- Military personnel embarking on a civilian career
- Those returning to the workplace after a long absence
- People closer to retirement than to the onset of their careers

The functional resume does present a major challenge for the writer. Because it focuses so strongly on skills and ability to contribute in a particular direction, you must have an employment objective clearly in mind. When this is achieved, such a resume can be very effective. Without this focus, however, or if you are looking for "a job, any job," this format loses its direction and tends to drift without purpose.

Though a functional resume is a bit more free-form than a chronological one, there are certain essentials that make it work. In addition to contact information and a job and/or career objective, these include the elements that follow.

- *A Functional Summary.* Different skills are needed for different jobs, so the functional summary is where you make the tough decisions to determine what goes in and what stays out. Consider the case of an executive sales secretary bored with her job but challenged by the excitement and money the sales force is enjoying. She will want to emphasize those abilities that lead to success in sales, such as written and verbal communication skills, and time management. On the other hand, she will almost certainly leave out references to her typing and short-hand abilities, because these skills don't contribute to her new goals.

- *Dates.* Strictly speaking, a functional resume needn't give dates. Up until a couple of years ago, you could still sometimes get away with omitting them. That is no longer the case. Today, a resume without dates waves a big red flag at every employer in the land. So, what if your employment history doesn't have all the stability it might? The functional resume is perfect for you, because dates can be deemphasized by their placement. You put them at the end of the resume, or perhaps on a second page, for example, in a small block type; and you use year dates omitting the details of day, week, and month. The idea is to force the reader's attention to your skills, not your history.

- *Education.* The inclusion of education and other optional categories is determined by the space available to you and the unique aspects of your background (see chapter 3).

The Combination Chrono-Functional Resume

For the upwardly mobile professional with a track record, this is becoming the resume of choice. It has all the flexibility and strength that come from combining both the chronological and functional formats. If you have a performance record, and are on a career track and want to pursue it, then this is the strongest resume tool available. This format, in addition to contact information and a job objective, incorporates a number of identifying factors, outlined below.

- *A Career Summary.* The combination resume, more often than not, has some kind of career summary. Here you spotlight a professional with a clear sense of self, a past of solid contributions, and a clear focus on future career growth. The career summary, as you might expect, will include a power-packed description of skills, achievements, and personal traits that fairly scream "Success!"
- *A Description of Functional Skills.* This is where the combination of styles comes into play. Following the summary, the combination resume starts out like a functional resume and highlights achievements in different categories relevant to the job/career goals, without any reference to employers.
- *A Chronological History.* Then it switches to the chronological approach and names companies, dates, titles, duties, and responsibilities. This section can also include further evidence of achievements or special contributions.
- *Education.* Then come the optional categories determined by the space available to you and *the* unique aspects of your background.

One of these styles is perfect for you. Pick one, and in the next chapter we'll begin to fill it in with the resume basics.

3 | The Basic Ingredients

It used to be that there were just a few set rules for writing a great resume. Everything was simple—you did this, you didn't do that. Now, however, many of the jobs for which those rules were made no longer exist—so many of the traditional hard and fast rules no longer apply.

New technologies are creating new professions overnight, and, with them, new career opportunities. The content of these new professions and careers is dramatically different from the employment world of a few short years ago. Times and the rules of the game have changed, and these changes require that we adopt a modern and flexible approach to resume writing.

What used to be strictly off-limits in all resumes is now acceptable in many and required in some. (The need for technical jargon to explain skills, for example, comes to mind.) Elements that were once always included, such as the mug shot, are now frowned upon in almost every instance. And so it goes on, creating a fog of confusion for everyone. What are the rules?

Today, writing a resume can be likened to baking a cake. In most instances, the ingredients are essentially the same. What determines the flavor is the order and quantity in which those ingredients are blended. There are certain ingredients that go into almost every resume. There are others that rarely or never go in, and there are those special touches that are added (a pinch of this, a dash of that), depending on your personal tastes and requirements.

Sound complicated? It really isn't. This chapter will explain it all. If a certain ingredient must always go in, you will understand why; the same goes for something that should never appear in your resume. In circumstances where the business world holds conflicting views, these views will be explained so that a reasoned judgment can be made. In these instances you will always get my reasoned opinion, based on my extensive experience and contact in the human resources field.

First, let's look at the ingredients that are part of the mix of every successful resume.

What Must Always Go In

Name

We start with the obvious, but there are other considerations about your name besides remembering to put it on your resume. Give your first and last name only. It isn't necessary to include your middle name(s). My name is Martin John Yate—but my resume says simply Martin Yate, because that is the way I would introduce myself in person. Notice also that it isn't M. J. Yate, because that would force the reader to play Twenty Questions about the meaning of my initials, and the average resume reader isn't looking for light entertainment. Even if you are known by your initials don't put them on your resume. If you use quotation marks or parentheses, those on the receiving end might think it a little strange. Better that it come out at the interview when the interviewer asks you what you like to be called: At the very least you'll have some small talk to break the tense interview atmosphere.

It is not required to place Mr., Ms., Miss, or Mrs. before your name. But what if your first name is Gayle, Carrol, Leslie, or any of the other names that can easily be used for members of either sex? While it isn't strictly necessary, in such instances it is acceptable to put Mr. Gayle Jones, or Ms. Leslie Jackson. The reasoning is based on human frailty and the ever-present foot-in-mouth syndrome: In contacting you to follow up on your resume, your interviewer is likely to make the mistake of asking to speak to Ms. Gayle Jones, or Mr. Leslie Jackson. Though it is a little mistake that is easily corrected, the possible future employer is immediately put in the awkward position of starting the relationship with an apology. If your name falls into the "gender-less" category, avoid the complication and employ a title.

Finally, for those who are the IInd, IIIrd, Junior, or Senior holders of their name: If you always add "Jr." or "III" when you sign your name or if that is the way you are addressed to avoid confusion, go ahead and use it. Otherwise, it is extraneous information on the resume, and therefore not needed.

Address

Always give your complete address. Do not abbreviate unless space restrictions make it absolutely mandatory—you want the post office to have every possible advantage when it comes to delivering those offer letters efficiently. If you do abbreviate—such as with St. or Apt.—be consistent. The state of your residence, however, is always abbreviated to two capitalized letters (for example, MN, WV, LA), according to post office standards. Always include the correct zip code.

The accepted format for laying out your address looks like this:

Maxwell Krieger
2 Caswell Place, Apartment 38
New York, NY 23456

Notice that the city, state and zip code all go on the same line, with a comma between city and state.

Telephone Number

Always include your telephone number: Few businesses will send you an invitation for an interview in the mail. Including your area code is important even if you have no intention of leaving the area. In this era of decentralization, your resume might end up being screened in another part of the country altogether!

Examples:

(202) 555-5555
202/555-5555

The inclusion or exclusion of a work telephone number is a little bit more of a problem.

> *The case for inclusion:* Featuring your daytime contact number allows prospective employers to reach you at a time of their convenience.
>
> *The case for exclusion:* Being pulled out of the Monday meeting every five minutes to take calls from headhunters and *Fortune 500* executives can ruin your whole day. The funny thing about employers is that they always prefer to lose you at their convenience rather than yours. In addition, keeping the company number off the resume adds to its life expectancy. Who needs another detail that may be obsolete in short order?
>
> *The solution:* Unless your current employer knows of your job search, leave the business number off the resume, but put it in your cover letter. Good cover letters do this with a short sentence that conveys the information and demonstrates you as a responsible employee. For example, something like this can work very well:

"I prefer not to use my employer's time taking personal calls at work, but with discretion you can reach me at 202/555-5555, extension 555, to initiate contact."

Job Objective

This section sometimes appears on resumes as:

Position Desired
Job Objective
Objective
Employment Objective

All are acceptable. Regardless of the heading, the job objective has traditionally meant one or two sentences about the kind of job you want and what you can contribute to the company in return for such a job. You will recall from chapter 2 that the use of a job objective in your resume will depend in part on the style of resume you employ to present your qualifications. Remember that the functional resume in particular almost demands one.

That notwithstanding, feelings run strong about whether or not to include a job objective in the resume, so let's review the cases for and against, then reach a considered conclusion.

The case for inclusion: Without a job objective, a resume can have no focus, no sense of direction. And if you don't know where you are going, you can't write a resume, because the body copy has nothing to support. The resume revolves around your objective like the earth around the sun.

The case for exclusion: A job objective is too constricting and can exclude you from consideration from countless jobs you might have been interested in, and for which you are qualified. And after creating a resume with the intent of opening as many doors as possible, you wouldn't want to have half of them slammed shut. Besides, employers are not generally believed to be overly concerned about what you want from them until they have a damn good idea about what they can get out of you.

The solution: You do need an objective, but it needn't fit the traditional definition. The best resumes have objectives written in broad, nonspecific terms. They are often little more than a categorization, such as:

Job Objective: Marketing Management

Sometimes these objectives appear at the top of a resume, as a headline and attention grabber. If they go beyond that, they focus on skills, achievements, and relevant personal characteristics that support the argument.

Job Objective: To pursue an accounting career

STAFF ACCOUNTANT—REAL ESTATE

To obtain a responsible position in a company where my experience, accomplishments, and proficiency will allow me the opportunity for growth.

This last approach is best, because it considers the forces at work in business these days. Including job objectives has as much to do with filing and retrieval systems and computers as it does with people. On the one hand, the resume reader is looking for a problem solver, so, by seeing that you fit into a general area, will want to rush on to the rest of the resume (where there are more specifics). Then what happens? In the best-case scenario, you will get a frantic call asking you to state your terms and a start date right away. But what happens when there isn't a need for your particular talents that day? Your resume gets filed or logged onto the company's database. The folks who file resumes aren't rocket scientists, just overworked functionaries trying to dispose of a never-ending flow of paper. They want to get rid of it as quickly as possible, so they will file your resume according to your instructions. And unless you give it the right help, it may not be filed under the right category; it may never see the light of day again. The broader your objective, the greater frequency with which it will be retrieved and reviewed in the future.

The same argument holds true for resumes sent to employment agencies and executive recruiters, who have been known to keep them on file for as long as ten years.

Just recently, in fact, I heard one of those wonderful tales of an eight-year-old resume that landed a job for its writer because it had a general objective. Why is this relevant? Had the specific job objective of an entry-level professional been on that resume, the writer would never have been considered.

Such considerations are encouraging many job seekers to include brief and nonspecific job objectives in their resumes. You will learn how to come up with the right tone for your specific needs later in the book.

Employment Dates

Resume readers are often leery of resumes without employment dates. If you expect a response, you can increase your odds dramatically by including them—in one form or another.

With a steady work history and no employment gaps you can be very specific (space allowing) and write:

January 11, 1997 to July 4,1998
or
1/11/97 to 7/4/98

or, to be a little less specific:
January 1997–February 1998

But if there are short employment gaps, you can improve the look of things:

1997–1998
instead of
December 12, 1997–January 23, 1998

There is no suggestion here that you should lie about your work history, but it is surprising just how many interviewers will be quite satisfied with such dates. There seems to be a myth that everything written on 20-lb. rag paper needs no further inquiry.

While this technique can effectively hide embarrassing employment gaps, and may be enough to get you in for an interview, you should of course be prepared with an adequate answer to questions about your work history once you sit down with the interviewer. Even if such questions are posed, you will have the opportunity to explain yourself—*mano a mano,* as it were—and that is a distinct improvement over being peremptorily ruled out by some faceless non-entity before you get a chance to speak your piece The end justifies the means, in this case.

Again, if you abbreviate months and years, do so consistently.

Job Titles

The purpose of a job title on your resume is not to reflect exactly what you were called by a particular employer, but rather to provide a generic identification that will be understood by as many employers as possible.

A job title should give the employer "something to hang his hat on." So if your current title is "Junior Accountant, Level Three," realize that such internal titling may well bear no relation to the titling of any other company on earth. I remember looking over the personnel roster of a New York bank and learning, to my astonishment, that it had over one hundred systems analysts. (The typical number for an outfit this size is about twelve.) Then I noticed that they had no programmers. The reasoning that I eventually unearthed was remarkably simple. The human resources department, finding people to be title-conscious in this area, obligingly gave them the titles they wanted. (Another perceived benefit was that it confused the heck out of the raiding headhunters, who got disgusted with systems analysts who couldn't analyze their way out of a wet paper bag!)

This generic approach to job titles also holds true as your job takes you nearer the top of the corporate ladder. The senior executive knows that the higher up the ladder, the more rarefied the air and the fewer the opportunities. After all, a company only has one Controller or one VP of Operations. Again, to avoid painting yourself into a career corner, you can be "specifically vague" with job titles like:

Administrative Assistant
instead of
Secretary

Accountant
instead of
Junior Accountant Level II

It is imperative to examine your current role at work, rather than relying on your starting or current title. Job titles within companies change much more slowly than the jobs themselves, so a job change can be the opportunity for some to escape stereotyping and the career stagnation that accompanies it. Take the typist hired three years ago, who has now spent two years with a word processor. Such a person could be identified thus:

Word Processor
instead of
Typist

This approach is important because of the way titles and responsibilities vary from company to company. Often, more senior titles and responsibilities are structured around a person's specific talents, especially so outside the *Fortune 1000.*

There are two situations, however, that don't lend themselves to this technique:

- When you apply for a specific job where you know the title and the responsibilities, and where the position's title is similar but not the same as your own. (Then the exact title sought should be reflected in your resume—as long as you are not being misleading concerning your capabilities.)
- When you apply for a job in certain specific professions, such as health care. (A brain surgeon wouldn't want to be specifically vague by tagging herself as a Health Aide.)

Company Name

The names of employers should be included. There is no need to include street address or telephone number of past or present employers, although it can be useful to include the city and state. The company will find the complete address on your employment application.

When working for a multiple-division corporation you may want to list the divisional employer: "Bell Industries" might not be enough, so you would perhaps want to add "Computer Memory Division." By the way, it is quite all right to abbreviate words like Corporation (Corp.), Company (Co.), Limited (Ltd.), or Division (Div.). Again, be consistent.

Here is how you might combine the job title and company name and address:

> DESIGN ENGINEER.
> Bell Industries, Inc., Computer Memory Div., Mountain View, CA.

The information you are supplying is relevant to the reader, but you don't wish it to detract from space usable to sell yourself. If, for instance, you live in a nationally known city, such as Dallas, you need not add "TX."

There is a possible exception to these guidelines. Employed professionals are justified in omitting current employers when their industry has been reduced to a small community of professionals who know, or know of, each other, and where a confidentiality breach is likely to have damaging repercussions. This usually happens to professionals on the higher rungs of the ladder. Of course, if you don't quite fit into this elite category but are still worried about identifying your firm, you are not obliged to list the name of your current employer.

One approach is simply to label a current company in a fashion that has become perfectly acceptable in today's business climate.

> A National Retail Chain
> An Established Electronics Manufacturer
> A Major Commercial Bank

You will notice that usually a company name is followed by a brief description of the business line:

> A National Retail Chain: Women and junior fashions and accessories.
>
> An Established Electronics Manufacturer producing monolithic memories.

This requirement is obviated when the writer can get the company's function into the heading.

> A Major Commercial Bank

The writer who can do this saves a line or two of precious space which can be filled with other valuable data.

Responsibilities

This is what is referred to as the meat, or body copy, of the resume, the area where not only are your responsibilities listed, but your special achievements and other contributions are also highlighted. This is one of the key areas that sets the truly great resume apart from the rest. This is a crucial part of the resume; it will be dealt with in detail in chapters 4 and 5.

Endorsements

Remember when you got that difficult job finished so quickly? And all the good things the boss said about your work? Well, in a resume you can very effectively quote him, even if the praise wasn't in writing (though of course it is best to quote directly). A line such as "Praised as 'most innovative and determined manager in the company'" can work wonders.

These third-party endorsements are not necessary, and they most certainly shouldn't be used to excess. But one or two can be a useful addition to your resume. Such quotes, used sparingly, can be very impressive; overkill can make you sound too self-important and reduce your chances of winning an interview.

Such endorsements become especially effective when the responsibilities have been qualified with facts, numbers, and percentages.

Accreditation and Licenses

Many fields of work require professional licensure or accreditation. If this is the case in your line of work, be sure to list everything necessary. If you are close to a particular accreditation or license (a C.P.A., for example), you would want to list it with information about the status:

Passed all parts of C.P.A. exam, September '97 (expected certification February '98).

Professional Affiliations

Your affiliation with associations and societies dedicated to your field shows your own dedication to your career. Membership is also important for networking, so if you are not currently a member of one of your industry's professional associations, give serious consideration to joining. Note the emphasis on "professional" in the heading. An employer is almost exclusively interested in your professional associations and societies. Omit references to any religious, political, or otherwise potentially controversial affiliations. They simply do not belong on a resume; you want yours to reflect a picture of your professional, not your personal, life.

An exception to this rule is in those jobs where a wide circle of acquaintances is regarded as an asset. Some examples would include jobs in public relations, sales, marketing, real estate, and insurance. In that case, include your membership in the Kiwanis or the Royal Lodge of the Raccoons.

By the same token, a seat on the village board, charitable cause involvement, or fundraising work are all activities that show a willingness to involve oneself and can often demonstrate organizational abilities. Space permitting, these are all activities worthy of inclusion because they show you as a sober and responsible member of the community.

These activities become more important as one climbs the corporate ladder of the larger companies. Those firms that take their community responsibilities seriously look for staff who feel and act the same way—an aspect of corporate culture applying itself at the most immediate levels.

Some corporations are committed to the idea that community activities are good public relations. Accordingly, such work may mark an individual for even greater responsibilities and recognition once in the company.

As for method of inclusion, brevity is the rule.

American Heart Association: Area Fundraising Chair

My personal observation is that these activities increase in importance with the maturity of the individual. Employers, quite selfishly perhaps, like to think of their younger staff burning the midnight oil solely for them.

Civil Service Grade

With a civil service job in your background, you will have been awarded a civil service grade. So, in looking for a job with the government, be sure to list it. In transferring from the government to the private sector, you are best advised to translate it into generic terms and ignore the grade altogether, unless you are applying for jobs with government contractors, subcontractors, or other specialized employers familiar with the intricacies of civil service ranking.

Publications and Patents

Such achievements, if they appear, are usually found at the end of the best resumes. Although they serve as positive means of evaluation for the reader, these achievements are of relatively minor importance in many professions.

Nevertheless, both publication and patents are manifestations of original thought and extended effort above and beyond the call of accepted professionalism. They tell the reader that you invest considerable personal time and effort in your career and are therefore a cut above the competition. Publication carries more weight in some industries and professions (where having literary visibility is synonymous with getting ahead); patents are a definite plus in the technology and manufacturing fields. You will notice in the resume examples how the writers list dates and names of publications, but do not usually include copyright information.

"New Developments in the Treatment of Chronic Pain."
1987. *New England Journal of Medicine.*

"Radical Treatments for Chronic Pain." 1986. *Journal of American Medicine.*

"Pain: Is It Imagined or Real?" 1987. *OMNI* Magazine.

Languages

Technology is rapidly changing our world into the proverbial global village. This means that today, as all companies are interested in client-based expansion, a linguistic edge in the job hunt could be just what you need. If you are fluent in a foreign language, you will want to mention it. Likewise if you understand a foreign language, but perhaps are not fluent, still mention it:

Fluent in French
Read and write Serbo-Croatian
Read German
Understand Spanish

Education

Educational history is normally listed whenever it helps your case, although the exact positioning of the information will vary according to the length of your professional experience and the relative strength of your academic achievements.

If you are recently out of school with little practical experience, your educational credentials, which probably constitute your primary asset, will appear near the beginning of the resume.

As you gain experience, your academic credentials become less important, and gradually slip toward the end of your resume. The exception to this is found primarily in certain professions where academic qualifications dominate a person's career—medicine, for instance.

You will notice that all examples for education are in reverse chronological order: The highest level of attainment (not necessarily a degree) always comes first, followed by the lesser levels. In this way, a doctorate will be followed by a master's degree, then a bachelor's. For degreed professionals, there is no need to go back further into educational history. (It is optional to list your prestigious prep school.) Those who attended school but did not graduate should nevertheless list the school in its proper chronological position, but should not draw attention to the fact that they did not receive a degree.

Those who did not achieve the higher levels of educational recognition will list their own highest level of attainment. A word on attainment is in order here. If you graduated from high school, attended college, but didn't graduate, you may be tempted to list your high school diploma first, followed by the name of the college you attended. That would give the wrong emphasis: it says you are a college drop-out and focuses on you as high school graduate. In this instance you would in fact list your college and omit reference to earlier educational history.

While abbreviations are frowned on in most circumstances, it is *acceptable* to abbreviate educational degrees (Ph.D., M.A., A.B., etc.), simply because virtually everyone understand them.

Those with scholarships and awards will list them, and recent graduates will usually also list majors and minors (space permitting). The case is a little more confused for the seasoned professional. Many human resources professionals say it makes life easier for them if majors and minors are listed, so they can further sift and grade the applicants. That's good for them, but it might not be good for you. All you want the resume to do is get you in the door, not slam it in your face. So, as omitting these minutiae will never stop you from getting an interview, I strongly urge you to err on the side of safety and leave 'em out.

If you are a recent entrant into the workplace, both your scholastic achievements and your contributions have increased importance. Certainly you will list your position on the school newspaper or the student council, memberships in clubs, and recognition for scholastic achievement; in short, anything that demonstrates your potential as a productive employee. As your career progresses, however, prospective employers care less and less about your school life and more and more about your work life. If you have five years of work experience and still feel compelled to list your chairmanship of the school's cafeteria committee, then you are not concentrating on the right achievements.

Changing times have also changed thinking about listing fraternities and sororities on resumes. A case could be made, I think, for leaving them off as a matter of course: If such organizations are important to an interviewer he or she will ask. My ruling, however, is that if the resume is tailored to an individual or company where membership in such organizations will result in a case of "deep calling to deep," then by all means, list. If, on the other hand, the resume is for general distribution, forget it.

Professional Training

Under the educational heading on smart resumes, you will often see a section for continuing professional education, focusing on special courses and seminars attended. Specifically, if you are computer literate, unlike many in the country, you will include this strong plus.

Summer and Part-time Employment

This should only be included when the resume writer is either just entering the work force or re-entering it after a substantial absence. The entry-level person can feel comfortable listing dates and places and times. The returnee should include the skills gained from part-time employment in a fashion that minimizes that "part-time" aspect of the experience—probably by using a Functional resume format.

What Can Never Go In

Some information just doesn't belong in resumes. Make the mistake of including it, and at best your resume loses power. At worst, you fail to land the interview.

Titles: Resume, Fact Sheet, Curriculum Vitae, etc.

Never use any of these variations on a theme as a heading. Their appearance on a resume is redundant: If it isn't completely obvious from the very look of your piece of paper that it is a resume, go back to square one. By the way, there is no difference in meaning between the above terms. "Curriculum Vitae" (or CV, as it is sometimes known) was an early term much favored in English and American academia—basically to prove that the users knew a little Latin. Its use today is outmoded and affected. "Fact Sheet," on the other hand, was a term developed by the employment agencies to imply they were presenting unvarnished facts. The phrase has never caught on.

Availability

Saying anything about your availability for employment on a resume is another redundancy. If you are not available, then why the heck are you wasting everyone's time and slowing down the mails? The only justification of the item's inclusion is if you expect to be finishing a project and moving on at such and such a time, and not before. But your view should be that intelligent human beings always have their eyes and ears open for better career opportunities—because no one else is going to watch out for them. If leaving before the end of a project could affect your integrity and/or references, O.K. There's a lot to be said for not burning your bridges, and as careers progress, it's surprising how many of the same people you bump into again and again.

Let the subject of availability come up at the face-to-face meeting. After meeting you, an employer will often be prepared to wait until you are available, and will probably appreciate your integrity. If, on the other hand, the employer just sees a resume that says you won't be available until next year—well, you'll just never get to a face-to-face meeting in the first place.

Reason for Leaving

There is no real point to stating your reasons for leaving a job on a resume, yet time and again they are included—to the detriment of the writer. The topic is always covered during an interview anyway. Mentioning it in advance and on paper can only damage your chances for being called in for that meeting.

References

It is inappropriate and unprofessional to list the names of references on a resume. You will never see it on a top example. Why? Interviewers are not interested in checking them before they meet and develop a strong interest in you—it's too time-consuming. In addition, employers are forbidden by law to check references without your written consent (thanks to the 1972 Fair Credit and Reporting Act), and they have to meet you first in order to obtain it, right?

Most employers will assume that references are available anyway (and if they aren't available, boy, are you in trouble). For that reason, there's an argument to be made for leaving that famous line—References Available Upon Request—off the end of the resume. I disagree, however. It may not be absolutely necessary to say that references are there for the asking, but those four extra words certainly don't do any harm and may help you stand out from the crowd. Including the phrase sends a little message:

"Hey, look, I have no skeletons in my closet."

A brief but important aside. If you have ever worked under a different surname, you must take this fact into account when giving your references. A recently divorced woman wasted a strong interview performance not too long ago because she was using her maiden name on her resume and at the interview. She forgot to tell the employer that her references would, of course, remember her by a different last name. The results of this oversight were catastrophic. Three prior employers denied ever having heard of anyone by that name the woman's interviewer supplied. She lost the job.

Written Testimonials

Even worse than listing references on a resume is to attach a bunch of written testimonials. It is an absolute no-no. No one believes them anyway.

Of course, that doesn't mean that you shouldn't solicit such references for your files. They can always be produced when references are requested and can be used as a basis for those third-party endorsements we talked about. This will be especially helpful to you if you are just entering the work force, or re-entering after a long absence, because the content of the testimonials can be used to beef up your resume significantly.

Salary

Leave out all references to salary, past and present—it is far too risky. Too high or too low a salary can knock you out of the running even before you hear the starting gun. Even in responding to a help-wanted advertisement that specifically requests salary requirements, don't give them. A good resume will still get you the interview, and in the course of your discussions with the company, you'll certainly talk about salary anyway. If you somehow feel obliged to give salary requirements, simply write "competitive" or "negotiable" (and then only in your cover letter).

Abbreviations

With the exceptions of educational attainments, and those required by the postal service, avoid abbreviations if at all possible. Of course, space constraints might make it imperative that you write "No. Wilshire Blvd." instead of "North Wilshire Boulevard." If that is the case, be sure to be consistent. If you abbreviate in one address, abbreviate in all of them. But bear in mind that you will always seem more thoughtful and professional if everything is spelled out. And anyway, your resume will be easier to read!

Jargon

A similar warning applies to industry slang. Your future boss might understand it, but you can bet your boots that neither his or her boss nor the initial resume screener will. Your resume must speak clearly of your skills to many different people, and one skill that we all need today is a sensitivity to the needs of communication.

If you are in one of the high-technology industries, however, avoiding jargon and acronyms is not only impossible, it is often inadvisable. All the same, keep the nontechnical resume screener in mind before you wax lyrical about bits and bytes.

Charts and Graphs

Even if charts and graphs are part of your job, they make poor use of the space available on a resume—and they don't help the reader. In fact, you should never even bring them out at an interview unless requested. The same goes for other examples of your work. If you are a copywriter or graphic artist, for example, it is all right to say that samples are available, but only if you have plenty of resume space to spare.

Mention of Age, Race, Religion, Sex, National Origin

Government legislation was enacted some years ago forbidding employment discrimination in these areas. If the government had to take action, you know things were bad. Although today it's much better, I urge you to leave out any reference to any of these areas in your resume.

Photographs

In days of old when men were bold and all our cars had fins, it was the done thing to have a photograph in the top right-hand corner of the resume. So, if you are looking for a job in the 1950s, include one; if not, don't. Today, the fashion is against photographs; including them is a waste of space that says nothing about your ability to do a job.

(Obviously, careers in modeling, acting, and certain aspects of the electronic media require photos. In these instances your face is your fortune.)

Health/Physical Description

Who cares? You are trying to get hired, not dated. Unless your physical health (gym instructor, e.g.) and/or appearance (model, actor, media personality) are immediately relevant to the job, leave these issues alone.

Early Background

I regularly see resumes that tell about early childhood and upbringing. To date, the most generous excuse I can come up with for such anecdotes is that the resumes were prepared by the subjects' mothers.

Weaknesses

Any weakness, lack of qualifications, or information likely to be detrimental to your cause should always be canned. Never tell resume readers what you don't have or what you can't or haven't had the opportunity to do yet. Let them find that out for themselves.

Demands

You will never see demands on a good resume. Don't outline what you feel an employer is expected to give or to provide. The time for making demands is when the employer has demonstrated sincere interest in you by extending a job offer with a salary and job description attached. That is when the employer will be interested and prepared to listen to what you want. Until then, concentrate on bringing events to that happy circumstance by emphasizing what you can bring to the employer. In your resume you should, to paraphrase the great man, ask not what your employer can do for you, but rather what you can do for your employer.

Exaggerations

Avoid verifiable exaggerations of your skills, accomplishments, and educational qualifications. Research has now proven that three out of every ten resumes feature inflated educational qualifications. Consequently, verification, especially of educational claims, is on the increase. If, after you had been hired, you were discovered to have told a sly one on your resume, it could have cost you your job and a lot more. The stigma of deceit will very likely follow you for the rest of your professional days. On the other hand, I don't notice 30 percent of the work force stumbling around with crippled careers. Matters are tightening up in this area, and ultimately it will be a personal judgment call. Ask yourself, "Do I have a defensible position, should this matter come under scrutiny now or at a later date?"

Judgment Calls

Here are some areas that fall into neither the do nor the don't camp. Whether to include them will depend on your personal circumstances.

Summary

The Summary, when it is included in a resume, comes immediately after the Objective. The point is to encapsulate your experience and perhaps highlight one or two of your skills and/or contributions. You hope, in two or three short sentences, to grab the reader's attention with a power pack of the skills and attributes you have developed throughout your career. Good summaries are short; you don't want to show all your aces in the first few lines! You can see examples of resumes with strong summaries in the resume section of this book.)

On the other hand, many experts feel that the content of the summary must be demonstrated by the body of the resume, and that therefore summaries are pointless duplications and a waste of space. The choice is yours. Used wisely and well, they can work.

Personal Flexibility, Relocation

If you are open to relocation for the right opportunity, make it clear. It will never in and of itself get you an interview, but it won't hurt. On the other hand, never state that you aren't open to relocation. After all, that factor usually comes into play only when you have a job offer to consider. Let nothing stand in the way of a nice collection of job offers!

Career Objectives

These are okay to include at the very start of your career, before your general direction has been confirmed by experience and track record. Inclusion is also acceptable if you have very clearly defined objectives and are prepared to sacrifice all other opportunities. If that is the case, state your goals clearly and succinctly, remembering not to confuse the nature of long-term career objectives with short-term ones of job objectives.

Beware, though, of the drawbacks. First of all, resume readers aren't famous for paying much attention to objectives. Second, I have seen these used on many occasions to make a hiring decision between two candidates. The resumes are compared, A has no objective, B has an objective that doesn't match the initial expectations. Result? A gets the job. Another consideration is that your resume may be on file for years, during which time your objectives are bound to change. You don't need last year's dusty dreams clouding over your bright tomorrows.

Marital Status

If you think mention of your marital status will enhance your chances (if you are looking for a position as a long-distance trucker, marriage counselor, or traveling salesperson, for example), include it. In all other instances leave it out. Legally, your marital status is of no consequences.

Military

Include your good military record with highest rank, especially if you are applying for jobs in the defense sector. Otherwise exclude it: It is no longer any detriment to your career not to have a military history.

Personal Interests

A recent Korn Ferry study showed that executives with team sports on their resumes were seen to be averaging $3,000 a year more than their more sedentary counterparts. Now, that makes giving a line to your hobbies worthwhile, if they fit into certain broad categories. These would include team sports (baseball, basketball), determination activities (running, swimming, climbing, bicycling), and "brain activities" (bridge, chess).

The rule of thumb, as always, is only to include activities that can in some way contribute to your chances. If you can draw a valid connection, include them; if not, don't.

Personal Paragraphs

Here and there throughout the resume section of this book you will see resumes that include—often toward the end—a short personal paragraph that gives you a candid snapshot of the resume writer as a person. Done well, these can be exciting, effective endings to a resume, but they are not to everyone's taste. Typically, they refer to one or two personal traits, activities, and sometimes, beliefs. These are often tied in with skills required for the particular job sought.

The idea is to make the reader say, "Heh, there's a real person behind those Foster Grants, let's get him in here; sounds like our kind of guy." Of course, as no one can be all things to all people, you won't want to go overboard in this area.

4 | Resumes That Knock 'em Dead

It has been theory up to now; this is where the rubber hits the road.

You have a sound idea of why you need a resume; you've had an overview of the different types available to you; and you know what belongs in a powerful resume and what doesn't. We now move from the abstract to the intensely practical side of resume writing.

This is the part of the book that requires you to do some thinking. I will ask questions to jog your memory about your practical experience. The outcome will be a smorgasbord of your most sellable professional attributes. The work we do together in this chapter will not only form the foundation of your resume but prepare you to turn those job interviews into job offers.

People change jobs for a multitude of reasons. Perhaps your career isn't progressing as you want it. Perhaps you have gone as far as you can with your present employer, and the only way to take another career step is to change companies. Maybe you have been in the same job for three or more years, without dramatic salary increases or promotions, and you know that you are going nowhere. You have been stereotyped, classified, and pigeonholed.

Whether you are a fast-tracker, recent graduate, work force reentrant, career changer, or what-have-you, if you are considering new horizons, you must take stock before stepping out.

You need to know where you've been, where you are, and where you're headed. Without this stock taking, your chances of reaching your ultimate goals are reduced, because you won't know how best to use what you've got to get what you want.

Believe it or not, very few people have a clear fix on what they do for a living. Oh, I know; you ask a typist what he or she does, and you get, "Type, stupid." You ask an accountant, and you hear, "Fiddle with numbers, what do you think?" And that is the problem. Most people don't look at their work beyond these simplistic terms. They never examine the implications of their jobs in relation to the overall success of the department and company. Most people miss not only their importance to an employer as part of the business, but also, their importance to themselves. Preparing your resume will give you a fresh and more lucid view of yourself as a professional and your role in your chosen profession.

Employers all want to know the same thing: How can you contribute to keeping their ship afloat and seaworthy? No one is hired merely to be a typist or an accountant—or anything else, for that matter. Companies hire only one type of person—a problem solver. Look at your work in terms of the problems you solve in the daily round, the problems that would occur if you weren't there.

Some people find the prospect of taking stock of their skills to be an ominous one. They feel it means judging themselves by others' standards, by the job title and salary assigned to by someone else. Then, knowing their own weaknesses too well, they look at other people in their position, of whom they see only the exterior, and are awed by those persons' seemingly superior competence, skills, and professionalism.

"Seemingly" is the key word here. You are as good as the next person, and to prove it, all you have to do is look yourself squarely in the eye and learn that you have a great deal more to offer than you may ever have imagined. You have solved problems. That's what this chapter is all about.

The Secret of Resume Writing

As a resume writer, you have a lot in common with journalists and novelists. Beginners in each field usually bring some basic misconceptions about how writing is done: I always thought that Stephen King or James Clavell sat down, wrote "Page 1," then three weeks later wrote "The End," and placidly returned the quill to the inkwell. In fact, many professional writers—and resume writers—have more in common with sculptors. What they really do to start the creative process is to write masses of notes. This great mass is the raw material, like a block of stone, at which you chip away to reveal the masterwork that has been hiding there all along.

The key is that the more notes you have, the better. Just remember that whatever you write in the note-making part of your resume preparation will never suffer public scrutiny. It is for your private consumption; from these notes, the finished work of art will emerge for public view.

This chapter is going to help you write those notes, as you recapture all those forgotten moments of glory that employers love to hear about.

The only difficult step to take is the first one. So pick up a pen and some paper, and plunge ahead right now; without even pausing for breath.

Questionnaire, Part One: Raw Materials

This questionnaire is set up to follow your entire career. In answering the questions as completely as you can, you are creating the mass of raw material from which you will sculpt the final work of art.

1. *Current or Last Employer:* This includes part-time or voluntary employment if you are a recent graduate or about to reenter the work-force after an absence. Try looking at your school as an employer and see what new information you reveal about yourself.
   Starting Date:
   Starting Salary:
   Leaving Date:
   Leaving Salary:
2. *Company Description:* Write one sentence that describes the product(s) your company made or the service(s) it performed.
3. *Title:* Write your starting job title (the one given to you when you first signed on with the company). Then write a one- or two-sentence description of your responsibilities in that position.
4. *Duties:* What were your three major duties in this position?
5. *Methods, Skills, Results:* Now, for each of the above three duties, answer the following questions:

   What special skills or knowledge did you need to perform this task satisfactorily?

   What has been your biggest achievement in this area? (Try to think about money saved or made, or time saved for the employer. Don't worry if your contributions haven't been acknowledged in writing and signed in triplicate, as long as you know them to be true without exaggeration.)

What verbal or written comments were made about your contributions in this area, by peers or managers?

What different levels of people did you have to interact with to achieve your job tasks? How did you get the best out of Superiors? Co-workers? Subordinates?

What aspects of your personality were brought into play when executing this duty? (For example, perhaps it required attention to detail, or determination, or good verbal and writing skills. Whatever, jot them all down.)

To help you address that last issue (it's a vitally important one), you should look over the following list of a number of personality traits that are in constant demand from all employers.

Analytical Skills: Weighing the pros and cons. Not jumping at the first solution to a problem that presents itself.

Chemistry: Your willingness to get along with others and get the job done.

Communication Skills: More than ever, the ability to talk with and write effectively to people at all levels in a company is a key to success.

Confidence: Poise, friendliness, honesty, and openness with all employees—high and low.

Dedication: Doing whatever it takes to get the job done.

Drive and Determination: A desire to get things done. Goal-oriented. Someone who does not back off when a problem or situation gets tough.

Economy: Most problems have an expensive solution and an inexpensive one that the company would prefer to implement.

Efficiency: Always keeping an eye open for inefficient uses of time, effort, resources, and money.

Energy: Extra effort in all aspects of the job, the little things as well as the important matters.

Honesty/Integrity: Responsibility for all your actions—both good and bad. Always making decisions in the best interests of the company, rather than on whim or personal preference.

Listening Skills: Listening, rather than just waiting your turn to speak.

Motivation: Enthusiasm, finding reasons to accept challenges rather than avoid them. A company realizes that a motivated person accepts added challenges and does that little bit extra on every job.

Pride: Pride in a job well done. Paying attention to detail.

Reliability: Follow-through, a willingness to keep management informed, and a predisposition toward relying on oneself—not others—to see your job done.

Sensitivity to Procedures: Following the chain of command, recognizing that procedures exist to keep a company functioning and profitable. Those who rush to implement their own "improved procedures" wholesale, or organize others to do so, can cause untold chaos in an organization.

6. *Supporting Points:* If you asked for a promotion or a raise while in this position, what arguments did you use to back up your request?

7. *Most Recent Position:* Write down your current (or last) job title. Then write a one- or two-sentence description of your responsibilities in that position, and repeat steps three through six. In this step it is assured that you have a title and responsibilities that are different from those you had when you first joined the company. If this is not the case, simply ignore this step. On the other hand, many people have held three or four titles with a specific employer, and gained breadth of experience with each one. In this instance, for each different intermediary title, repeat steps one through six. The description of responsibilities should be reserved for your departing (or current) title.

8. *Reflecting on Success:* Make some general observations about work with this employer. Looking back over your time with this employer, what was the biggest work-related problem that you had to face? What solution did you find? What was the result of the solution when implemented? What was the value to the employer in terms of money earned or saved and improved efficiency? What was the area of your

greatest personal improvement in this job? What was the greatest contribution you made as a team player? Who are the references you would hope to use from this employer, and what do you think they would say about you?

9. *Getting All the Facts:* Repeat the last eight steps for your previous employer, and then for the employer before that, and so forth. Most finished resumes focus on the last three jobs, or last ten years before that, and so forth. In this developmental portion of the process, however, you must go back in time and cover your entire career. Remember that you are doing more than preparing a resume here: you are preparing for the heat of battle in the interview preparation, throughout any telephone screening interviews, and especially before that crucial face-to-face meeting, you can use this Questionnaire to prepare yourself for anything the interviewer might ask. One of the biggest complaints interviewers have about job candidates, and one of the major reasons for rejection, is unpreparedness: "You know, good as some of this fellow's skills are, something just wasn't right. He seemed—slow somehow. You know, he couldn't even remember when he joined his current employer!" You won't have that problem.

Questionnaire, Part Two: Details, Details, Details

The hard work is done and it's all downhill from here. Just fill in the facts and figures relating to the following questions. Obviously, not everything will apply to you. The key is just to put it all down; you can polish it later.

Military History

Include branch of service, rank, and any special skills that could further your civilian career.

Educational History

Start with highest level of attainment and work backward. Give dates, schools, majors, minors, grade-point averages.

Specify any scholarships or other special awards.

List other school activities, such as sports, societies, social activities. Especially important are leadership roles: Any example of how you "made a difference" with your presence could be of value to your future. Obviously, this is important for recent graduates with little work experience.

Languages

Specify fluency and ability to read and write foreign languages.

Personal Interests

List interests and activities that could be supportive to your candidacy. For example, an internal auditor who plays chess or bridge would list these and probably use them in a resume, because they support the analytical bent so necessary to work.

Computer Literacy

If you are computer literate, let's have the details. (If not, maybe it's time to wake up and smell the coffee: A knowledge of computers could be critical to your professional survival.)

Patents

Include patents that are both pending and awarded.

Publications

If you have published articles, list the name of the publication, title of article and the publication date. If you have had books published, list the title and publisher.

Professional Associations

Include membership and the details of any offices you held.

Volunteer Work

Also include any volunteer work you performed. It isn't only paid work experience that makes you valuable.

Miscellaneous Areas of Achievement

All professions and careers are different. Use this section to itemize any additional aspects of your history where you somehow "made a difference" with your presence.

Questionnaire, Part Three: Where Are You Going?

Knowing where you want to go will determine both the wording and the layout of your resume. There is an old saying that if you don't know where you are going, you have no hope of getting there. Remember that there is a difference between valid objectives and pipedreams. Dreams aren't bad things to have, but they mustn't be confused with making a living.

Your first step is to write down a job title that embraces your objectives. Having taken this simple step, you need to note underneath it all the skills and qualifications needed to do that job successfully. List them like this:

Job Title

1. First skill
2. Second skill
3. Third skill
4. Fourth skill
5. Fifth skill

But remember that your thoughts on what it takes may not jibe with the employer's thoughts. And what if you are simply not sure what it takes to do the job at all? Simple. Take a trip to the library and ask to see a copy of the *Dictionary of Occupational Titles*. It gives you endless job titles, as you might expect, and brief job descriptions. Make notes by all means, but don't copy it out word for word. The book is full of dead prose that's copper-bottom guaranteed to send the average resume reader to sleep in three seconds flat. You want to avoid letting any of this soporific stuff sneak into the final draft of your resume.

When you have decided on an objective, and defined what it takes to do that job, go back through the first part of the questionnaire and flag all the entries you can use to build a viable resume. Just underline or highlight the appropriate passages for further attention when the time comes for putting pen to paper.

The chances are that you will find adequate skills in your background to qualify you for the job objective. And remember: Few people have all the qualifications for the jobs they get!

If you still aren't sure, develop a "Matching Sheet" for yourself. List the practical requirements of your job objective on one side of a piece of paper and match them on the other side with your qualifications. A senior computer programmer, looking for a step up to a systems analysis position with a new job in financial applications, might develop a Matching Sheet that looks like this:

Job Needs	*My Experience*
Mainframe IBM experience	6 yrs. experience
IBM COBOL	COBOL, PL/1, Assembler
Financial experience	6 yrs. in banking
Sys. dev. methodology	Major sys. dev., 3 yrs.
Communication	Ongoing customer service work OS/MVS, TSO/SPF, CICS, SNAOS/MVS, TSO/SPF, ROSCOE, IMS, DB/DC, SAS

But what about the junior accountant who had VP of finance as a goal? Naturally, at this stage, many of the needed skills—and much of the experience—aren't in place. If you fall into this category, don't worry. You just happened upon a career objective rather than a job objective. To solve the dilemma, list all the title changes between your present position and your dream job. This will show you how many career steps stand between you and your ultimate goal. Your job objective is simply the title above your own, the first achievable stepping stone toward the ultimate goal.

At best, job and career objectives are simply a tool to give you focus for writing the resume, and to give the reader something to take sightings on. The way the world is changing, by the time you can reasonably expect to reach your ultimate career goal, that particular position may not even exist.

Be content with a generalized objective for the next job. And don't be afraid of what objective—you aren't taking holy order, you're identifying a job you'd like to win. Who knows what the next few years will hold for you?

(Note: You will find an example of a completed questionnaire on page 271. You'll also find examples of chronological, functional, and combination resumes based on the completed questionnaire on pages 102–105.)

5 | Writing the Basic Resume

Advertisements and resumes have a great deal in common.

You will notice the vast majority of advertisements in any media can be heard, watched, or read in under thirty seconds. That is not accidental. The timing is based on studies relating to the limit of the average consumer's attention span.

And that is why you sometimes notice that both resumes and advertisements depart from the rules that govern all other forms of writing. First and last they are an urgent business communication, and business likes to get to the point.

Before putting pen to paper, good advertising copywriters imagine themselves in the position of their target audience. They imagine their objective—selling something. Then they consider what features their product possesses and what benefits it can provide to the purchaser.

You will find a similar procedure beneficial in your own writing. Fortunately, your approach is simplified somewhat, because you can make certain generalizations. You can assume, for instance, that the potential employer has a position to fill and a problem to solve, and that he or she will hire someone who is able to do the job, who is willing to do it, and who is manageable.

For the next fifteen minutes, imagine yourself in one of your target companies. You are in the personnel department on resume detail. Fortunately it is a slow morning, and there are only thirty that need to be read. Go straight to the example section now and read thirty resumes without a break, then return to this page.

Now you have some idea of what it feels like. Except that you had it easy— the resumes you read were good, interesting ones; resumes that got real people real jobs. Even so, you probably felt a little punch drunk at the end of the exercise. But I know that you learned a very valuable lesson: Brevity is to be desired above all other things.

41

Preparation

There is nothing worse than sitting down with the old quill pen, ready to create words of deathless prose, only to discover you forgot the parchment. Getting everything you'll need together first will help you beat that other enemy of the muse—procrastination. Collect:

- A pad of 8 1/2" x 11" paper
- Pens, pencils, a computer or typewriter—whatever is your chosen method of writing
- A dictionary. Even your kids' dictionary is O.K. (At least it will restrain you from using those confusing nineteen cent words.)
- An old resume, some generic job descriptions, and, of course, the completed Questionnaire.
- A ruler—it's useful for keeping things aligned as you lay out and write your resume.

Now, just write. Don't even try for style or literacy—you can tend to that later. Think of yourself as speaking on paper. You'll find your personal speech rhythms will make for a lively resume, once they have been edited.

Choose a Layout

You have seen the basic examples of chronological, functional, and combination resumes in chapter 2, and certainly you have browsed through the dozens of actual resumes. Find one that strikes your fancy and fits your needs, and use it as your model. It need not reflect your field of professional expertise. Obviously, you will have to tinker with any model, adding or deleting jobs and making other subtle adjustments as necessary, to fashion it for your background.

This first step is just like painting by numbers. Go through the model and fill in the obvious slots—name, address, telephone number(s), employer names, employment dates, educational background and dates, extramural activities and the like. Shazam! Now the first half of your resume is complete.

Filling in the Picture: Chronological Resumes

Objectives

You can have a simple nonspecific objective, one that gives the reader a general focus, such as, "Objective: Data Processing Management." It gets the message across succinctly; and if there is no immediate need for someone of your background, it encourages the employer to put your resume in the file where you feel it belongs. That's important, because even if you are not suitable for today's needs, there's a good chance that the resume will be pulled out when such a need does arise.

If you choose to use an expanded, detailed objective, refer to chapter 3. You will of course:

- Keep it short, just one or two sentences.
- Express your objective in the fewest possible words that can bring a picture to the reader's mind.
- Not get too specific—no one is that interested.
- Focus the objective on what you can do for the company and avoid mention of what you want in return.
- State exactly the job title you seek, if the resume is in response to a specific advertisement.
- Keep your objectives general to give yourself the widest number of employment options, if the resume will be sent out "blind" to a number of companies.

Of course, with your resume either written or produced on a computer, your objective can go through subtle variations for each specific job.

If you want to use both a nonspecific and a detailed objective, headline the resume with the nonspecific title, and then follow with the more detailed one.

Company Role

Now, for each employer, edit your response from step two of the Questionnaire, which outlines that company's services or products. Make it one short sentence: Do not exceed one line or ten words.

Job Titles

Remember what we said in chapter 3. There is nothing intrinsically wrong with listing your title as "Fourth-Level Administration Clerk, Third Class," as long as you are prepared to wait until doomsday for it to be considered by someone who understands what it means and is able to relate it to current needs. With this in mind:

- Be general in your job title. All companies have their particular ways of dispensing job titles, and they all vary. Your title with employer A will mean something entirely different to employer B, and might not make any sense at all to employer C.
- Whenever possible, stay away from designations such as trainee, junior, intermediate, senior—as in Junior Engineer—and just designate yourself as Engineer, Designer, Editor, or what have you.

Responsibilities

In a chronological resume, the job title is often followed by a short sentence that helps the reader visualize you doing the job. Get the information from the completed questionnaire and do a rough edit to get it down to one short sentence. Don't worry about perfection now; the polishing is done later.

The responsibilities and contributions you list here are those functions that best display your achievements and problem-solving abilities. They do not necessarily correspond with how you spent the majority of your working day, nor are they related to how you might prefer to spend your working day. Problems sometimes arise by mistakenly following either of these paths. It can perhaps best be illustrated by showing you part of a resume that came to my desk recently. It is the work of a professional who listed her title and duties for one job like this:

> Sales Manager: Responsible for writing branch policy,
> coordination of advertising and advertising agencies.
> Developed knowledge of IBM PC. Managed staff of six.

Is it any wonder she wasn't getting responses to her resume-mailing campaign? Here, she has explained where she was spending her time when the resume was created. The explanation, however, has nothing to do with the major functions of her job. She has mistakenly listed everything in the reverse chronological order, not in relation to the items' relative importance to a future employer. Let's look at what subsequent restructuring achieved:

> Sales Manager: Hired to turned around stagnant sales force. Successfully recruited, trained, managed and motivated a consulting staff of six. Result: 22 percent sales gain over first year.

In the rewrite of this particular part of the resume, notice how she thought like a copywriter and quickly identified the problem she was hired to solve.

> Hired to turn around stagnant sales force. (Demonstrates her skills and responsibilities.)

> Successfully recruited, trained, managed and motivated a consulting staff of six. Result: 22 percent sales gain over first year. (Shows what she subsequently did about them, and just how well she did it.)

By doing this, her responsibilities and achievements become more important in the light of the problems they solved.

Some More about Contributions

Business has very limited interests. In fact, those interests can be reduced to a single phrase: Making a profit. Making a profit is done in just three ways: By saving money in some fashion for the company; by saving time through some innovation at the company, which in turn saves the company money and gives it the opportunity to make more money in the time saved; or by simply making money for the company.

That's all there is to any business, when you reduce things to their simplest forms.

That does not mean that you should address only those points in your resume and ignore valuable contributions which cannot be quantified. But it does mean that you should try to quantify as much as you can.

If you find it difficult to recall and prioritize your responsibilities at a given company, go to the library and consult the *Directory of Job Descriptions*. But, as I have said before, be careful. If you do resort to this as a memory jogger be careful not to copy out the appropriate entry in its entirety—the prose is deadly boring.

Achievements

Your achievements will be listed in step five of the first part of the Questionnaire. The achievements you take from step five will not necessarily be the greatest accomplishments that can help you reach your stated (or unstated) employment objective. Concentrate solely on those topics that relate to your objectives, even if it means leaving out some significant achievement; you can always rectify the situation at the interview.

Pick two to four accomplishments for each job title and edit them down to bite-size chunks that read like a telegram. Write as if you had to pay for each entry by the word—this approach can help you pack a lot of information into a short space. The resulting abbreviated style will help convey a sense of immediacy to the reader.

Responsible for new and used car sales. Earned "Salesman of the Year" awards, 1996 and 1997. Record holder for:

- Most Cars Sold in One Month
- Most Cars Sold in One Year
- Most Board Gross in One Month
- Created an annual giving program to raise operating funds. *Raised $2,000,000.*
- Targeted, cultivated, and solicited sources including individuals, corporations, foundations, and state and federal agencies. *Raised $1,650,000.*
- Raised funds for development of the Performing Arts School facility, capital expense, and music and dance programs. *Raised $6,356,000.*

Now, while you may tell the reader about these achievements, you should never explain how they were accomplished. After all, the idea of the resume is to pique interest and to raise as many questions as you answer. Questions mean interest, and getting that interest satisfied requires talking to you!

You probably have lots of great accomplishments to share with the reader that will tempt you to add a second page, or even a third. Your resume, however, is designed to form the basis for tantalizing further discussions, so just be content with showing the reader a little glimpse of the gold vein—and let him or her discover the rest of the strike later. Very often the information discovered by the interviewer's own efforts takes on greater value than information offered free of charge on paper. Also, you have saved some of your heavy firepower for the interview, so that the meeting will not be an anticlimax for the interviewer. And that, in turn, will lend you some leverage and control in the discussions.

Prioritize the listing of your accomplishments as they relate to your job objective, and be sure to quantify your contributions (that is, put them into tangible, profit-oriented terms) wherever possible and appropriate.

Now is the time to weave in one or two of those laudatory quotes (also from step five). Don't include every one, but do incorporate enough to show that others think well of you.

- Sales volume increased from $90 million to $175 million. Acknowledged as "the greatest single gain of the year."
- Earnings increased from $9 million to $18 million. Review stated, "always a view for the company bottom line."
- Three key stores were each developed into $30-million units. Praised for "an ability to keep all the balls in the air, all the time."

Functional or Combination Resumes

These resumes are similar to chronological ones in content; often it's just the order of information that is different. Employers and employment dates are downplayed by relegating them to the end of the paragraphs, or to the bottom of the resume. Job titles and job responsibilities for specific jobs are sometimes omitted altogether.

In a functional or combination resume, you will have identified the skills and attributes necessary to fulfill the functions of the job objective, and will highlight the appropriate attributes you have to offer. In this format, you will have headings that apply to the skill areas your chosen career path demands, such as: Management, Training, Sales, etc. Each will be followed by a short paragraph packed with selling points. These can be real paragraphs, or the introductory sentence followed by the bullets usually recommended for the chronological formats. Here are examples of each style.

COLLECTIONS:
Developed excellent rapport with customers while significantly shortening pay-out terms *through application of problem-solving techniques.* Turned impending loss into profit. Personally salvaged and increased sales with two

multi-million dollar accounts by providing remedial action for their sales/financial problems.

COLLECTIONS:

Developed excellent rapport with customers while significantly shortening pay-out terms:

- Evaluated sales performance, offered suggestions for financing/merchandising.
- Performed on-the-spot negotiations; turned impending loss into profit.
- Salvaged two multi-million-dollar problem accounts by providing remedial action for their sales/financial problems. Subsequently increased sales.

Keep each paragraph to an absolute maximum of four lines. This ensures that the finished product has plenty of white space so that it is easy on the reader's eye.

Editing and Polishing

Sentences gain power with verbs that demonstrate an action. For example, one client—a mature lady with ten years at the same law firm in a clerical position—had written in her original resume:

I learned to use a Wang 220VS.

After discussion of the circumstances that surrounded learning how to use the Wang 220VS, certain exciting facts emerged. By using action verbs and an awareness of employer interests, this sentence was charged up, given more punch. Not only that, for the first time the writer fully understood the value of her contributions, which greatly enhanced her self-image:

I analyzed and determined need for automation of an established law office. Responsible for hardware and software selection, installation and loading. Within one year, I had achieved a fully automated office.

Notice how the verbs show that things happen when you are around the office. These action verbs and phrases add an air of direction, efficiency and accomplishment to every resume. They succinctly tell the reader why you did and how well you did it.

Now look at the above example when a third party endorsement is added to it:

> I analyzed and determined need for automation of an established law office. Responsible for hardware and software selection, installation and loading. Within one year, I had achieved a fully automated office. Partner stated, "You brought us out of the dark ages into the technological age, and in the process neither you nor the firm missed a beat!"

Action Verbs

Here are over 175 action verbs that will see which ones you can use to give punch to your resume writing.

accomplished
achieved
acted
adapted
addressed
administered
advanced
advised
allocated
analyzed
appraised
approved
arranged
assembled
assigned
assisted
attained
audited
authored
automated
balanced
budgeted
built
calculated
catalogued
chaired
clarified
classified
coached
collected
compiled
completed
composed
computed
conceptualized
conducted

consolidated
contained
contracted
contributed
controlled
coordinated
corresponded
counseled
created
critiqued
cut
decreased
delegated
demonstrated
designed
developed
devised
diagnosed
directed
dispatched
distinguished
diversified
drafted
edited
educated
eliminated
enabled
encouraged
engineered
enlisted
established
evaluated
examined
executed
expanded
expedited

explained
extracted
fabricated
facilitated
familiarized
fashioned
focused
forecast
formulated
founded
generated
guided
headed up
identified
illustrated
implemented
improved
increased
indoctrinated
influenced
informed
initiated
innovated
inspected
installed
instigated
instituted
instructed
integrated
interpreted
interviewed
introduced
invented
launched
lectured
led

maintained
managed
marketed
mediated
moderated
monitored
motivated
negotiated
operated
organized
originated
overhauled
oversaw
performed
persuaded
planned
prepared
presented
prioritized
processed
produced
programmed
projected
promoted
provided
publicized
published
purchased
recommended
reconciled
recorded
recruited
reduced
referred
regulated
rehabilitated

remodeled
repaired
represented
researched
restored
restructured
retrieved
revitalized
saved
scheduled
schooled
screened
set
shaped
solidified
solved
specified
stimulated
streamlined
strengthened
summarized
supervised
surveyed
systemized
tabulated
taught
trained
translated
traveled
trimmed
upgraded
validated
worked
wrote

Use these words to edit and polish your work, to communicate, persuade, and motivate the reader to take action.

This stage is most challenging, because many people in different companies will see and evaluate your resume. Keep industry "jargon" to a minimum; there will be some who understand the intricacies and technicalities of your profession, and some who don't. And you need to share your technical or specialist wisdom with the nonspecialists, too.

Varying Sentence Structure

Most good writers are at their best writing short punchy sentences. Keep your sentences under about twenty words; a good average is around fifteen. If your sentence is longer than the twenty mark, either shorten it by restructuring, or make two sentences out of the one. The reader on the receiving end has neither the time nor the inclination to read your sentences twice to get a clear understanding.

At the same time, you don't want the writing to sound choppy, so vary the length of sentences when you can. You can also start with a short phrase and follow with a colon:

- Followed by bullets of information,
- each one supporting the original phrase.

All these different techniques are designed to enliven the reading process. Here's an example of how the above suggestions might be put into practice.

Analyzed and determined need for automation of an established law office:

- Responsible for hardware and software selection;
- Coordinated installation of Wang 220VS and six work stations;
- Operated and maintained equipment, and trained other users;
- Achieved full automation in one year.

Partner stated, "You brought us out of the dark ages, and neither you nor the firm missed a beat!"

Just as you use short sentences, use common words. They communicate quickly and are easy to understand. Stick to short and simple words wherever possible without sounding infantile. Of course, you need action words and phrases. But the real point is to stay away from obscure words.

> *Short words for short sentences*
> *help make short, gripping paragraphs:*
> *Good* for *short attention spans!*

Within your short paragraphs and short sentences, beware of name and acronym dropping, such as "Worked for Dr. A. Witherspoon in Sys. Gen. SNA 2.31." This is a good way to confuse (and lose) readers. Such coinage is too restricted to have validity outside the small circle of specialists to whom they speak. Your resume deserves the widest possible readership. Apart from the section on the resume that includes your educational qualifications, stay away from jargon unless you work in a highly technical field.

Voice and Tense

The voice you develop for your resume depends on a few important factors: getting a lot said in a small space; being factual; and packaging yourself in the best way.

The voice you use should be consistent throughout the resume. There is considerable disagreement among the experts about the best voice, and each of the leading options have both champions and detractors.

Sentences can be truncated (up to a point) by omitting pronouns—I, you, he, she, it, they—and articles—a or the. In fact, many authorities recommend the dropping of pronouns as a technique that both saves space and allows you to brag about yourself without seeming boastful. It gives the impression that another party is writing about you. Many people feel that to use the personal pronoun ("I automated the office") is naive and unprofessional. These experts suggest you use either the third person ("He automated the office") or leave the pronoun out altogether ("Automated office").

At the same time, there are others who recommend that you write in the first person because it makes you sound more human. Use whatever style works best for you. If you do use the personal pronoun, though, try not to use it in *every* sentence—it gets a little monotonous and takes up valuable space on the page.

A nice variation I have seen is a third-person voice used through the resume and then a final few words in the first person appended to the end of the resume, to give an insight into your values. Here is an example:

Regular third person:
James Sharpe is a professional who knows Technical Services from the ground up. He understands its importance in keeping a growing company productive, and takes pride in creating order in the chaos of technology.

Abbreviated third person:
Responsible for machine and system design, production scheduling, procurement and quality control. Redesigned conveyors and simplified maintenance while improving quality. Instituted a system of material control to account for all materials used.

First person:
I am accustomed to accepting responsibility and delegating authority; and am capable of working with, and through people at all levels. Am able to plan, organize, develop, implement, and supervise complex programs and special projects. All of this requires a good sense of humor and a personal dedication to producing timely, cost-effective results.

Many people mistake the need for professionalism in a resume with stiff-necked formality. The most effective tone is one that mixes both the conversational and the formal, just the way we do in our offices and on our jobs. The only overriding rule is to make it readable, so that another person can see the human being shining through the pages.

Length

If you are writing in longhand, it can be difficult to judge how your pages of writing will convert to typescript. As a rule of thumb, two and a half pages of double-spaced handwriting usually make one page of typescript.

The accepted rules for length are one page for every ten years of your experience. If you have more than twenty years under you belt, however, you won't want to appear to be too steeped in the annals of ancient history, and so will not want to exceed the two-page mark.

Occasionally a three- or four-page resume can be effective, but only when:

- You have been contacted directly by an employer about a specific position and have been asked to prepare a resume for that particular opportunity.
- An executive recruiter who is representing you determines that the exigencies of a particular situation warrant an extensive dossier. Usually, such a resume will be prepared exclusively by the recruiter.

You'll find that thinking too much about length considerations while you write will hamper you. Think instead of the story you have to tell, then layer fact upon fact until it is told. When that is done, you can go back and ruthlessly cut it to the bone.

Ask yourself these questions:

- Can I cut out any paragraphs?
- Can I cut out any sentences?
- Can I cut out any superfluous words?
- Where have I repeated myself?

If in doubt, cut it out—leave nothing but facts and action words!

And if you find at the end that you've cut out too much, you'll have the additional pleasure of reinstating text!

The Proofreading Checklist for Your Final Draft

There are really two proofing steps in the creation of a polished resume. The first you do at this point, to make sure that all the things that should be in are there—and that all the things that shouldn't, aren't. The final proofing is done after typesetting, and is addressed later in the book.

In the heat of the creative moment, it's easy to miss critical components or mistakenly include facts that give the wrong emphasis. Check your resume against these points:

Contact Information

- Is the pertinent personal data—name, address, and personal telephone number correct? (Later, when the resume is typed or printed, you will want to make sure that this personal data is on every page.)
- Is your business number omitted unless it is absolutely necessary and safe to include it?

Objectives

- Does your objective briefly state your employment goals without getting too specific and ruling you out of consideration for many jobs?
- If you gave a detailed objective (up to—but no more than—two sentences), does it focus on what you can bring to the employer, rather than what you want from the employer?
- Is your stated objective supported by the facts and accomplishments stated in the rest of your resume?

Summary

- If you choose to include a summary, is it no more than two or three sentences long?
- Does it include at least one substantial accomplishment that supports your employment goals?
- Does it include reference to some of your personality or behavioral traits that are critical to success in your field?

Body of Resume

- Is your most relevant and qualifying work experience prioritized throughout the resume to lend strength to your application?
- Have you avoided wasting space with inessential employer names and addresses?
- Have you been suitably discreet with the name of your current employer?
- Have you omitted any reference to reasons for leaving a particular job?
- Have you removed all references to past, current, or desired salaries?
- Have you removed references to your date of availability?

Education

- Is education placed in the appropriate position? (It should be at the beginning of the resume if you have little or no work experience; at the

end if you are established in your field and your practical experience now outweighs your degree.)
- Is your highest educational attainment shown first?
- Have you included professional courses that support your candidacy?

Chronology
- If you've done a chronological resume, is your work history stated in reverse chronological order, with the most recent employment coming at the head of the resume?
- Within this reverse chronology, does each company history start with details of your most senior position?
- Have you avoided listing irrelevant responsibilities or job titles?
- Does your resume emphasize the contributions, achievements, and problems you have successfully solved during your career? Is this content made prominent by underlining, bolding, italicizing, etc.?
- Does the body copy include at least one, and possibly two or three, laudatory third-party endorsements of your work?
- Have you avoided poor focus by eliminating all extraneous information? (This category includes anything that doesn't relate to your job objective, such as captaining the tiddlywinks team in kindergarten.)
- Have you included any volunteer or community service activities that can lend strength to your candidacy?
- Is the whole thing long enough to whet the reader's appetite for more details, yet short enough not to satisfy that hunger?
- Have you left out lists of reference and only included mention of the availability of references (if, of course, there is nothing more valuable to fill up the space)?
- Have you avoided treating your reader like a fool by highlighting the obvious (i.e., heading your resume, "RESUME")?

Writing Style
- Have you substituted short words for long words? And one word where previously there were two?
- Is your average sentence ten to twenty words? Have you made sure that any sentence of more than twenty words is shortened or broken into two sentences?
- Have you kept every paragraph under five lines, with many paragraphs considerably shorter?

- Do your sentences begin, wherever possible, with the powerful action verbs and phrases from earlier in the chapter and from the resume examples?
- If you are in a technical field, have you weeded out as much of the jargon as possible?

Crossing the T's, Dotting the I's

Before you have your resume typed or printed (a topic covered in the next chapter), you have to make sure that your writing is as clear as possible. Three things guaranteed to annoy resume readers are incorrect spelling, poor grammar, and improper syntax. Go back and check all these areas. If you feel uneasy about your resume's syntax, you had better get a third party involved.

An acquaintance of mine recently came up with an eminently practical solution to the "style" problem. She went around to the local library, waited for a quiet moment, and got into conversation with the librarian, who subsequently agreed to give her resume the old once-over for spelling, grammar, and syntax. You say you're on bad terms with the library because of all those overdue books? Surely you know someone whose opinion you trust in these matters. Enlist him or her. The point is that you must do everything you can to make the resume a "perfect" document before it is typed, printed, or copied.

It simply isn't possible for even the most accomplished professional writer to go directly from final draft to print, so don't try it. Your pride of authorship will blind you to the blemishes, and that's a self-indulgence you can't afford.

You need some distance from your creative efforts to gain detachment and objectivity. There is no hard and fast rule about how long it takes to come up with the finished product. Nevertheless, if you think you have finished, leave it alone as long as you can—at least overnight. Then you can come back to it fresh and read almost as if it were meeting your eyes for the first time.

More Than One Resume?

Do you need more than one type of resume? It depends. Some people have a background that qualifies them for more than one job. If this applies to you, the process is as simple as changing your objective for various employers and rewriting along the lines directed in this chapter.

There is a case for all of us having resumes in more than one format. I was once engaged in an outplacement experiment for a group of professionals. With just a little extra work, we developed chronological, functional, and combination resumes for everyone. The individuals concerned sent out the resume of their choice. Then, in those instances where there was no response, a different version of the resume was sent out. The result from just a different format: 8 percent more interviews.

What's Next?

Almost home now. Save your notes, early drafts, and, of course, the completed Questionnaire. This "legwork" represents essential material you'll need in updating or revising future versions of your resume.

6 | The Final Product

When it comes to clothes, style has a certain look. It has a feel that everyone recognizes but few can define accurately. Fortunately, with resumes, the situation is considerably simplified. There are definite rules to follow.

What Do You Mean I Need TWO Resumes?

One of these rules is that in today's job market you can't get by with just one perfect resume any more. Why not? Because an astounding 78 percent of resumes are read not by humans but by machines. Your resume may be an aesthetic marvel, beautiful to behold, but if it goes into the computer as gobbledy-gook, it won't do you much good. That's why you need two. This chapter will cover "the traditional" resume—the resume designed for human eyes. The other kind, the "computer-friendly" resume, is custom-designed to get through a computer scanner with data intact. It is such a hot topic in today's job market that I have devoted a separate chapter to it (see chapter 7, "Is Your Resume Computer-Friendly?"). Of course, the two kinds of resume do have certain basics in common. Let's start with those.

The Circular File

A lot of resumes get trashed without ever being properly read.

The average resume arrives on a desk with dozens of others, all of which require screening. Stand in the shoes of a day-in, day-out resume reader, and you can expect that your resume will get a maximum of thirty to forty seconds of initial attention. And that's only if it's laid out well and looks clear.

What are the biggest complaints about those resumes that reach the trash can in record time?

Impossible to read. They have too much information crammed into the space and are therefore very difficult to read and hard on the eyes.

Messy. They exhibit amateurish typing.

No coherence. Their layout is unorganized, illogical, and uneven. In other words, they look shoddy and slapdash—and who wants an employee like that?

Typos. They are riddled with misspellings.

Here are some tips garnered from the best resumes in America that will help yours rise above the rest.

Typewriter or Computer?

If you plan to be employable in the year 2000, you'd better wake up and smell the coffee—computer literacy is a must. Typing on typewriters doesn't cut it any more. Typing your resume or using a typing service is the equivalent of carving your resumes in tablets of stone. It looks old-fashioned, and it must be done from start to finish every time you need to send one to someone else or customize it for another purpose. If you cannot now prepare your resume in a computer, engage the services of a good word-processing outfit while you get up to speed.

The crucial difference between typing on a typewriter and word processing on a computer is the computer's ability to store information on a disk. This means that every resume can be immediately customized for every different job. A word-processing service will give you free (or very cheap) changes in these instances. You can target endless variations of your resumes to fit the special nuances of all the different jobs you come across in your search.

Once stored on disk, your entire series of resumes is ready for updating as long as you live. Logic and the short odds say that some fine day you will need to use them again. Hold onto the disks.

Hard Copy

With a computer, the printing unit is separate from the box that does the actual word processing. Is that important? Yes, because just as all typewriters are not created equal, neither are all printers; and while printers are not the business end of the machine, they are the end that business sees! When you use a computer or a word-processing service, insist that your letters are printed on a letter-quality printer or a laser printer; either of these will give you high-quality print. You must never accept what is known as dot matrix, thermal, or near-letter-quality (NLQ) printers, because they lack the razor sharpness you need. *Don't let anyone tell you otherwise—ever.*

If you use thermal, dot matrix, or near-letter-quality printers, IT COULD COST YOU THE JOB, today or next year. The reason: Companies are increasingly adopting new scanning technology, allowing a computer to look at a letter or resume (through a copier-type peripheral) and store the data in memory. So a growing number of companies will be storing your communications not on paper but on disk. Many scanners are incapable of reading the output of NLQ, thermal, and dot matrix printers.

Typefaces/fonts

If you are using a laser printer, remember—you don't have to use those boring old pica and elite typefaces that scream "typewriter." A laser printer gives you a vast choice of print styles and quality fonts. Business is rapidly coming to accept the likes of Bookman, New York, and Palatino as the norm, and these typefaces are only available through laser printer output or professional typesetting. By the way, when choosing your typeface, stay away from heavy and bold for your body copy (although you may choose to take a more dramatic approach with key words or headlines). Bold type takes up too much space, and if it needs to be copied on the receiving end, it can blur and look dreadful. Avoid "script" faces similar to handwriting; while they look attractive to the occasional reader, they are harder on the eyes of the person who reads any amount of business correspondence. Capitalized copy is tough on the eyes too; we tend to think it makes a powerful statement when all it does for the reader is cause eye strain.

How to Brighten the Page

Once you decide on a typeface, stick with it, because more than one on a page looks confusing. You can do plenty to liven up the visual impact of the page within the variations of the typeface you have chosen.

Most typefaces come in a selection of regular, bold, and italic. Good traditional-style resumes try to take advantage of this—they can vary the impact of key words with italics, underline important phrases, or use boldface or capital letters in titles for additional emphasis. (Computer-friendly resumes, by contrast, keep type variations to a minimum.)

You will notice from the examples in this book that the best resumes pick two or three typographical variations and stick with them. For example, a writer who wants to emphasize personality traits might italicize only those words or phrases that describe these aspects; this way the message gets a double fixing in the reader's mind.

Proofing

When you have the typed or typeset resume in hand, you *must* proofread it. Typists are not perfect. Check everything, from beginning to end.

- Is everything set up the way you want it?
- Are there any typographical errors?
- Is all the punctuation correct?
- Has everything been underlined, capitalized, bolded, italicized, and indented, exactly as you specified?

Once you read the resume, try your best to get someone else to review it as well. A third party will always provide more objectivity than you can, and can catch errors you might miss.

Appearance Checklist

- Have you remembered that the first glance and the first feel of your resume can make a powerful impression?
- Have you used only one side of the page?
- If you have employed more than one page for your resume, did you check to make sure that your name, address, and telephone number are on every page?

- If more than one page, did you paginate your resume ("1 of 2" at the bottom of the first page, and so on)?

Choosing Your Paper

Quality and care have a look and a feel to them that are loud and clear. Quality paper always makes a favorable impression on the person holding the page.

Beyond the aesthetics, there are plenty of reasons to use quality paper for your copies. The right paper will take the ink better, giving you clean, sharp print resolution.

While you should not skimp on paper cost, neither should you be talked into buying the most expensive available. Indeed, in some fields (health care and education come to mind), too ostentatious a paper can cause a negative impression. The idea is to create a feeling of understated quality.

Paper can come in different weights and textures. Good resume-quality paper has a weight designation of between 16 and 25 lbs. Lighter, and you run the risk of appearing nonchalant, unconcerned about the personal "I-printed-this-especially-for-you" aspect of the resume. Heavier, and the paper is unwieldy, like light cardboard.

As for color, white is considered to be the prime choice. Cream is also acceptable, and I'm assured that some of the pale pastel shades can be both attractive and effective. Personally, I think that most professionals just don't show up in the best light when dressed in pink—call me old-fashioned if you will.

Such pastel shades were originally used to make resumes stand out. But now that everyone is so busy standing out from the crowd in Magenta and Passionate Puce, you might find it more original to stand out in white or cream. Both colors reflect the clean-cut, corporate conservatism of our time. White and cream are straightforward, no-nonsense colors.

Cover letter stationery should always match the color and weight of your resume. To send a white cover letter—even if it is written on your personal stationery—with a cream resume is gauche, and detracts from the powerful statement you are trying to make.

A good idea, in fact, is to print some cover-letter stationery when you produce your finished resume. The letterhead should be in the same typeface and on the same kind of paper, and should copy the contact data from your resume. With the advent of word processing, it can take less than five minutes to create the letterhead of your choice.

Copies

Every resume should be printed on standard, 8 1/2" x 11" (letter-size) paper. If the original is set up like this, you will be able to take it to a good-quality copy shop for photocopying. Technology has improved so much in this area that as long as the latest equipment is used, you should have no problems. (Bear in mind, though, that the computer-friendly resume is always an original—to ensure a clean scan.)

If you choose to have your resume printed—rather than photocopied—for whatever reason, you must go to a multi-lith or photo-offset printer. Both produce really smart, professional copies. Of the two—unless you are printing more than two-hundred copies—photo-offset will be proportionately more expensive. Shop around for prices, as printers vary quite dramatically in their price structures. While you are shopping, ask to see samples of their resume work—they are bound to have some. If not, keep shopping.

Word-processing services can produce not only the resume and cover letter stationery but also the required number of copies of both, as can a multi-lith or offset printer. There are both local and national companies that can provide these services.

The Final Checklist

- Have you used a good-quality paper, with a weight of between 16 and 25 lbs.?
- Does the paper size measure 8 1/2" x 11"?
- Have you used white, off-white, or cream-colored paper?
- If your resume is more than one page, have you stapled the pages together (one staple in the top left-hand corner)?
- Is your cover letter written on stationery that matches your resume?

7 | Is Your Resume Computer-Friendly?

Computers have infiltrated human resources offices across America. Here's how they'll affect your job search.

PART ONE: Is Your Resume Scanner-Friendly?

Review Your Resume

You say you already have a great resume. After all, it helped you land your most recent job, and the one before that, and the one before that. Now all you have to do is update it—add your latest job title, your responsibilities, the beginning and end dates of your employment, special projects you worked on, advanced training you received, and the like—and your resume will be ready to send in the mail, or put into your briefcase.

Right?

Well, it may not be that simple. If your resume looks exactly as it did a few years ago, then merely updating the information and keeping the old format may not be good enough. The resume that opened corporate doors for you five years ago, or even last year, may not work for you now. In fact, it *may not even get read.*

Resumes in the Computer Age

Computers are being used to scan and store your resume electronically; they are being used to read help-wanted advertisements on Web site databases, and to search the resume banks on those same Web sites. In fact, the next HR professional to scan your resume is likely to be a PC or Mac instead of a mortal. The problem is that computers look at things differently than we do, which creates the new challenge of making your resume attractive to digital eyes.

Since the mid-1980s, when the technology was first introduced, the number of companies using computer-based automated tracking systems has climbed steadily. The technology has become so pervasive that by mid-1997, 85 percent of companies surveyed had some sort of automated resume-tracking system in place.

The Way It Was

It seems like only yesterday that most companies manually read, assessed, coded, and filed all of the resumes they received. When a position opened up, an HR representative would look through all the files for likely prospects. The most promising candidates would then be invited for an interview.

In it's day, this was a pretty good system. It was especially nice when you, the applicant, made the short list of prospects. Of course, sometimes the manual system didn't work in your favor. Once in a while, an HR professional who didn't like your choice of stationery, or thought that your alma mater wasn't covered in quite enough ivy, would code your resume unfavorably or even put it in the circular file. Or perhaps a recruiter thought of you immediately when a job opened up, but couldn't lay his hands on your resume quick enough to call you before the position was filled—perhaps because another supervisor, who was winging her way to Europe, had the resume in her briefcase.

Often, under the manual tracking system, resumes were misplaced, miscoded, or misfiled, never to be found again. Frequently, a perfectly good resume was buried under so much paper that it just wasn't worth anybody's trouble to unearth it. It used to be common to trash all resumes every six months.

The problems with manual resume tracking became especially apparent when corporate cutbacks caused companies to reduce their HR staff. With three people doing the job of ten, it simply wasn't possible to access, code, file, and retrieve resumes in an orderly, effective fashion. Corporations sometimes missed their chance to hire the best candidate for the job because the appropriate resume didn't make it to the top of the heap, out of the file cabinet, or sometimes even out of the envelope.

So What's New?

These days, solicited and unsolicited resumes alike are increasingly likely to be filed in electronic databases rather than in metal cabinets. Under this system, no matter how large the computerized stack of resumes, any computer user can pull up appropriate ones with a few keystrokes or clicks of a mouse. The challenge for you is to get your resume into a shape and style that:

- Can be scanned, digitized, and stored electronically, once received through the mail.
- Can be transmitted, via e-mail, to specific individuals or companies.
- Can be loaded onto public resume databases.

In the first instance, your printed/hard copy resume would wing through the mail to a company. There, a functionary in the HR department runs it through a scanner (which, if you haven't seen one yet, looks just like a small copying machine); this digitizes your resume and allows it to be stored electronically in the company's database.

In the second instance, you create a digitized resume yourself. You use this electronic/digitized version of your resume to e-mail to companies at their Web sites, to specific executives at their e-mail addresses, and to log it into the proliferating array of resume banks. We'll discuss digitized resume formats in greater detail later in this chapter.

The Computer Recruiter

What should you know about the technology that just might be responsible for deciding whether or not you're invited to that next job interview?

Like their human counterparts, computers have their good traits and their bad. The good part is that computers don't care what school you went to, whether or not you're married, or how old you are. In a computerized search for qualified candidates, there's no room for human prejudice or error. Your name either pops up or it doesn't. Either way, it's nothing personal; it's strictly an automated decision. The bad news is that, if you're using a traditional resume that isn't computer-friendly (and, as you'll see, most traditional resumes aren't), your name probably won't pop up. A resume that was perfectly fine before automated tracking and the advent of the Internet will most likely leave you in the dust today.

New Resume Rules

If you want to impress a human recruiter before he or she even reads your resume, make sure that your envelope matches your stationery, that the address is well-typed, and that the layout catches the eye. Similarly, if you want to impress a computerized recruiter, you want to first be confident that optical character recognition (OCR) software can properly read the font in which your resume was written. This is because resumes are scanned, not typed, into databases, because scanning is a quicker and more efficient method. A computer can scan a resume in a couple of minutes. The danger is that if your resume was constructed to fit the old rules of resume writing (the more eye-catching, the better), the scanner and OCR software may get confused and miss some critical information.

The human resources person who is assigned to check the resume once it's scanned may or may not have the time, or the know-how, to undo the damage; he or she may not even notice that critical elements are missing or distorted. It's therefore your responsibility to make sure the computer scans your resume properly. The rules that apply to making your resume scannable will also apply to the creation of your electronic resume; again, we'll discuss this later in the chapter.

Keep It Simple

Here's how you can help the computer (that is, the scanner and OCR software) do its job.

- Always send a clean, crisp, original resume. Even photocopies that look fine to your eye may be too fuzzy to scan.
- Put your name on the first line of your resume, with nothing else before it. If you put your address first, then your new moniker might well be "555 Bayville Drive!"
- Use a laser jet rather than a dot matrix printer so that you get the best possible print quality.
- When choosing a typeface, stick to common ones, such as Times, Universe, Palatino, Optima, Courier, Futura, ITC Bookman, and New Century Schoolbook. Avoid exotic or serif typefaces that the OCR software might confuse or might not recognize.
- Keep the point sizes between 10 and 14. Type that is too large or too small may not scan properly.
- If you want to use boldface, save it for headings. While most OCR software can read boldface, some can't, so don't take the risk of using it for your name, address, or telephone number.

- Leave out decorative lines, particularly vertical lines. Or, if you use them, do so judiciously, leaving at least a quarter of an inch of space around them. Otherwise, you're liable to confuse the software, which often can't tell the difference between lines and letters.

Here are some things that are guaranteed to make your resumes computer-unfriendly and that you should always avoid:

- Double columns and other complicated layouts. The scanner can only read from left to right—and it's not going to appreciate your creativity.
- Colored paper. Use white or light beige paper; save the pink and blue stuff for personal letters announcing your new job. A key to scannability is to get the greatest possible amount of contrast between the background and the letters.
- Odd-sized paper. You should always use 8 1/2 x 11-inch sheets.
- Graphics, shading, ellipses, brackets, or parentheses.
- Italics, script, or underlining.
- Compressing letters. It isn't worth cramming a lot of information onto one page if the computer can't scan it.
- Stapling, folding, or faxing your resume. Send your resume, unstapled and unfolded, in a 9 x 12-inch envelope—or hand-deliver it.

Getting the Computer's Attention

If you've taken care to update your resume so that the computer can read it, the next step is to be sure the computer can find you when it's looking for somebody with your skills.

A computer isn't able to interpret your resume and make judgments about your suitability—you have to convince it. And the way to do that is by using keywords.

Here's the Key

A keyword is a word or phrase the software will search for when looking for job candidates. It is any label that can be used to describe you, or the job. The keywords are first chosen by the software user.

Also known as "talents," keywords are not action words like "oversaw," "initiated," and "installed," with which we've all saturated resumes in the past. They are nouns used to label the job and yourself. They encompass technical jargon, specific skills that relate to the job, degrees you hold, job titles, personal traits, and other buzzwords.

If you're in doubt about which keywords to include on your resume, then check the classifieds for positions similar to the one you're looking for, and take note of which nouns crop up repeatedly—skills, traits, and so on. Keep a running list of possibilities from which you can pick and choose, depending on the job you're applying for. Also, be open to collecting new keywords while reading the want ads (or during interviews) to add to your resume. If employers are looking for an Engineer of Excellence with a diploma in Delightfulness who can attack a Wonderwidget to a Maximachine, then those are your keywords!

How to Use Keywords

Of course, it behooves you to make sure that your keywords describe who you are and what you know, and that you're not just fudging it. Telling the computer anything it might want to hear, regardless of whether it's fact or fiction, isn't the best policy. At worst, you could tip off a prospective employer who might wonder why somebody with an engineering degree is also an expert in education, psychology, business, theater, law, and medicine.

Scanning software has limits on how many keywords it can retain, so keep the list down to a reasonable length—say, eighty words or so. And make sure the most important words go first. The scanning software won't weight your placement of keywords, but the subsequent human eyes will.

The art of making computer-friendly resumes is still brand new, and we are all feeling our way, to a certain extent. One neat technique that people are just starting to use (and are apparently finding very effective) is to place a box filled with applicable keywords/talents that might not appear in the body of your resume either near the top or at the bottom of your resume. There is absolutely no hard and fast rule on this yet, but you might find including it at the bottom of a resume less intrusive. For example, here's the talent box used by a HR professional who was able to reveal an additional bunch of skills, and make her resume more computer-friendly.

> Talents: team leader, people and communication skills, hardware needs evaluation, database management, client orientation, word-processing, spreadsheets, arbitration, manual writing, union negotiation, downsizing.

Part Two: Is Your Resume Internet-Friendly?

Is the Internet the answer to a job seeker's prayer, or the emperor's new suit of clothes? Some tout it as a speedy way to end your job hunt, since it gives you global exposure. ("But," you say, "I only want to work in Michigan!") Others discount the Internet, claiming you have about one chance in a hundred of getting a job this way. Neither view is right, the issue isn't that simple or clear-cut, since little in the modern world of work is unarguably right or wrong.

The most practical way to look at the Internet, in the context of your job hunt, is as a means of communication that simply gives you a handful of new ways to get in contact with potential employers and headhunters. You can:

- Meet and talk electronically with other job hunters, or even job hunting and career experts.
- Network with your professional peers in newsgroups. Newsgroups are ongoing discussion groups with a narrow focus aimed at people who share a common interest. There are newsgroups for every profession, from accountants to zoologists.
- Approach potential employers through their own Web sites. This method may get your resume closer scrutiny, since the flow of applicants online is much lighter that through traditional methods. By the same token, you might also get a much swifter response, since your manipulation of the new technology can tag you as a more potentially desirable employee. Remember that even if a company has job openings but isn't advertising specifically for your skill sets, you can still query it.
- Scan the job banks. These are nothing more than the help-wanted section of newspapers published in an electronic medium. Instead of reading the ads for an hour, your computer can generate matching jobs in seconds or minutes, which makes life easier for you.
- Load your resume into a resume bank, which functions just like HELP AVAILABLE ads in your local newspaper. Although in the past I have been strongly against advertising your availability in print, since no employer or headhunter has the time or inclination to read these ads, using this same technique in this new medium changes the picture in

two ways. First, the VP of Human Resources for your local First National Bank is still unlikely to peruse these data banks, but he now has electronic servants who will. Second, headhunters do scan the resume banks as yet another way of digging up that hard-to-find professional for a client.

The electronic world can give you a number of practical ways to pursue your job hunt. But keep in mind that the headhunters use this new medium as just another way of completing a job search—and you should do the same.

The rest of this chapter will concern itself with how electronic resumes can help you in your job search.

The Technical Side of an Electronic Resume

The oldest, most common, and soon-to-be outmoded method of compiling an electronic resume is to write and save it in a text format (often referred to as ASCII). The benefit of this format is that there are no formatting commands, so anyone can read the document, regardless of the software application/program they are using. You can also cut and paste parts of a text document into the information boxes you'll find on many resume bank Web sites. To create a text/ASCII format resume, create a new resume in whatever application that you are using (or make a copy of an existing one). Then, as you exit the document, us the "Save As" option to save it in text/ASCII format. Depending on the application you are using, the computer may advise you that your actions will destroy the formatting; ignore the warning and save it as text/ASCII anyway.

After this, your resume will now look like a dog's dinner. Unfortunately, there are only a few things you can do to improve the look of a text resume. You can use a text editor to edit your resume to look more like your real resume. Since e-mail allows no more than seventy characters to a line, you will most likely have to reformat your document. Similarly, if you have created space on your resume using the tab key, you'll want to redo it using the space bar instead. Apart from these guidelines, the dos and don'ts are the same that apply to making your resume scanner-friendly, which were addressed earlier in the chapter.

HTML

HTML is the acronym for Hypertext Markup Language, the wave of the electronic resume future. HTML allows you to create sharply designed and formatted resumes. It does this by placing your wording between tags, parenthesis, and slashes that indicate certain kinds of formatting. These tags allow another person's (read: human resource recruiter) electronic browser to translate the accompanying data into words, graphics, format, and even color, either on a screen or as a printout. This makes HTML extremely useful in electronic resume writing since, when printed, your electronic resume will stack up against traditionally printed and mailed resumes.

HTML uses two different types of tags: those that identify and format the content of your resume so that it looks good, and those that allow you to condense your resume into its critical essentials, so that the search engines other people use when searching the resume databases will pick you out of the crowd. These condensed essentials, called metatags, will not be seen on your actual resume, and are only visible to the search engine (read: the software that searches the resume database). While HTML coding might only seem like a good idea for computer science majors, it is in fact getting easier and easier to create your own HTML resume. (You might even remember, if not admit to, an era when "WYSIWYG" seemed equally obscure.) Many current word processors allow you to save text in HTML format, and software developers have made a whole bunch of tools available to HTML wanna-bes.

Want HTML to be even easier? Come visit me on the Monster Board at www.monster.com, in the *Knock 'em Dead* resume area at www.knockemdead.com, and at the Career City website at www.careercity.com, and you'll find complete sample code for this format on screen just waiting to be downloaded, *and* it's absolutely free. Download the HTML format and you will literally be able to fill in the blanks, just put your own words between the tags, and *voila*, you'll have one pretty neat-looking HTML resume.

Final Considerations

One issue to consider is that of confidentiality. As with any distribution medium, once the resume is out of your hands, you no longer have control over what happens to it. So it's wise to evaluate the relative compatibility of your needs and how they match the operational realities of the different databases.

For example, if you don't want people to know where you live, or to be able to contact you directly at home or work (it's never a good idea to have a work contact number on a resume), act accordingly. Get a voice mail service for telephone calls. Don't imagine for a moment that recruiters are going to use your e-mail address, though; if you look like a good fit, the phone is still the quickest means of cutting to the chase. Conversely, if e-mail is your only means of contact, you can expect to miss hearing about a few opportunities. And just as you would never use your current employer's time or phone to pursue a job contact, don't use their e-mail either. Depending on where you live, it is quite legal for an employer to monitor your e-mail.

If you are employed, identify your current employer as "a major bank," "a mid-sized service company," or "an international pharmaceutical conglomerate." Not only will you not get unwanted calls at work, but you won't run the risk of your current boss learning of your search before it suits your needs.

Other confidentiality considerations can be answered at each individual site. When you get to a particular Web site, one of the first things you will do is to look for FAQs (frequently asked questions) to find out:

- Who can access this database?
- Can you block access to certain employers or people?
- Are you notified when someone downloads your resume?

Apart from the confidentiality issue, you will want to know if you can get access to your resume to update it, change it, or delete it. If not, you'll want to know the procedure for achieving each of these ends. Some resume banks will charge you for updates.

Internet Myths

This question of updating your resume brings us to three areas of Internet lore you need to be aware of:

1. You will be told that a *good* database will delete your resume after three to six months if you don't update it. This is absolute drivel! Constant resume updating is driven by commercial concerns. No one on God's earth needs a resume updated every ninety days! The other argument for deleting resumes that aren't updated is that, once employed, you won't want to get calls from other employers. Again, absolute drivel! Happily employed or not, wouldn't you rather hear about exciting

new jobs that fit your skill sets, and have the opportunity to pursue or reject them, *rather than never hear about them at all?* Of course you'll want to hear about every opportunity, if not for today, then for tomorrow, if your current employment no longer suits your career needs, or your company is about to downsize. You want to get your resume out there, period! And there's no reason to limit your resumes to services that limit your exposure.

2. You will be told that a one-page resume is no longer the rule. Now, while one of the strengths of the Internet as a publishing medium is that space is limitless, that does not in any way affect the dictum that when it comes to resumes, shorter is better. Yes, your resume can be longer, but that won't stop human eyes from getting bored by the end of page two, just as resume screeners have always done. So no matter who tells you this, use your common sense and keep it short and succinct.

3. You will also be told to put your resume on only two to four resume databases, because employers are frustrated at finding the same candidates at every database they check. Excuse me? Am employer can check a hundred databases, but you can only use a maximum of four? Here are the facts: as an employer, if I like your background, I'll be happy to find you. If I like your background and I find you in a number of places, it will make recruiting you more difficult since I'll likely have more competition from other employers. On the other hand, if I keep finding your resume and you *don't* match my needs, it shouldn't matter if I find you in two or two hundred databases.

If you want to take advantage of the Internet as a means of resume creation and/or distribution, there are services out there that will take care of this business for you for a fee. If you choose to do this, there are a handful of questions you'll need to answer for yourself to make an informed decision.

- Exactly what is the service? Will they write the resume for you? Will it be in text, HTML, or multimedia? (You really don't need multimedia unless you are in graphic design and want to show your command of the new technology, in which case you'll have to walk the walk and talk the talk. On the other hand, HTML is state of the art and will show you in your best light.)
- How much will everything cost?
- Is there a charge to edit or update your resume once it is created, or to create a slightly different resume that emphasizes other skill sets? Once you have been in the job market for a few years, you're probably

qualified for more than one job, which means that you'll need a separate resume that will highlight those skills.

- How is your resume marketed? Find out how many sites the company will post your resume on, and whether or not they will repost it if that site trashes your resume after a predetermined period of time.
- What, if anything, will you be charged if you get a job as a result of the service?

To get you started with these services, try:

- Resumes on the Web   www.resweb.com
- Job Center   www.jobcenter.com
- Resume Creator   www.ipt.com/internetworking/create.htm
- The Resume Place   www.resume-place.com/jobs
- Job Lynx   www.joblynx.com
- AAA Resume Posting   www.infi.net/-resume
- Superior Resumes, Inc.   www.mindtrust.com

Internet Resume Etiquette

Sending out your resume through another medium (e-mail rather than regular mail) requires that you adhere to a few simple rules if you want that resume to be seen and acted upon.

1. While some companies will advertise their positions electronically, they don't all accept electronic resume submissions. So when you see a position and want to apply for it, read the instructions carefully and follow them.
2. If you are applying for a job listed in a job bank, it will always be headed with a job title, and will often have a reference number as well. Be sure to use these in your cover letter. For example:

Ref: Internal Auditor, Ref #123, Monster Board Job Bank

Make reference to the same in the first paragraph of your cover letter. For example:

Dear Ms. Jones:

   I have long admired the work of Pzifer, Inc., so when I came across your ad for an Internal Auditor (Ref #123) on the Monster Board Job Bank, it took me two seconds to decide I had to throw my hat in the ring.

3. When you send a resume in more traditional circumstances, you will typically send two documents: the cover letter and the resume. When e-mailing two documents, they are guaranteed to become separated; so send the cover letter and resume as one document. It is also courteous and wise to mention that you will forward a copy of your communication through the mail. Remember to do so! Of course, your mail version will be compatible with its format: that is two repeat documents, a cover letter and a resume.

Still Confused?

If you are still confused, ask. Most people on the Web are new to it, and you'll find that nearly everyone (except some of those old-time elitist Web Neanderthals) is pleasant and helpful.

   You might also use these in-print resources:

- *The Guide to Internet Job Searching* by Margaret Riley is published by VGM. This is the best book on the topic at the moment, written by a woman who has my professional respect and that of the rest of the career management community. She also has a Web site (see below).
- *Career Crossroads* by Crispin and Mehler. This self-published book reviews about five hundred employment-related sites.

   Both of these books may be difficult to find in book stores. But since both organizations have Web sites, you can get purchasing information directly from them.

   On the Internet, try:

- The Riley Guide   www.jobtrak.com

This is Margaret Riley's site. She is a very knowledgeable resource. Do her and yourself a favor by reading her FAQs carefully.

- Career Crossroads   mmc@careerxroads.com

Double Trouble

Now that you know how to get the computer's attention, be sure you don't get the computer's attention more than once because you've sent one too many resumes.

Suppose that, in the old days, you wanted to work for Big Boston Publishing. You might have sent one resume to the Editorial Director in application for a job as an editorial assistant; another to the Operations Manager, touting yourself as the best warehouse worker ever; and still another to the Customer Service Manager, revealing your years of intensive telemarketing experience.

So why not send three resumes to Big Boston Publishing now? Because the resume-tracking computer in the Human Resources Department is a know-it-all and a tattletale.

While the human supervisors of old might have read their copies of your resumes and never compared notes, the computer is all-knowing. With too many resumes and too many work histories in its files, the computer is likely to peg you as somebody who is at best unfocused about his or her career direction—and at worst a pathological liar.

If you do want to submit more than one resume in application for multiple jobs and you're unsure of whether or not the company is using a computerized tracking system, minimize the risks. Be sure that you don't follow up the resume that sells you as an experienced reference book editor with another that delineates your years of experience as an expert book packer.

8 | Cover Letters

Do you ever receive junk mail? Of course you do. Who doesn't?

Junk mail. Tons of it have probably made it into your mailbox over the years. Now, what do you do with the stuff marked "Occupant"? Either junk it without reading, or junk it after a quick glance. That's why they call it junk mail! It never gets the attention a personal letter does.

The days when you could dash your resume off to "Personnel," with a clear conscience and no personal note, are long gone. It will be read by the lowest of the low, someone who probably can't even spell "professional." You will be consigning it to the mass resume graveyard that all other impersonally addressed resumes reach.

Your cover letter is the personalizing factor in the presentation of an otherwise essentially impersonal document—your resume. A good cover letter sets the stage for the reader to accept your resume as something special.

So your first effort with a cover letter is to find an individual to whom you can address it. That shows you have focus, and guarantees that a specific individual will open and read it. It also means you have someone to ask for by name when you do your follow-up—important when you are interview hunting.

Your target is someone who can either hire you or refer you to someone who can—and management rather than personnel offers you a much better chance of achieving that goal.

Your cover letter will either be sent to someone as a result of a prior conversation, or sent "cold"—with no prior conversation. You will see how to handle both these eventualities as we progress through the chapter.

When the envelope is opened, your cover letter is the first thing seen. It can make an indelible first impression. I'm not saying that it will get you the job (or even land you the interview), but it will help you along the way by getting that resume read with something akin to serious attention.

The higher up the professional ladder you climb, the more important cover letters become. For the person using written communication in the execution of daily duties (and who doesn't these days?), this letter becomes a valuable vehicle for demonstrating needed job skills.

Cover Letter Rules

Cover letters are brief, never more than a page. Write more, and you will be labeled as an unorganized windbag. You should always try to follow accepted business letter protocol, with the date, employer's name and address first. Space can be at such a premium, however, that you can dispense with the formality and begin with a normal salutation: "Dear _____." Stick with the protocol when you can, ignore it when you have to.

The following four steps will help you create the body of the letter.

Step One

Grab your reader's attention. Do this by using quality stationery. If you don't have personal stationery, use some of the sheets you have bought to have your resume printed on. That way, letter and resume will match and give an impression of balance and continuity. Basic business letters should be laid out according to the accepted standards, like this:

[YOUR ADDRESS/LETTERHEAD
AND TELEPHONE NUMBER]

[DATE]

[ADDRESSEE ADDRESS]
[SALUTATION]

Recently I have been researching the leading local companies in data communications. My search has been for companies that are respected in the field, and who provide ongoing training programs. The name of DataLink Products keeps coming up as a top company.

I am an experienced voice and data communications specialist with a substantial background in IBM environments. If you have an opening for someone in this area you will see that my resume demonstrates a person of unusual dedication, efficiency, and drive.

My experience and achievements include:

- The complete redesign of a data communications network, projected to increase efficiency companywide by some 12 percent.
- The installation and troubleshooting of a Defender II call-back security system for a dial-up network.

I enclose a copy of my resume, and look forward to examining any of the ways you feel my background and skills would benefit DataLink Products. While I prefer not to use my employer's time taking personal calls at work, with discretion you can reach me at 213/555-5555 to initiate contact. Let's talk!

Yours,

[SIGNATURE]
[TYPED NAME]

Step Two

Generate interest with the content. You do this by addressing the letter to someone by name and quickly explaining what you have to offer: The first sentence grabs attention, the rest of the paragraph gives the reader the old one-two punch. The rule is: Say it strong and say it straight; don't pussy-foot around.

A little research, for example, can get your letter off to a fast start.

> I came across the enclosed article in *Newsweek* and thought it might interest you. It encouraged me to do a little research on your company. The research convinced me of two things: You are the kind of people I want to be associated with, and I have the kind of qualifications you can use.

Of course, in the real world, we don't all apply for jobs with companies that are featured in the big magazines. Here are some other examples:

I have been following the performance of your fund in *Mutual Funds Newsletter*. The record over the last three years shows strong portfolio management. Considering my experience with one of your competitors, I know I could make significant contributions.

Recently, I have been researching the local _____ industry. My search has been for companies that are respected in the field and that provide ongoing training programs. The name _____ keeps coming up as a top company.

With the scarcity of qualified and motivated *(your desired job title)* that exists today, I felt sure that it would be valuable for us to communicate.

I would like the opportunity to put my _____ years of _____ experience to work for _____.

Within the next few weeks I will be moving from New York to San Francisco. Having researched the companies in my field in my new home town, I know that you are the people I want to talk to.

The state of the art in _____ changes so rapidly that it is tough for most professionals to keep up. I am the exception. I am eager to bring my experience to bear for your company.

I am applying for a position with your company because I know you will find my background and drive interesting.

This letter and the attached resume are in application for employment with _____.

If you are looking for summer jobs.

In six weeks I shall be finishing my second year at John Carroll University. I am interested in working for your firm during the summer because...

As the summer season gets under way, I know you will be looking for extra help.

I am a high school senior looking for some real world experience during the summer break.

I am very interested in becoming one of your summer interns.

If you are writing as the result of a referral, say so and quote the person's name if appropriate:

Our mutual colleague, John Stanovich, felt my skills and abilities would be valuable to your company.

The manager of your San Francisco branch, Pamela Bronson, has suggested I contact you regarding the opening for a _____.

I received your name from Henry Charles last week. I spoke to Mr. Charles regarding career opportunities with _____ and he suggested I contact you. In case the resume he forwarded is caught up in the mails, I enclose another.

Arthur Gold, your office manager and my neighbor, thought I should contact you about the upcoming opening in your accounting department.

If you are writing as the result of a newspaper advertisement, you should mention both the publication and the date—and remember not to abbreviate advertisement to "ad."

I read your advertisement in the *Daily Gotham* on October 6th and after researching your company, felt I had to write.

I am responding to your recent advertisement offering the opportunity to get involved with automated accounting practices.

In re: Your advertisement in the *Columbus Dispatch* on Sunday, the eighth of November. As you will notice, my entire background matches your requirements.

Your notice regarding a _____ in the *Detroit News* caught my eye, and your company name caught my attention.

This letter and attached resume is in response to your advertisement in the *Boston Globe.*

If you are writing to an executive search firm:

(**Note:** In a cover letter to executive search firms, unlike any other circumstances, you *must* mention your salary and, if appropriate, your willingness to relocate.)

I am forwarding my resume to you because I understand you specialize in representing clients in the _____ field.

Please find the enclosed resume. As a specialist in the _____ field, I felt you might be interested in the skills of a _____.

Among your many clients may be one or two who are seeking a candidate for a position as a _____.

My salary is in the mid-20s, with appropriate benefits. I would be willing to relocate for the right opportunity.

Step Three

Now turn that interest into desire. First, make a bridge that ties you to a general job category or work area. It starts with phrases like:

I am writing because…

My reason for contacting you is…

This letter is to introduce me and to explore any need you might have in the _____ area.

…should this be the case, you may be interested to know…

If you are seeking a _____, you will be interested to know…

I would like to talk to you about your personnel needs and my ability to contribute to your department's goals.

If you have an opening for someone in this area, you will see
that my resume demonstrates a person of unusual dedication,
efficiency, and drive.

Then call attention to your merits with a short paragraph that highlights one
or two of your special contributions or achievements:

I have an economics background (Columbia) and a strong
analytical approach to market fluctuations. This combination has
enabled me consistently to pick the new technology flotations
that are the backbone of the growth-oriented mutual fund.

Similar statements applicable to your area of expertise will give your letter
more personal punch. Include any qualifications, contributions, and attributes
that qualify you as someone with talent to offer. If an advertisement (or a
conversation with a potential employer) revealed an aspect of a particular job
opening that is not addressed in your resume, it can easily be covered in the
cover letter.

I notice from your advertisement that audio and video training
experience would be a plus. In addition to the qualifications
stated in my enclosed resume, I have over five years' experience
writing and producing sales and management training materials
in both these media.

Whether you bullet or list your achievements in short, staccato sentences
will be determined in part by the amount of space available to you on the page.

Step Four

Here's where your letter turns that desire into action. You want to make the
reader dash straight to your resume, then call you in for an interview. You
achieve this with brevity.

Your one-page letter shouldn't be longer than four or five paragraphs, or
two hundred words. Leave the reader wanting more. This final step tells the
reader that you want to talk. It explains when, where, and how you can be
contacted. Then tell the reader that you intend to follow up at a certain point in
time if contact has not been established by then. This can encourage a decision
on the reader's part to initiate action, which is what you want.

Useful phrases include:

I look forward to discussing our mutual interests further.

It would be a pleasure to give you more data about my qualifications and experience.

I will be in your area around the 20th, and will call you prior to that date to arrange a meeting.

I hope to speak with you further and will call the week of the 20th to follow up.

The chance to meet with you would be a privilege and a pleasure. To this end I will call you on the 20th.

I look forward to speaking with you further and will call in the next few days to see when our schedules will permit a face-to-face meeting.

May I suggest a personal meeting where you can have the opportunity to examine the person behind the resume?

My credentials and achievements are a matter of record that I hope you will examine in depth when we meet.

I look forward to examining any of the ways you feel my background and skills would benefit your organization. I look forward to hearing from you.

Resumes help you sort out the probables from the possibles, but they are no way to judge the true caliber of an individual. I should like to meet you and demonstrate that I have the personality that makes for a successful _____.

My resume can highlight my background and accomplishments. My drive, willingness and manageability, however, can come out only during a face-to-face meeting. With this in mind, I shall call you on the 20th, if I don't hear from you before.

After reading my resume, you will know something about my background. Yet you will still need to determine whether I am the one to help with the current problems and challenges. I would like an interview to discuss my ability to contribute.

I am anxious to meet and discuss any potential opportunities further. I will make myself available for an interview at a time convenient to you.

I expect to be in your area on Tuesday and Wednesday of next week and wonder which day would be best for you. I will call to find out.

With my training and hands-on experience, I know I can contribute to your company, and want to speak with you about it in person. When may we meet?

I feel certain that I can contribute and that I can convince you I can. I look forward to a meeting at your convenience.

You can reach me at 202/555-1212 to arrange an interview. I know that your time investment in meeting with me will be amply repaid.

Thank you for your time and consideration. I hope to hear from you shortly.

May I call you for an interview in the next few days?

I am sure that our mutual interests will be served by speaking further, and am convinced a personal meeting will assure you of my ability, willingness, and manageability. I look forward to meeting with you.

A brief phone call will establish whether or not we have mutual interest. Recognizing the demands of your schedule, I will make that call within the week.

As many employed people are concerned about their resumes going astray, you may wish to add:

> In the meantime, I would appreciate my application being treated as confidential, as I am currently employed.

Just as you worked to get the opening right, labor over the close. It is the reader's last remembrance of you, so make it strong, make it tight, and make it obvious that you are serious about entering into meaningful conversation.

Writing the Cover Letter

Keep your sentences short—an average of fourteen words per sentence is about right. Likewise, your paragraphs should be concise and to the point. In cover letters, paragraphs can often be a single sentence, and should never be longer than two or three sentences. This makes the page more inviting for the harried reader, by providing adequate white space to ease eye strain.

Short words work best here also. They speak more clearly than those polysyllabic behemoths that say more about your self-image problems than your abilities. A good approach is to think in terms of sending a telegram, where every word must work its hardest.

While abiding by accepted grammatical rules, you should punctuate for readability rather than strictly following E. B. White or the *Chicago Manual of Style*. Get by on commas, dashes—and periods. And in between the punctuation marks use the action verbs and phrases that breathe life into your work.

Cover Letter Examples

Notice that the italicized areas come directly from the previous examples. You too can write a dynamite cover letter with the old "cut and paste" technique. Then all you have to do is make the minor adjustments necessary to personalize your letter:

James Sharpe   November 16, 19__
1234 La Cienga Boulevard
Los Angeles, CA 93876

Dear Mr. Bell,

Recently I have been researching the leading local companies in data communications. My search has been for companies that are respected in the field. and who provide on-going training programs. DataLink Products *keeps coming up as a top company.*

I am an experienced voice and data communications specialist with a substantial background in IBM environments. *If you have an opening for someone in this area you will see that my resume demonstrates a person of unusual dedication, efficiency, and drive.*

My experience and achievements include:

- complete redesign of a data communications network, projected to increase efficiency companywide some 12 percent;
- The installation and troubleshooting of a Defender II call-back security system for a dial-up network.

I enclose a copy of my resume, and look forward to examining any of the ways you feel my background and skills would benefit DataLink Products. While I prefer not to use my employer's time taking personal calls at work, with discretion I can be reached at 213/555-5555 to initiate contact. Let's talk!

Yours truly,

James Sharpe

James Sharpe

In response to an advertisement, here is an example using a different selection of phrases.

Jane Swift   November 16, 19__
376 Jaguar Lane
Sunnyside, NY 11104

Dear Ms. Pena,

I have always followed the performance of your fund in Mutual
Funds Newsletter.

*Recently, your notice regarding a Market Analyst in Investors Daily
caught my eye—and your company name caught my attention—
because your record over the last three years shows exceptional portfolio management. With my experience with one of your competitors, I
know I could make significant contributions.*

I would like to talk to you about your personnel needs and how I
would be able to contribute to your department's goals.

*An experienced market analyst, I have an economics background
and a strong analytical approach to market fluctuations. This
combination has enabled me to consistently pick the new technology
flotations that are the backbone of the growth-oriented mutual fund.*

For example, I first recommended Fidelity Magellan six years ago.
More recently, my clients have been strongly invested in Pacific Horizon
Growth (in the high-risk category), and Fidelity Growth and Income (for
the cautious investor).

Those following my advice over the last six years have owned shares
in funds which consistently outperformed the market.

I know that *resumes help you sort out the probables from the
possibles, but they are no way to judge the personal caliber of an
individual. I would like to meet with you and demonstrate that, along
with the credentials, I have the personality that makes for a successful
team player.*

Yours faithfully,

Jane Swift

Jane Swift

The Executive Briefing

Here is a variation on the traditional cover letter. It has been developed most effectively by the recruiting fraternity for use in relation to a specific opening.

Behind the executive briefing is the belief that the initial resume screener might have little understanding of the job in question. So a format was developed that dramatically increased the odds of your resume getting through to the right people. In addition, it customizes your general-purpose resume to each specific opening you discovered. It looks like this:

EXECUTIVE BRIEFING
for a
CREDIT/LOAN SUPERVISOR
as advertised in the *Gotham Daily News*

Jane Swift   November 16, 19__
9 Central Avenue
Mesa, AZ 85201
602/964-5652

To help you evaluate the attached resume and manage your time effectively today, I have prepared this executive briefing. It itemizes your needs on the left and my skills on the right. The attached resume will give you additional details.

Job Title:	My Current Title:
CREDIT AND LOAN SUPERVISOR	CREDIT AND LOAN SUPERVISOR
Required Experience:	Relevant Experience
• Five years in consumer banking	• Five years with a major Arizona consumer bank
• Knowledge of Teller Operations	• Four years in Teller Operations, as teller and supervisor
• Three years Consumer Loans and Mortgage Loans	• Five years Consumer & Commercial and Mortgages
• Extensive Customer Service experience	• Four years in customer service. Reviewed as "having superior communication skills."

An executive briefing sent with a resume provides a comprehensive picture of a thorough professional, plus a personalized, fast, and easy-to-read synopsis that details exactly how you can help with an employer's current batch of problems.

The Broadcast Letter

The broadcast letter is nothing but a simple variation on the cover letter. All the information you would need is available to you from the achievements section of your questionnaire. The intent is to get around sending a resume. Practically speaking, it can often get you into a telephone conversation with a potential employer, but that employer is usually likely to request a proper resume before seeing you anyway. A broadcast letter might have a place in your campaign, but do not use it as a resume substitute. Here is an example of a broadcast letter, in this instance sent in response to a blind newspaper advertisement:

Dear Employer,

For the past seven years I have pursued an increasingly successful career in the sales profession. Among my accomplishments I include:

SALES
As a regional representative, I contributed $1,500,000, or 16 percent of my company's annual sales.

MARKETING
My marketing skills (based on a B.S. in Marketing) enabled me to increase sales 25 percent in my economically stressed territory, at a time when colleagues here were striving to maintain flat sales. Repeat business reached an all-time high.

PROJECT MANAGEMENT
Following the above successes, my regional model was adopted by the company. I trained and provided project supervision to the entire sales force. The following year, company sales showed a sales increase 12 percent above projections.

The above was based and achieved on my firmly held zero price discounting philosophy. It is difficult to summarize my work in a letter.

The only way I can think of for providing you the opportunity to examine my credentials is to talk with each other. I look forward to hearing from you.

Yours sincerely,

James Sharpe

James Sharpe

As you can see, the letter is a variation on a theme, and as such might have a place in your marketing campaign.

Here is an example of a cover letter sent as a result of a conversation.

Dear Ms. _____,

I am writing in response to our telephone conversation on Friday the 10th regarding a new- and used-car sales management position.

With a successful track record in both new- and used-car sales, and as a sales manager, I believe I am ideally suited for the position we discussed. My exposure to the different levels of the sales process (I started at the bottom and worked my way up), has enabled me to effectively meet the challenges and display the leadership you require.

I am a competitive person professionally. Having exercised the talents and skills required to exceed goals and set records as a Sales Manager, I believe in measuring performance by results.

I would appreciate your consideration for a meeting where I could discuss in more detail my sales and management philosophy, and capabilities. Please call me at your earliest convenience to arrange a personal meeting.

Sincerely yours,

James Sharpe

James Sharpe

Finally, here is an example of the somewhat different cover letter you would send to a corporate headhunter:

Dear Mr. _____,

As you may be aware, the management structure at XYZ Inc. will be reorganized in the near future. While I am enthusiastic about the future of the company under its new leadership, I have elected to make this an opportunity for change and professional growth.

My many years of experience lends itself to a management position in any medium-sized service firm, but I am open to other opportunities. Although I would prefer to remain in Detroit, I would be amenable to relocation if the opportunity warrants it. I am currently earning $65,000 a year.

I have taken the liberty of enclosing my resume for your review. Should you be conducting a search for someone with my background—at the present time or in the near future—I would greatly appreciate your consideration. I would be happy to discuss my background more fully with you on the phone or in a personal interview.

Very truly yours,

James Sharpe

James Sharpe

9 | What Do You Do with It?

Creating one of the best resumes in America is a major part of your job hunt, but nevertheless, only a part. It won't get you a job by sitting on your desk like a rare manuscript. You have to do something with it.

Companies are always looking for employees. Even a company with no growth rate can still be expected (based on national averages) to experience a 14 percent turnover in staff over the course of a year. In other words, every company has openings, and any one of those openings could have your name on it.

The problem is, you won't have the chance to pick the very best opportunity unless you check them all out. The intelligent job hunter will use a six-pronged approach to cover all the bases. This process incorporates different ways to use:

- Newspapers
- Employment agencies
- Executive recruiters
- Vocational and college placement offices
- Business and trade publications
- Personal and professional networking

Newspapers

A first step for many is to go to the want ads and do a mass mailing. But beware. If this is the first idea that comes to *your* mind, hitting the want ads will probably be at the front of everyone else's mind, too.

A single help-wanted advertisement can draw hundreds of responses. And that's not counting all the other unsolicited resumes that come in every day. So your approach must be more comprehensive than that of the average applicant. The following tips might be helpful.

- Newspapers tend to have an employment edition every week (usually Sunday, but sometimes mid-week), when, in addition to their regular advertising, they have a major drive for help-wanted ads. Make sure you always get this edition of the paper.
- Look for back issues. Just because a company is no longer advertising does not necessarily mean that the slot has been filled. The employer may well have become disillusioned and gone on to hire a professional recruiter to work on the position.
- Cross-check the categories. Don't rely solely on those ads seeking your specific job title. For example, let's say you are a graphic artist looking for a job in advertising. Any advertising or public relations agency with any kind of need should be flagged. On the basis that they are actively hiring at the moment, simple logic leads you to the conclusion that their employment needs are not restricted to that particular title.

Newspapers represent an important part of your marketing campaign; you should follow up all your resumes with a phone call about a week after they have been sent.

Employment Agencies

There are essentially three categories: State employment agencies, private employment agencies, and executive recruiters.

State Employment Agencies

These are funded by the state's labor department and typically carry names like State Employment Security, State Job Service, or Manpower Services. The names vary, but the services remain the same. They will make efforts to line you up with appropriate jobs and will mail resumes out on your behalf to interested employers who have jobs listed with them. It is not mandatory for employers to list jobs with state agencies, but more and more are taking advantage of these free services. Once the bastion of minimum-wage jobs, positions listed with these public agencies can reach fifty to sixty thousand dollars a year for some technical positions.

If you are moving across the state or across the country, your local employment office can plug you into a computer bank accessing major employers on a national basis (often referred to as a national "job bank").

Insiders agree, however, that it can take up to a month for a particular job from a local office to hit the national system. The most effective way to use the services is to visit your local office and ask for an introduction to the office in your destination area.

Private Employment Agencies

Here we have a definitely for-profit sector of the employment marketplace. There are some major questions that you should get answered before signing up with any particular agency. Chief among them: Are the fees to be paid by the client or by you as the job candidate? The answer distinguishes employer paid fee (or EPF) agencies from applicant paid fee (or APF) agencies. *In all but the most dire emergencies you are strongly recommended to work only with EPF companies.* Apart from the expense, you simply don't want to be known as someone who has to pay to get a job.

You are best advised to call first, verify the fee status, and then visit. Be prepared to leave a copy of your resume for their files and for possible review by interested clients.

Here are some practical ways for you to check on the professional standing of your agent. Be sure to ask:

- When was the firm established? If the company has been in town ever since you were in diapers, the chances are good that it is reputable.
- Is the agency a member of the state employment association? State associations have strict codes of behavior and ethics and provide ongoing training for their members. And as in all industries, people and companies who are actively involved in enhancing their profession invariably have an edge on the competition.
- Does your particular agent have a CPC designation? That stands for Certified Personnel Consultant, a title achieved only after considerable time and effort. Employment consultants with this designation come straight from the top drawer, so you can trust them and should listen attentively to their advice.
- Is the agency part of a franchise chain or independent network? Knowing this can be valuable to you, because both kinds of organizations provide considerable training for their associates, a feature that can enhance the level of service you receive. In addition, other members of the network may have a job suitable for you if the one you've located doesn't.

Finally—don't get intimidated. Remember, you are not obliged to sign anything. Neither are you obliged to guarantee an agency that you will remain in any employment for any specified length of time. Don't get taken advantage of by the occasional rogue in an otherwise exemplary and honored profession.

Executive Recruiters

These people rarely deal at salary levels under seventy thousand dollars a year. All the above advice regarding employment agencies applies here, although you can take it for granted that the headhunter will not charge you a fee. He or she will be more interested in your resume than in seeing you right then and there, unless you match a specific job the recruiter is trying to fill for a client. Executive recruiters are far more interested in the employed than in the unemployed. An employed person is less of a risk (headhunters often guarantee their finds to the employer for up to a year) and constitutes a more desirable commodity. Remember, these people are there to serve the client, not to find you a job. They neither want nor expect you to rely on them for employment counseling, unless they specifically request that you do—in which case you should listen to them closely.

Vocational and College Placement Offices

If you're leaving school, you should take advantage of this resource. (If you don't, you're crazy.) Many of the larger schools have alumni placement networks, so even if you graduated some time ago, you may want to check with the alma mater and tap into the old-boy and old-girl network.

Business and Trade Publications

Two uses here. The articles about interesting companies can alert you to growth opportunities, and individually can provide neat little entrees in your cover letters. Of course, there's also the welcome fact that most of these magazines carry a help-wanted section.

Networking

A fancy word from the seventies that means talking to everyone you can get hold of in your field, whether you know them or not.

The Encyclopedia of Associations (published by R.R. Bowker) tells you about associations for your profession. Networking at the meetings and using an association's directory for contacts are wise and accepted uses of membership.

At the Library

The business reference section can give you access to numerous research books that can help, including:

- *Standard and Poor's*
- *The Thomas Register*
- *The National Job Bank*
- *The Directory of Directories*

Follow-Up

It is no use mailing off tens or even hundreds of resumes without following up on your efforts. If you are not getting a response with one resume format, you might want to consider redoing it another way, as discussed in chapter 5. Of course, in doing so, you should never mention your previous submission. Be satisfied with one of your baits catching a fish.

Always take five or six copies of your resume with you to interviews. Often you can attach it to those annoying application forms and then just write on the form "See attached resume." You can have one on your lap during the interview to refer to, as the interviewer does.

It is always wise to offer copies to subsequent interviewers. This is because they have very often been inadequately briefed and may have no idea about your background and skills. It's also a good idea to leave extra copies of your resume behind with managers for their personal files (which travel with them through their careers from company to company). That person may not need you today, but could come up with a dream job for you sometimes in the future. I know of people who have landed jobs years later as a result of a resume left judiciously with the right person. Who is the right person? Potentially, anyone who holds on to your resume.

The job you ultimately accept may not be your picture of perfection. Nevertheless, any job can lead to great things. You can make the opportunities for yourself in any job if you make the effort. A job becomes what you choose to make it.

In the job hunt there are only two kinds of "yes" answers: Their "yes-we-want-you-to-work-for-us," and your "yes-I-can-start-on-Monday." The joy is in the hunt, with every "no" bringing you closer to the big "yes." Never take rejections of your resume as rejections of yourself; just as every job is not for you, you aren't right for every job. Keep things in perspective.

Good luck!

10 | The Resumes

And now, without further ado...the stars of our show.

The resumes on the following pages are based on the genuine articles, the ones that really did the trick for someone who had to translate his or her fantastic skills and background into a single, compelling document. Whether or not your background is represented in the following sample, use the resumes reproduced here as a starting point for composing your own.

Which Style Is Best for You?

The first three resumes in this section are based on the completed questionnaire you'll find on page 271. Each has been written in a different format—chronological, functional, and combination—to show the dramatic changes you can achieve using each of the recommended resume styles.

Chronological

Jane Swift, 9 Central Avenue, Quincy, MA 02169. (617) 555-1212

SUMMARY: Ten years of increasing responsibilities in the employment services industry. Concentration in the high-technology markets.

EXPERIENCE: Howard Systems International, Inc.   1995-Present
Management Consulting Firm
Personnel Manager

Responsible for recruiting and managing consulting staff of five. Set up office and organized the recruitment, selection, and hiring of consultants. Recruited all levels of MIS staff from financial to manufacturing markets.

Additional responsibilities:

- Coordinated with outside advertising agencies.
- Developed P.R. with industry periodicals—placement with over 20 magazines and newsletters.
- Developed effective referral programs—referrals increased 32%.

EXPERIENCE: Technical Aid Corporation   1988-1995
National Consulting Firm. MICRO/TEMPS Division

Division Manager   1993-1995
Area Manager   1990-1993
Branch Manager   1988-1990

As Division Manager, opened additional West Coast offices. Staffed and trained all offices with appropriate personnel. Created and implemented all divisional operational policies responsible for P & L. Sales increased to $20 million dollars, from $0 in 1984.

- Achieved and maintained 30% annual growth over 7-year period.
- Maintained sales staff turnover at 14%.

As Area Manager, opened additional offices, hiring staff, setting up office policies, and training sales and recruiting personnel.

Additional responsibilities:

- Supervised offices in two states.
- Developed business relationships with accounts—75% of clients were regular customers.
- Client base increased 28% per year.
- Generated over $200,000 worth of free trade-journal publicity.

As Branch Manager, hired to establish the new MICRO/TEMPS operation. Recruited and managed consultants. Hired internal staff. Sold service to clients.

EDUCATION: Boston University
B.S. Public Relations, 1987.

Functional

Jane Swift
9 Central Avenue
Quincy, MA 02169
(617) 555-1212

OBJECTIVE: A position in Employment Services where my management, sales, and recruiting talents can be effectively utilized to improve operations and contribute to company profits.

SUMMARY: Over ten years of Human Resources experience. Extensive responsibility for multiple branch offices and an internal staff of 40+ employees and 250 consultants.

SALES: Sold high-technology consulting services with consistently profitable margins throughout the United States. Grew sales from $0 to over $20 million a year.

Created training programs and trained salespeople in six metropolitan markets.

RECRUITING: Developed recruiting sourcing methods for multiple branch offices.

Recruited over 25,000 internal and external consultants in the high-technology professions.

MANAGEMENT: Managed up to 40 people in sales, customer service, recruiting, and administration. Turnover maintained below 14% in a "turnover business."

FINANCIAL: Prepared quarterly and yearly forecasts. Presented, reviewed, and defended these forecasts to the Board of Directors. Responsible for P & L of $20 million sales operation.

PRODUCTION: Responsible for opening multiple offices and accountable for growth and profitability. 100% success and maintained 30% growth over seven-year period in 10 offices.

WORK EXPERIENCE:

1995 to Present   HOWARD SYSTEMS INTERNATIONAL, Boston, MA
National Consulting Firm
Personnel Manager

1988-1995   TECHNICAL AID CORPORATION, Needham, MA
National Consulting & Search Firm
Division Manager

EDUCATION: B.S., 1987, Boston University

REFERENCES: Available upon request.

Combination

Jane Swift
9 Central Avenue
Quincy, MA 92169
(617) 555-1212

OBJECTIVE:

Employment Services Management

SUMMARY: Ten years of increasing responsibilities in the employment services marketplace.
            Concentration in the high-technology markets.

SALES: Sold high technology consulting services with consistently profitable margins throughout the
            United States. Grew sales from $0 to over $20 million a year.

PRODUCTION: Responsible for opening multiple offices and accountable for growth and profitability. 100%
            success and maintained 30% growth over seven-year period in 10 offices.

MANAGEMENT: Managed up to 40 people in sales, customer service, recruiting, and administration. Turnover
            maintained below 14% in a "turnover business." Hired branch managers and sales and
            recruiting staff throughout the United States.

FINANCIAL: Prepared quarterly and yearly forecasts. Presented, reviewed, and defended these forecasts
            to the Board of Directors. Responsible for P & L of $20 million sales operation.

MARKETING: Performed numerous market studies for multiple branch opening. Resolved feasibility of
            combining two different sales offices. Study resulted in savings of over $5,000 per month in
            operating expenses.

EXPERIENCE: Howard Systems International, Inc.   1995-Present
            Management Consulting Firm
            Personnel Manager

            Responsible for recruiting and managing consulting staff of five. Set up office and organized
            the recruitment, selection, and hiring of consultants. Recruited all levels of MIS staff from
            financial to manufacturing markets.

            Additional responsibilities:

            - developed P.R. with industry periodicals—placement with over 20 magazines and
              newsletters.
            - developed effective referral programs—referrals increased 320%.

Technical Aid Corporation   1988-1995
National Consulting Firm. MICRO/TEMPS Division

Division Manager   1993-1995
Area Manager   1990-1993
Branch Manager   1988-1990

As Division Manager, opened additional West Coast offices. Staffed and trained all offices with appropriate personnel. Created and implemented all divisional operational policies. Responsibilities for P & L. Sales increased to $20 million dollars, from $0 to 1984.

- Achieved and maintained 30% annual growth over seven-year period.
- Maintained sales staff turnover at 14%.

As Area Manager, opened additional offices, hiring staff, setting up office policies, and training sales and recruiting personnel.

Additional responsibilities:

- Supervised offices in two states.
- Developed business relationships with accounts—75% of clients were regular customers.
- Client base increased 28% per year.
- Generated over $200,000 worth of free trade journal publicity.

As Branch Manager, hired to establish the new MICRO/TEMPS operation. Recruited and managed consultants. Hired internal staff. Sold service to clients.

EDUCATION: B.S., 1987, Boston University

Accountant

Jane Swift
9 Central Avenue
Baltimore, MD 21207
(301) 555-1212

CAREER OBJECTIVE: To work in an Accounting/Business position that offers advancement opportunities.

EMPLOYMENT

1994-Present
An established health care company.
ACCOUNTANT

- Responsible for Accounts Payable for five companies
- Responsible for Payroll of all companies. Time saving of 11% across the board
- Maintain personnel records
- Administrator of Employee Benefits
- Prepare Cost Analysis for development projects of Real Estate Division
- Assisted in implementation of computerized accounting system

1991-1994
National Service Corporation, Baltimore
JUNIOR ACCOUNTANT

- Preparation of month-end reports
- Processing of all expense reports, educational assistant applications, and accounts payable
- Processing of Region Payroll

1989-1991
Casson Inc., Baltimore
ADMINISTRATIVE SECRETARY

- Data collection and analysis for market research projects
- Project budgeting and cost containment
- Processed departmental accounts payable and expense reports
- Maintained market research library
- Assisted with implementation of and transition to computerized system

EDUCATION:
University of Baltimore (Baltimore, MD)
Associate in Science Degree
Major: Accounting

Accountant (Entry-Level)

Jane Swift

9 Central Avenue • San Francisco, CA 94127 • (415) 555-1212

Objective: Entry-level accounting position with a CPA firm

Summary of Qualifications

- Fundamental accounting knowledge of financial statements, taxation, etc., through studies at San Francisco State University School of Accounting
- Strong analytical and problem-solving abilities
- Lotus 1-2-3, WordPerfect, Microsoft Word, and accounting software, including Lacerte and Class
- Motivated self-starter with a aptitude for learning new tasks quickly

Education

B.S. Degree in Accounting anticipated December 1998
San Francisco State University, San Francisco, California

Employment
March 1997 to
Present

Accounting Internship
Chinn Accountancy Corporation, San Francisco

- Quarterly payroll tax returns and sales tax returns preparation for various clients
- Assisted Certified Public Accountants with financial statements and tax returns for individuals, partnerships, and corporation

Summer 1996

Accounting Internship
Accounting Office, Holiday Inn, Fisherman's Wharf, San Francisco

- Exposed to all aspects of hotel accounting, including monthly Balance Sheet consolidation, food and beverage control accounting, general cash functions, auditing of income, direct billing, and application of payments and accounts payable procedures
- Filled Accounts Receivable position while clerk was on vacation

January to
March 1997

Volunteer Income Tax Assistance
Chinese American Association, California

- Tax return preparation for low-income, non-English-speaking, and disabled people
- Taught tax payers to fill out future income tax returns by "walking through" the return line-by-line with them

1996 to
March 1997

Student Assistant
Admissions Office, San Francisco State University

- Assisted international students with overseas transactions for proper documentation of student records
- Data entry of student records
- Filing, typing, copying, and other office support duties
- Worked independently to manage daily office activities

Accounting (Entry-Level)

JAMES SHARPE
9 Central Avenue, Brooklyn, NY 11432
(212) 555-1212

OBJECTIVE   To obtain a challenging entry level position in accounting that would provide an opportunity for advancement within the firm and put my abilities to the test.

EDUCATION   YORK COLLEGE, Jamaica, New York
Bachelor of Science in Accounting, December 1997
Courses included:

- Financial Accounting
- Auditing
- Cost Accounting
- Taxation
- Business Law

- Business Finance
- Money and Banking
- Statistics
- Calculus

- Dean's List (all semesters)
- Member of Student Accounting Society

EXPERIENCE
12/96 to 8/97   SEA CREST LINEN CO., Brooklyn, New York
- Accurately entered totals of delivery size, quantity and payments (data-entry). Interfaced with customers regarding orders.
- Updated records on a daily basis working with approximately 100 accounts.
- Handled all computerized billing, generating daily invoices and capably reconciling account balances.
- Reported to the Office Manager.

1992 to 1996   FOREST INDUSTRIES DEVELOPMENT CO., LTD., Jamaica, West Indies
Senior Accounting Clerk
- Handled Accounts Receivable and prepared monthly customer statements, generated reports and reconciled account balance to G/L.
- Reconciled Payables to G/L, verifying payments made against invoices.
- Check preparation and setting up new accounts (over 100).
- Completed bank reconciliations, entering all information into system and sorting our discrepancies.
- Reconciliation of expense accounts—utilities, supplies, etc.
- Prepared financial statements at month's end for Parent Company and its Subsidiary.
- Worked as a *Junior Accountant* for one year before receiving promotion.
- Reported to *Controller.*

PRIOR EDUCATION and ADDITIONAL TRAINING
In 1996 completed H & R Block training in **Individual Income Tax Preparation.**

COLLEGE OF ARTS SCIENCE AND TECHNOLOGY
Diploma: Business Administration, 1992

COMPUTERS   Lotus 1-2-3, WordPerfect, Dbase III.

REFERENCES   Available upon request.

Accounting (Entry-Level)

JANE SWIFT

10 Darcy Street   Boston, MA 02116   (617) 555-1212

Objective: Entry level accounting position with a CPA firm

Summary of Qualifications

- Basic accounting knowledge of financial statements, taxation, etc., through studies at Bentley College
- Strong problem solving abilities
- Lotus 1-2-3, Microsoft Office, Microsoft Word and accounting software
- Motivated team member or independent worker with an aptitude for quickly learning new tasks

Education

B.S. Degree in Accounting anticipated December 1998
Bentley College, Waltham, Massachusetts

Employment

January 1998 to Present — **Accounting Internship**
H & R Block, Boston

- Prepared quarterly payroll tax returns and sales tax returns
- Assisted Certified Public Accountants in preparing financial statements and tax returns for individuals

Summer 1997 — **Accounting Internship**
Accounting Office, Holiday Inn Fisherman's Wharf, San Francisco

- Exposed to all aspects of hotel accounting including monthly Balance Sheet consolidation, food and beverage control accounting, general cash functions, auditing of income, direct billing and application of payments and accounts payable procedures
- Filled Accounts Receivable position while clerk was on vacation

January to March 1997 — Volunteer Income Tax Assistance
Chinese American Association, California

- Tax return preparation for low income, non-English speaking and disabled people
- Taught taxpayers to fill out future income tax returns by "walking through" the return line-by-line with them

1996 to March 1998 — **Student Assistant**
Admissions Office, Bentley College

- Assisted transfer students with course orientation
- Data entry of student records
- Office support duties: filing, copying

Accounting (Medical)

Jane Swift
(415) 555-1212 or 555-1213

9 Central Avenue
San Francisco, CA 94124

Objective: **Accounting department position in the medical field.**

HIGHLIGHTS OF QUALIFICATIONS

- 13 years hospital accounting experience in accounts receivable, following up on past due accounts, billing, posting accounts, and adjustments due to contracts with insurance HMOs.
- Adept as cashier, financial counselor, and secretary.
- Successful track record of positions which demanded high responsibility and a reputation as a dependable and accountable employee.

PROFESSIONAL EXPERIENCE

- Balanced and reconciled accounts using 10-key by touch.
- Successfully tracked high volumes of patient accounts in varying stages of their collection.
- Comprehensive knowledge of patient accounting procedures and handling of receivables as well as dealing with medical benefits.
- Financial counseling experience acting as liaison between patients, the hospital, and insurance companies.
- Computer knowledge including word-processing; Type 55 wpm.
- Extensive public contact and experience with heavy phones and cashiering.

EMPLOYMENT HISTORY

1987 to 1998   **California Pacific Medical Center** *(Formerly Children's Hospital)*
Patient Financial Service Representative

1985 to 1987   **Kaiser Foundation Hospital,** Santa Clara, California
Patient Financial Service Representative

1971 to 1985   **El Camino Hospital,** Mountain View, California
Nurse Assistant (5 years) and Psychiatry Secretary (3 years)

References available upon request

Accounting Customer Service Specialist

Jane Swift
9 Central Avenue
Merrick, NY 11516
(516) 555-1212

OBJECTIVE

A challenging position, utilizing abilities developed through my experience and education, with the opportunity for professional growth based on performance.

EXPERIENCE

1995-Present   CHUBB INSURANCE COMPANY, CARLE PLACE, NY
Accounting Customer Service Specialist

- Prepared daily correction for suspense reports
- Balanced billing statements
- Handled customer inquiries concerning coverage changes, rebills, renewal rates, and reinstatement procedures
- Prepared requisitions for overpayment refund checks
- Investigated premium posting errors

1993-1995   NATIONAL CREDIT UNION, BROOKLYN, NY
Accounting Service Coordinator

- Consolidated daily transactions of all Automatic Teller machines in the state (50)
- Processed applications for the ATM
- Transferred funds through First Carolina Corporation for external users

Member Service Representative/Teller

- Opened new accounts for members; handled inquiries
- Participated in cross-selling the services of the Credit Union
- Performed data entry of daily loan transactions
- Provided paying/receiving functions
- CRT and 10 key calculator skills

1990-1993   IBM CORPORATION, PORT WASHINGTON, NY
Word Processor

- Performed word processing, typing, filing, and other general office duties; set appointments

EDUCATION

Bachelor of Business Administration
North Carolina Central University, Durham, NC

Accounting Clerk

Jane Swift
9 Central Avenue
Huntington Valley, PA 19006
(215) 555-1212

JOB OBJECTIVE   To pursue an accounting career

EXPERIENCE
6/93 to Present   ACCOUNTS PAYABLE CLERK. Fast Markets, Huntington Valley, PA

- Recorded daily accounts receivable checks. Normal day: 50 checks with total value of $70,000
- Computerized complete accounts payable system, for a saving of 80 man hours a week
- Computed daily bank deposits
- Reconciled monthly bank statements
- Recorded general ledger entries
- Maintained automated billback accounts receivable system including daily data entry into IBM Systems 38 computer
- Coordinated regular meetings with wholesaler and merchandise representatives to reconcile their accounts receivable

1/87 to 6/93   ACCOUNT SERVICE REPRESENTATIVE. Sales Department

- Performed general clerical duties
- Catalogued product orders for military accounts
- Responsible for customer order status information

4/82 to 1/87   ACCOUNTING OFFICE CLERK. Jack Rabbit Foods, Huntington Valley, PA

- Responsible for all basic accounting functions: Coding and distribution of invoices, classified transactions, and processed distribution center invoices

EDUCATION   HOLYOKE COMMUNITY COLLEGE, Holyoke, MA.
Degree in Accounting. Graduated 9-81.

REFERENCES   Available upon request

Accounts Payable Supervisor

Jane Swift
9 Central Avenue
Detroit, MI 48204
(313) 555-1212

OBJECTIVE   To obtain a supervisory position in an Accounts Payable department that will utilize
accounting skills and provide the opportunity for professional development.

EXPERIENCE
Feb. 1993 to   Sweetrest Beds   Detroit, MI
Present   Accounts Payable Supervisor

- Supervised accounts payable personnel and reviewed their daily work.
- Utilized IBM System 11 computer system for various accounting functions.
- Managed, calculated, and maintained weekly payroll records for 300 employees.
- Prepared weekly Federal, FICA, and State withholding deposits.
- Delegated monthly bank reconciliations and reviewed work.
- Prepared monthly account analysis (detailing and verifying the general ledger balance
  sheet accounts).

Aug. 1984 to   Wagstaff Kitchens   Detroit, MI
Feb. 1993   Accounts Payable Clerk

- Prepared and entered vendor invoices into IBM and Wang computers
- Responsible for writing checks for vendors and operating expenses
- Handled all vendor inquiries and reconciled vendor statements
- Designed a more efficient vendor information apron, which was approved by management
- Analyzed weekly vendor aging reports
- Prepared monthly insurance expenses for payroll
- Trained new personnel
- Assisted in the supervision of departmental staff

EDUCATION   City University Detroit, MI. Bachelor of Science in Business Administration, May 1993.
Major: Accounting

Expenses financed through part-time employment, financial aid, and parental contributions.

INTERESTS   Personal Computing, Chess

REFERENCES   Available upon request

Administrative Assistant

Jane Swift
9 Central Avenue
Glendale, CA 91209
(818) 555-1212

SUMMARY OF EXPERIENCE

Degenhart Aluminum Recycling Co., Glendale CA. Personnel Assistant (7/91-present)

Administrative Assistant to the Personnel Manager. Served as liaison between company and employees.
Duties included:

> Taking shorthand and the use of the IBM Displaywriter Word Processor.

> Dictaphone transcription, preparation of correspondence.

> Assisting employees in field locations in complying with administrative procedures.

> Maintaining up-to-date employee records and compiling reports, working directly with employees and answering questions regarding benefits and medical claims, and assisting them with necessary paper work.

> **Employer comments: "Extremely organized…exceedingly proficient."**

Degenhart Aluminum Recycling Company. Benefits Coordinator (1986-1991)

> Processed medical claims for employees. Began employment as a statistical typist and was promoted to the Claims Department.

> **Employer comments: "Willingness to work till the job is done…Easy to work with."**

Bank of Glendale, Mastercard Division, Glendale, CA. Typist (1985-1986)

> Dictaphone transcription for the Collection Department.

> **Employer comments: "Tactful and considerate…takes initiative."**

EDUCATION

Prioy High School, Philadelphia, PA: June 1977

Admissions Representative

James Sharpe
9 Central Avenue
Philadelphia, PA 19046
(215) 555-1212

CAREER OBJECTIVE
A position in education, recruitment, or personnel development.

CENTRAL PHILADELPHIA COLLEGE, PA
ADMISSIONS REPRESENTATIVE: 1997-Present

- Performed telemarketing procedures to set private interviews, schedule career workshops in 100 area high schools.
- Conducted personal interviews with prospective students.
- Designed and implemented career education and motivation workshops for high-school students. Led to 8% application increase.
- Designed brochures and handouts to accompany workshop presentations.
- Exceeded lead generation quota by 16%.
- Successfully addressed parent and student groups on Financial Aid.
- Coordinated student-faculty participation in recruitment activities.

CHARLES HAID, M.D., PHILADELPHIA. SECRETARY, 1995-1997

- Coordinated a number of administrative activities in this busy practice; implemented office automation system ahead of schedule, increasing personal and office productivity.

TEACHER OF ART AND MUSIC, MADISON, WI. 1984-1995

- Successfully taught in elementary and secondary schools in the midwest for ten years, specializing in art and music.

EDUCATION:
B.A. Notre Dame in Liberal Arts cum laude.
Computer Science Studies, Philadelphia College

EXTRACURRICULAR
Speakers Bureau, 88-96, Philadelphia College

Applications Programmer Analyst

James Swift
9 Central Avenue
Wilmington, MA 01887
(617) 555-1212

SUMMARY: A seasoned P/A with experience comprising all facets of the applications development cycle, working in online, database, and batch processing environments.

HARDWARE/ SOFTWARE: 43XX, OS/MVS/XA, COBOL, VISUAL BASIC, CICS, DL/1, VSAM. ICCF, ROSCOE, EASYTRIEVE, SOFT/MERGE, MSA A/P, TSO/SPF, EDGAR, VOLLIE

EXPERIENCE: *First Bank of Boston. Programmer/Analyst.* 1/94 to Present

Responsible for installation and maintenance of MSA Accounts Payable System. Member of a team that designed and coded a front-end system to MSA Payroll that allowed online daily input, employee inquiry and accompanying batch reports including labor distribution. Analyzed, coded, and maintained COBOL and CICS Command Level programs, applications included: Profit Sharing, General Ledger, Gross Profit Forecasting, Billing and Sales Reporting.

Shearson, Programmer/Analyst. 10/89 to 1/94

Promoted to Programmer/Analyst after eight months as a Documentation Analyst. As a Programmer, was a member of the Customer Support Group for the Integrated Financial Information System. Resolved client software problems, coded and installed software modifications at client sites. Analyzed and coded program modifications as required. Responsibilities included: Reconciliation, Accounts Payable and General Ledger.

EDUCATION: *Drexel University*
B.S., Accounting/Computer Systems Management (May, 1990)

Assistant Manager Trainee

James Sharpe
9 Central Avenue
Overland Park, KS 66212
(913) 555-1212

OBJECTIVE   An administrative/managerial position in which I can utilize my skills and abilities.

EXPERIENCE
1994 - Present   UNION SAVINGS BANK   Overland Park, KS
Administrative Assistant/Assistant Manager Trainee
Monitored cash flow and alarm systems, supervised Customer Service Department, Payroll Department and tellers. Regularly reported to the Assistant Vice President. Fifteen people reported to me on a daily basis. Assumed responsibilities of Branch Manager in the absence of the Assistant Vice President.

Supervisor to Customer Service Department
Drafted weekly and monthly financial reports, monitored safe-deposit boxes, handled new accounts for branch, updated department personnel on bank policies and products. Five people reported to me.

Customer Service Representative
Provided customers with information, bank products, and bank services, such as brokerage accounts, certificates, and savings and checking accounts.

1990 - 1994   TELECOMMUNICATIONS, INC.   Overland Park, KS
Administrative Assistant
Worked closely with the editor and staff of *Computer Magazine*, a monthly computer magazine. Responsibilities included interacting with readers and vendors, handling correspondence, making travel arrangements, assisting editors and reporters in story research, and other projects.

EDUCATION
9/95 - 12/95   WORD PROCESSING
Overland Adult Education Program
Comprehensive word-processing course. Hands-on experience with Digital Rainbow and Apple IIE (Bank Writer and PFS:WRITE).

PERSONAL   Member of Kansas Coalition for Literacy. Enjoy reading, scuba diving, camping. Well-developed ability to delegate assignments and convey job goals. Work well with people.

REFERENCES   Available upon request.

Associate (Legal)

Jane Swift
9 Central Avenue
New York, NY 10017
(212) 555-1212

EDUCATION

Legal: Columbia Law School, J.D., 1992: Grade Average: B+

Bar Admission: New York, 1992; United States Federal District Court (Manhattan), 1993

College: Yale University, B.A. with Honors, 1989. GPA: 3.5

Secondary: Waldorf School, 1982-1985

EMPLOYMENT

1994-Present: Associate with Skasky Brant of New York. General corporate representation of early-stage, growth-oriented hi-tech companies, usually in computer industry. Concentration on negotiation and drafting of technology-related contracts, distributorship, proprietary rights, and employee agreements. Regular involvement in private financings of high-technology companies.

September, 1992 - March, 1994: Associate with Kliernan, Peabody & Schraft of New York. General corporate work, acquisitions, private financings, negotiation and drafting of computer and other contracts. Experience in real estate and litigation.

Summer, 1991: Summer associate with deJong & Kelsey of San Jose, CA. Hi-tech corporate representation.

Summer, 1990: Intern with Environmental Protection Bureau of New York State, Attorney General's Office.

PERSONAL DATA

Skills: Scientific background; familiar with Spanish and Chinese.

Automobile Salesperson

JAMES SHARPE
9 Central Avenue
Melrose, MA 02176
(617) 555-1212

OBJECTIVE: New-Car Sales Manager

**PRINCIPAL
SKILLS:** New Car Sales Manager; Automobile/Professional Sales and Finance

EXPERIENCE: TOYOTA OF MELROSE, 1993 - Present, **Sales Manager**
Initially hired as **Salesman**. Proved professional skills and talents for working and dealing effectively with the public, and desire and ability in training and influencing others. Promoted (after one year) to **Sales Manager**. Responsible for 24 new- and used-car sales. Achievements include:

- New-car sales increase 12% in 1994, 27% in 1995
- Staff turnover reduced 14%
- Cost of sales remained constant

MELROSE AUTO SALES. 1987 - 1993. **Salesman**
Responsible for new- and used-car sales. Earned "Salesman of the Year" awards, 1991 and 1992. Record holder for:

- Most Cars Sold in One Month
- Most Cars Sold in One Year
- Most Board Gross in One Month
- Most Board Gross in One Year

CAREFREE ADVERTISING AGENCY. 1983 - 1987
Direct Commercial Advertising Sales

U.S. ARMY. 1974 - 1983
Helicopter Flight Engineer
Served in Vietnam, April 1974 to November 1975.
Awarded the Bronze Star Medal, the Air Medal, and the Army Commendation Medal.
Honorable Discharge.

EDUCATION: University of Massachusetts
Completed 30 credit hours: College Accounting I and II, Personnel Management and related courses.

Professional Courses and Seminars:
Dr. Norman Vincent Peal—Self-Starter Sales
Zig Zigler—Motivation and Sales
Jackie Cooper—Making the Sale/Closing the Sale
Toyota Sales Society

REFERENCES: Furnished upon request.

Automotive Management Specialist

James Sharpe
9 Central Avenue
Raleigh, NC 27612
(919) 555-1212

Employment Experience

Service Manager. Capucci Chevrolet. Raleigh, NC. 1992-present
Supervised 22 mechanics, customer service relations, processing of warranty claims. I/M program coordinator, trained mono-lingual mechanics, safety coordinator, paid sublet repair shops, authorized check requests, analyzed employee production, produced reports for entire car dealer department operations.

Adjunct Professor. Raleigh Community College. 1988-1993
Teacher of Automotive Technology for A.A.S. (34 credits). Prepare lessons and evaluate class performance. Spanish and English courses.

Licenses

North Carolina State Inspectors License, Type F & E
New York City Board of Education Auto Mechanic

Certificates

Certificate of Competence: Sponsored by the National Institute for Automotive Service Excellent of Washington, D.C. (Certification)

Front End   Engine Performance
Brake Systems   Heating & Air Conditioning
Electrical Systems   Engine Tune-Up

Certificate of Training: Given by the Consumer Relations and Service Staff of General Motors Corporation

Driveability Diagnosis Computer Command Control
Electronic Fuel Injection
Computer Command Control Engine Performance

Certificate of Training: Given by the Monroe Auto Equipment Company

Principles of Shock Absorbers
Theory or Automotive Suspension

Certificate of Training: Given by the United Delco Training Program

Hydraulic System and Disk Brakes
Power Service Emissions Control
Power Service Fuel Systems

Education

Raleigh Community College
A.A.S. Electrical Technology

References furnished upon request.

Bank Teller

James Sharpe
9 Central Avenue
Kansas City, MO 64108
(816) 555-1212

OBJECTIVE: Seek a responsible position with growth opportunities in the field of Financial Management.

PROFESSIONAL EXPERIENCE:

| May 1994 to Present | FIRST SAVINGS BANK | Kansas City, MO |

Bank Teller
Duties include computing figures with speed and accuracy, maintaining proper activity in customer accounts, operating computer to retrieve processed data, controlling and supervising large amounts of cash flow, and obtaining accountability of transactions.

| January 1993 to May 1994 | NATIONAL WESTMINSTER BANK (internship) | Kansas City, MO |

Assistant to Retirement Accounts Manager
Duties include recording of contributions to new and existing accounts, assisting customers with information regarding benefits of IRA's and KEOGH's, calculating specific year-to-date interest and tax deduction advantages, assisting manager with form procedures to complete transactions.

Special research project as to the feasibility of funding retirement accounts with zero coupon bonds obtained currently by brokers and anticipating the participation of financial institutions, specifically banks.

EDUCATION:

B.B.A., City University College, May 1994. Concentration in Management Techniques, interest in Finance.

SPECIAL ACTIVITIES: Student Academic Affairs Committee, attention to improving balance within the academic environment at the college.

REFERENCES: Furnished upon request.

Banking Portfolio Manager

James Sharpe, 9 Central Avenue, Kansas City, MO 64112. (816) 555-1212. Page 1 of 2

SUMMARY

A track record of outstanding performance in the sophisticated environments of Trust and Investment Banking. Management of both personal and institutional portfolios with total values exceeding $700 million. An adept analyst of such diverse industries as energy, metals, automobile, insurance, banking, electrical, and consumer goods.

OBJECTIVE

An opportunity where a professional whose successful loss control/profit preservation approach to portfolio management can make a meaningful contribution.

CAREER HIGHLIGHTS

An Investment Banking Company: Vice President, *Institutional Portfolio Management*. 1992-Present.

Heads investment management activities of the firm's 170-account Kansas office. Reporting to Chairman. Created more effective marketing and management of large accounts, by initiating a program that resulted in:

- Upgrading and expansion of professional staff.
- Personal management of firm's 17 largest accounts.
- Effective supervision of all staff activities and performance.
- Elevation to position as member of Corporate Board of Directors and Chair of Investment Strategy and Policy Group.

Kansas Trust Company: *Vice President & Senior Portfolio Manager*. 1988-1992.

Managed a broadly diversified account base of over 395 personal and institutional accounts with total value in excess of $950 million. Improved performance of accounts supervised, shortened turn-around time of customer requests for investment reviews, cementing relations with clients. Developed effective computerized methods for rapid analysis of investment diversification.

- Program consistently outperformed the S&P index, distilled stock guidance list of 500 firms to a value-oriented 20-35 companies.
- Reduced turn-around time on investment reviews by 30%.
- Reduced time spent in review analysis by 25% while improving review quality.

Morgan Guaranty (New York): *Portfolio Manager*. 1985-1988.

Initially recruited as a Senior Investment Analyst in the energy stock area, was promoted to Portfolio Manager within 10 months.

- Hired, trained, supervised, and directed activities of additional analysts in related research coverage.
- Dramatically reduced energy stock holdings in November 1988, a move that produced sizable realized capital gains while avoiding the sell-off that followed.
- Instituted automation and software for analytical staff. Increased the number of potential investment opportunities by 21% without additional cost.

EDUCATION AND PERSONAL

MBA, Columbia Business School	Finance and Marketing
MA, John Carroll University	Economics
BA, John Carroll University	Economics

Willing to relocate. References are available upon request.

Bookkeeper

James Sharpe
9 Central Ave
Wilmington, DE 19850
(302) 555-1212

OBJECTIVE
To pursue a career in the accounting field, utilizing my proven capabilities in payroll, general bookkeeping, cost, and accounting.

EXPERIENCE

Leader Instrument Corporation, Wilmington, DE
Bookkeeper, 1/94 - Present

Responsibilities include accounts receivable, accounts payable and payroll. Reconcile bank statements and accounts. Maintain depreciation schedules and monthly analysis. Prepare payroll for 100 employees, W-2 forms, quarterly returns, and other related payroll functions. Calculate employee sales commissions and employee production bonuses. Involved in major W.P. conversion and upgrade.

John Dalig, Wilmington, DE
Payroll Clerk, 9/90 - 1/94

Responsibilities included payroll returns, writeups, reconciliations, analysis work, and depreciation schedules. Figured timecards (overtime and shift); checked suspect entries with applicable supervisor. Performed other payroll-related activities. Assisted in the supervision and training of all new department members.

The Chubb Life Insurance Company, Wilmington, DE
Cost Accounting Systems Coordinator, 9/88 - 6/90

Controlled all input and analyzed all output to the functional Cost System and EDP Cost Allocation System. Prepared analytical information based on functional costs; calculated and distributed expense accounts departmentally. Reconciled the system to all company ledgers to assure the system was in complete balance.

EDUCATION

Wilmington Junior College, Wilmington, DE. Business Administration, 1979

REFERENCES

Furnished upon request

Broadcast Management Professional

Jane Swift
9 Central Avenue
Clifton, NJ 07013
(201) 555-1212

**PROFESSIONAL
INTEREST**   Marketing Management, Broadcast Management

**WORK
EXPERIENCE**   **MARKETING DIRECTOR** - A major provider of satellite communication services for broadcasting and private business networks. 1994-present.

- Member of policy-making corporate management team.
- Manage company's strategic position to effectively penetrate the multimillion-dollar corporate/organizational private satellite network market.
- Increased corporate visibility in the satellite industry through developing corporate image, producing new and comprehensive sales materials, and strengthening public relations and advertising efforts in trade magazines.
- Identified new market segments and reached these segments with successful direct mail campaigns.

PRODUCT DEVELOPMENT MANAGER - Viewcom International, Los Angeles, CA. 1993-1994.

- Supervised market research, market segmentation analysis, and product management.
- Designed and assisted in the composition of a Prospectus for use in attracting potential investors in the Company.

MARKETING VICE PRESIDENT'S ASSISTANT - KNEW TV & AM, Los Angeles, CA. 1988-1993.

- Supervised all activities (i.e., tours, printed and electronic advertising, hiring, catering, etc.) for successful two-week Grand Opening of multimillion-dollar Headquarters.
- Planned and supervised all marketing and promotional activities at KNEW.

PUBLIC RELATIONS DIRECTOR - KPIX, Los Angeles, CA. 1985-1988

- Supervised and designed corporation's first external newsletter for use in market development.
- Designed photo layout for use in advertising and press releases.

**ADDITIONAL
INFORMATION**

- Speak, read, and write Spanish fluently.
- Vice-President, American Marketing Association, NY Chapter, 1992-1993.
- Publications Vice-President, MBA Student Association.

EDUCATION   **M.B.A.**, Marketing Emphasis, Northwestern University. 1985.
B.A., Public Relations, John Carroll University. 1983.

REFERENCES   Available upon request.

Buyer

James Sharpe
9 Central Ave
Manhattan, NY 10012
(212) 555-1212

EXPERIENCE

3/94 - Present Ohrbach's (New York, NY), **Buyer***, Boyswear*

Responsible for purchasing boyswear sold in boys departments at 45 stores chainwide, with yearly sales exceeding $5.5 million. Branch managers report to this position. Visit wholesale showrooms on a weekly basis.

- Analyze daily sales data and inventories to plan promotions and make adjustments.
- Prepare and maintain budgets. Redistribute merchandise between stores.
- Travel to branch stores to direct departmental start-ups and solve problems.
- Train and evaluate assistant buyers.

2/93-3/94 **Assistant Buyer***, Silverware/Cookware/Junior Knits*

- Promoted through three different lines. Consistently exceeded quota.
- Assisted buyers in selection of merchandise.
- Prepared orders, budgets, and inventories.
- Planned and created newspaper advertisements.
- Organized and promoted annual Housewares Exposition.

8/91-2/93 **Sales Manager**

- Managed four separate departments in two stores, exceeded projections 14%.
- Trained, scheduled, and supervised salespeople; turnover dropped 20%.
- Met daily sales quotas, handled all merchandising.

EDUCATION

B.A. Merchandising: New York Fashion Institute of Technology (1990)

All education self-financed through working in Manhattan retail outlets throughout college years.

Capital Equipment Salesperson

6 Central Avenue
Beaverton, OR 97005
(503) 555-1212

JAMES SHARPE

OBJECTIVE   Challenging position in MARKETING/SALES offering an opportunity for growth.

SUMMARY   B.S. Degree in Business Administration plus six years' experience marketing capital equipment to the health care market.

EMPLOYMENT
EXPERIENCE   A major U.S. multinational corporation in the life sciences industry
1997-Present   ***Northwest Territory Area Sales Representative.***
Responsibilities include marketing X-ray equipment and ancillary products through X-ray dealers and OEM's to the Health Facilities market in western states. Routine interface between end-users, planning consultants, architects, and dealer salespeople on systems sale.

2/1991-3/1996   Beale Company, Sacramento, CA
Western Sales Representative.
Responsible for marketing sterilizers and surgical lighting fixtures directly to Health Facilities market and through dealer network to the laboratory market. Achievements include:

- Rookie of the Year Award, 1993
- Million Dollar Club (annual sales exceed 1 million) '93, '94 & '96
- Summit Club '93, '94, '95 & '96
- Hawaii Sales Contest Winner, 1995; Gold Ounce Sales Winner, 1996

10/1988-2/1991   Mead Paper, Dayton, OH
Major U.S. multinational corporation in the forest products industry.
Corporate Trainee.
Started as Assistant to the Division Manager in Dayton working primarily on an inventory control system prior to computer start-up. Accepted transfer to strengthen sales force with responsibilities for 42 retail accounts and business development within a specific territory.

- Doubled sales volume within six months.

EDUCATION
1984-1988   Bachelor of Science, School of Business Administration
Major concentration in Marketing with emphasis on Promotional Strategies and Consumer Behavior
University of Connecticut, Storrs, CT

PERSONAL AND PROFESSIONAL REFERENCES AVAILABLE UPON REQUEST

Chemical Salesperson

James Sharpe
9 Central Avenue
Dallas, TX 75379-1906
(214) 555-1212

OBJECTIVE:
To work for a growing company where my background in sales can be used to good advantage.

SUMMARY OF EXPERIENCE:
Wide-ranging background in agricultural chemicals and fertilizer sales. Experience gained through employment with large chemical companies. I feel that being a strong self-starter has helped me obtain many of my goals.

EMPLOYMENT HISTORY:
A Major Chemical Company, Dallas, TX <u>1994-Present</u>:
A sales representative for an agricultural chemical company. Sales territory has achieved 18-23% sales increases over past four years. Responsibilities include: Sales forecasting, sales planning, and inventory control.

- Promote impregnation of agricultural chemicals on dry fertilizer. In 1995 I increased sales with those 22 dealers that impregnated by 28%.
- Conduct 30 to 40 grower, dealer, and distributor meetings a year.
- Work one-on-one with 20% of the dealers that do 80% of the business, presenting marketing and incentive programs. Sales increase of 2.4 million dollars over last three years.
- I designed a marketing program offering free insecticide banders for those customers using our product. This idea is now a national program.
- Made presentations to sales force on impregnation, complaint handling, and setting up dealer calls.

Chevron, Tulsa, OK <u>1987-1994</u>
Sales representative calling directly on large plantations and dealers. Increased sales 25% in 1991, 24% in 1992, 33% in 1993, and 20% in 1994.

EDUCATION:

North Carolina State University, B.S. Agriculture

SPECIAL TRAINING:

Training offered by major agricultural chemical companies.

Agsell
Professional Selling Skills
Action Management
Customer Complaints as Sales Opportunities

Claims Representative

Jane Swift
9 Central Avenue
Sacramento, CA 95691
(916) 555-1212

Objective: Seeking a position utilizing my extensive knowledge and successful experience in planning, organizing, and following up multi-faceted, complex activities; and a position offering opportunities for personal contribution and professional growth.

SUMMARY OF QUALIFICATIONS

Offering comprehensive experience and expertise in the following areas of responsibility:

- Extensive experience planning, organizing, evaluating, and following up varied responsibilities in a timely and complete manner.
- Proficient in developing excellent relationships with clients and consultants.
- Experienced in knowledge of and in analyzing provisions and exclusions of policies in order to decide eligible benefits.
- Skilled at organizing work and resolving problems that arise in day-to-day activities.

EXPERIENCE HIGHLIGHTS

1991 to Present   **Claims Representative**   *Farmers Fund Insurance Co.*, Sacramento, CA
Responsible for meeting with policyholders, claimants, and attorneys to examine, evaluate, and decide upon claims for property damage and personal injury.

- Planning, organizing, evaluating and approving up to 100 active claims in process.
- Taking statements of witnesses and performing on-site inspections. Analyzing reports and statements of policyholders, witnesses, and claimants.
- Receiving and evaluating medical reports. Performing analytical reports of bodily injury claims.
- Negotiating claims settlements with individuals and attorneys.

1989 to 1990   **Management Trainee**   *PizzaTime Theaters*, Sacramento, CA
Participated in Management Training Program and assisted in interviewing, hiring, training and supervising personnel. Managed operations in absence of Manager.

1988 to 1989   **Administrative Assistant**   *Eastern Illinois University*, Charlestown, IL
Responsible for assisting Alumni Fund Director in fund-raising projects. Maintained daily and monthly reports of fund-raising activities. Organized and coordinated meetings and luncheons.

Education: B.A., Eastern Illinois University, Charleston, IL. 1988. Majored in Speech Communication/Business Management.

Licenses: Casualty License, including Auto Physical Damage and Liability, and General Liability issued by Texas Board of Insurance.

Strengths: Highly motivated, accurate, thorough and precise in attention to details. Excellent analytical and organizational skills. Major strength is completing multi-faceted tasks within time constraints allotted. Skilled in public relations, loyal, dependable, and willing to do whatever is needed to meet established goals.

References furnished upon request

Compensation/EEO Specialist

James Sharpe, 9 Central Avenue, Atlanta, GA 30301, (404) 555-1212. Page 1 of 2

OBJECTIVE

A career opportunity in Personnel Management that will implement skills gained through successful, broad-based experience and utilize expertise in organization and management and the ability to structure a responsive, well-accepted personnel function.

SKILL SUMMARY

Compensation

Responsible for all phases of salary administration. Developed, implemented complete compensation programs, including international, sales, and executive compensation. Formulated basic concepts, prepared proposal for corporate approval, formalized policies and procedures.

Designed and participated in wage and salary surveys, evaluated the comparative level of overall compensation.

Modified and/or developed salary ranges. Established and administered salary increase forecasts as well as merit and promotional budgets. Initiated programs and criteria for employee performance evaluation.

Administered salaries correlating potential percent of increase with quality of performance. Developed bonus and incentive plans as appropriate. Hands-on knowledge of the Hay system, factor-comparison and point-factor systems, etc. Designed, developed, implemented a Personal Data system and a Skills Inventory system.

Equal Employment Opportunity

Developed, revised, updated, and implemented Affirmative Action Plans according to company requirements.

Conducted compliance reviews, worked with inspection teams or individuals; negotiated where necessary.

Maintained appropriate files on protected classes in company; reviewed new job requisitions to ensure equal considerations and promotion commensurate with performance. Organized and ran training sessions for supervisors and managers on training and upgrading of minorities.

Employment

Directed all aspects of professional, technical, and administrative recruiting. Administered employee relations programs; counseled employees concerning personal or job-related problems, established effective relocation procedures.

Training, Development/Manpower Planning

Introduced management-by-objective concepts, developed programs and processes, implemented system on national basis.

Identified manpower planning needs, designed and implemented staffing and forecasting plans, using top-to-bottom participative process integrated with sound business strategy. Designed and taught a variety of programs for all levels of management, exempt and non-exempt personnel.

Benefits

Developed requirements, selected and administered group life health insurance plans, long-term disability, travel and accident programs. Negotiated with insurance carriers to secure competitive benefit levels at lowest possible cost.

COMPANY AFFILIATIONS

1992-present	Coca Cola, Atlanta, GA
	Director of Personnel
1987-1992	CITIBANK, New York, NY
	Manager, Salary Administration
1984-1987	LAURA ASHLEY, Trenton, NJ
	Manager, Salary Administration
1976-1984	PALL CORPORATION, Long Island, NY
	Personnel Manager

PROFESSIONAL ASSOCIATIONS

American Society for Personnel Administration
American Compensation Association
New York Personnel Management Association
New York Compensation Association

EDUCATION

New York University, 1972-1976

Computer Programmer (Entry-Level)

James Sharpe
9 Central Avenue
Tallahassee, FL 32301
(904) 555-1212

OBJECTIVE
To obtain employment at the entry-level with a company offering opportunities for advancement.

EDUCATION
ST. JOHN'S UNIVERSITY, Jamaica, New York. **Bachelor of Science**, May 1998
Major: Computer Science
Courses included:

- Structured Programming Concepts
- Computer Arch and Assembler Language
- Data Base Management Systems
- The C Programming Language
- Computers and The Law
- Matrix Methods
- Theory of Programming Language
- Advanced Business Programming
- Data Security and Cryptography

Minor: Business
Courses: Accounting, Management, Marketing, and Economics
Languages studied and related lab work:
C++, Visual C++, Visual Basic, COBOL, Prolog, LISP

Examples of programs and purposes:
Wrote a payroll program in Visual C++ language, utilizing two files and keeping track of names, addresses, etc. (business-oriented). Team effort.

Working on a limited basis with Prolog/LISP—Artificial intelligence language created a program enabling one to follow information and find solutions and answers to complex questions.

WORK HISTORY
BIG M CAR WASH, West Hempstead, New York   1994 - Present
Assistant Manager
Duties and responsibilities center on assisting with daily activities, ensuring that the business is profitable. Oversee the tasks performed by approximately twelve people. Keep daily log books, recording volume of business, and calculate weekly and monthly totals for Accountant. Prepare payroll and distribute pay to employees; make daily deposits at local bank; make withdrawals from business account in order to make purchases; open the establishment and set up cash register; handle customer complaints; ensure that work force is adequate and able to handle between 500 and 800 cars a day; oversee inventory and deal with all vendors: Syndet, Jobe, Echo Brush Co., Rodi, Elevation Corp., Tony Abrescis Distribution Co., and Music Galore.

REFERENCES
Available upon request.

Consultant

James Sharpe

9 Central Avenue • Novi, Michigan 48374 • Ph: (810) 555-1212 • Pager: (313) 555-1213

Executive Summary

An innovative and seasoned **Senior Executive** and **Consultant** with a successful background in **crisis resolution, turnaround and start-up situations**. More than 15 years successful, progressive experience in all phases of Strategic Planning, Operations and Financial Management. Recognized as a hands-on, pro-active **troubleshooter** who can rapidly identify business problems, formulate strategic plans, initiate change and implement new processes in challenging and diverse environments. Exceptional ability to **execute income enhancement strategies** and cost control actions.

Areas of Effectiveness

- Capital & Operational Budgeting
- Production & Inventory Management
- Financial & Operational Cost Control
- Business Valuation
- Sales/Marketing Strategies
- Corrective Action Planning
- P&L Responsibility
- Crisis Management
- Liquidation Management

Significant Accomplishments

- Recruited as a **Turnaround Consultant for A.C.I.,** to create spending accountability in all areas, resulting in cost reductions of $1 million annually. Facilitated successful negotiations with vendors, customers, the Internal Revenue Service, various state authorities and banks for lines of credit.
- As the **President of Dash Mobile Electronics**, orchestrated the start-up and growth of a subsidiary organization. Within just four years successfully established 18 retail stores, 3 warehousing/distribution locations and sales exceeding $10 million. Additionally created a wholly owned subsidiary for acquisitions and acquired 21 stores through bulk sale and transfer.
- Within 9 months, as the **Divisional Controller for Highland Superstores**, selected and implemented a fully integrated Purchase Order Management Systems enabling the centralization of national purchasing contracts and staff reductions resulting in a cost savings exceeding $2 million.
- Promoted to **Plant Comptroller**, for the **fifth largest facility in the U.S., at ITT** in less than three years (the standard was seven years). Effectively negotiated with and administered 4 unions and 15 different locals. Responsibilities for this 600 employee facility included: standard cost, budgets, sales forecasting, multi-state distribution, and capital projects.
- Developed and implemented internal controls and security measures to successfully resolve an inventory shortage that exceeded $1 million per month. Additional operational improvements resulted in a 25% increase in deliveries as well as a 20% reduction in staff.
- As the **Acquisition Manager**, spearheaded the acquisition of a 95-unit, 350-employee organization. This included the creation of a new company for the bankruptcy purchase, due diligence, negotiations with creditors, inventory valuation, employee termination and selective rehiring.
- Directed the closure of a manufacturing facility: transferred assets, handled MESC, workers' compensation and union issues, dismissed staff, idled plant, absorbed production.

Education

B.B.A., *Business Management & Accounting*
Walsh College

Counseling

JANE SWIFT

9 Central Avenue • New York, NY 10017 • (212) 555-1212

OBJECTIVE A Counseling Position in Alcohol Addiction and Substance Abuse…fulfill personal and professional commitment to make a contribution to patients/clients and to the treatment facility by utilizing my education and training, experience and skills on their behalf.

SUMMARY OF QUALIFICATIONS
- More than 500 hours of Alcoholism Counseling training including Counseling, Case Management, Addiction, Psychology, Sociology and all aspects of Human Relations.
- A comprehensive 400 hour internship working with single and dual diagnosis patients involved in Detoxification, Rehabilitation, Partial Hospitalization, Outpatient Group, Individual and Family Counseling…working knowledge of Crisis Intervention, Relapse Prevention, accurate documentation and various Fellowship programs.

PROFESSIONAL EDUCATION, EXPERIENCE & AFFILIATIONS

ST. JOSEPH'S COLLEGE, Patchogue, NY
B.S. Degree, Community Health & Human Resources, anticipated 1998.

SOUTH OAKS INSTITUTE OF ALCOHOLISM & ADDICTIVE BEHAVIOR STUDIES, Amityville, NY
Alcohol Counselor Training, Completed June, 1996
Alcohol Counselor Internship, Completed July, 1996
Credentialed Alcoholism Counselor Candidate for 1997 Examination

DALE CARNEGIE INSTITUTE, Hauppauge, NY
Certificate, Effective Speaking & Human Relations, 1989

Alcoholism Counselor, SOUTH OAKS HOSPITAL, Amityville, NY
Hired immediately after internship on a per diem basis to work with Detoxification, Rehabilitation and Partial Hospital units. Presented educational films and lectures, led group and one-on-one counseling…with single and dual diagnosis patients…1996 to present.

Affiliated with:
New York State Coalition for Children of Addictions
New York Foundation of Alcoholism & Chemical Dependency Counselors
Long island Council on Alcoholism and Drug Dependency

PREVIOUS EXPERIENCE & ACCOMPLISHMENTS
Sales Representative, COLDWELL BANKER, Smithtown, NY
Member, Multi-million Dollar Club and Winners' Circle. Top producer in annual sales; achieved **"Agent of the Month"** designation at least once each quarter…1993 to 1996.

Sales Representative, CENTURY 21, Patchogue, NY
A key contributor to agency's growth, through powerful sales and marketing campaigns, to #1 market share position within first 6 months; personally generated $2 million in sales during a declining market…1991 to 1993.

President/Sales Representative, HEALY-BOYD PRODUCTIONS, New York City, NY
Designed and provided a wide diversity of creative marketing and public relations services for small businesses and large corporations…1987 to 1991.

REFERENCES & ADDITIONAL DATA AVAILABLE UPON REQUEST

Credit/Loan Supervisor

Jane Swift
9 Central Avenue
Mesa, AZ 85201
(602) 555-1212

OBJECTIVE

A supervisory position providing the opportunities to further develop and apply skills and experience in bank operations.

SUMMARY OF EXPERIENCE

Nearly three years' progressively responsible experience in banking; familiarity in teller operations with the subsequent transfer to loan operations, including consumer loans, mortgages, and commercial loans. Extensive customer service experience.

EXPERIENCE
April 1997-
Present

Mesa Savings, Mesa, AZ
Assistant Credit Supervisor, Commercial Loan Department

- Responsible for the smooth day-to-day running of department of 5
- Review new loans for application to computer system and subsequent balancing
- Handle customer inquiries and solve billing problems
- Assist in billing, receipt, application to computer of payments
- Prepare various reports and information for loan officers
- Participate in the training and development of staff
- Assist supervisor with all other pertinent duties
- Participated in a recent computer conversion

April 1995-
April 1997

Bank of Arizona, Flagstaff, AZ
Assistant Commercial Loan Operations Manager. April 1997

- Managed a staff of 3; assisted in their training and development
- Oversaw daily functions, including customer servicing, billing, and computer input and its subsequent balancing
- Controlled collateral areas; reviewed loan documentation
- Prepared various reports and information for loan officers
- Organized a tickler and filing system

Loan Operations Clerk (March 1995 - April 1996)

- Performed various duties assigned by the Loan Manager, including credit investigations and inquiries, computer input and settlement, maintenance of files, and typing of reports and letters

EDUCATION

American Institute of Banking, Worcester, MA
Athol - Warren Koch High School, Flagstaff, AZ. Graduated 1989

Customer Service Manager

JAMES SHARPE, 9 CENTRAL AVENUE, MIAMI, FL 33152. (305) 555-1212

EXPERIENCE

CUSTOMER SERVICE MANAGER

A TELECOMMUNICATIONS SATELLITE COMPANY   5-94 to Present

Hired and developed a staff of forty people to service the customer service needs of our highest revenue commercial accounts. Maintained an account retention percentage of 99%, while keeping revenue loss through credits to less than 2%.

CUSTOMER SERVICE - TELEMARKETING MANAGER

MCI - S.E. Region Customer Service Center, Miami, FL   3-92 to 5-94

Hired and developed a staff of sixty customer service - telemarketing representatives and supervisors.

Managed a mixture of inbound and outbound call activities with job responsibilities including: sales, customer service, customer correspondence and special projects.

Responsible for a budget of close to one million dollars.

CUSTOMER SERVICE SUPERVISOR

NYNEX, New York, NY   1-91 to 3-92

Supervision of a division customer service staff. Responsibilities include: providing support for our sales force and sales management, implementing new policy and procedures for customer service, and monitoring to see that all our sales and service objectives are met.

CUSTOMER SERVICE REPRESENTATIVE

NYNEX   6-86 to 1-91

Involved in all aspects of customer service, including: answering questions, problem solving, interfacing with our sales force, and working with new customers to implement SPRINT services.

EDUCATION

B.A. 1986, Florida State University.

TRAINING

Leadership and Management of Change. Results Oriented Management. Managing Management Time.

REFERENCES AVAILABLE ON REQUEST

Data Processing Supervisor

James Sharpe
9 Central Avenue
Lakewood, CO 80228
(303) 555-1212

OBJECTIVE:
To make a contribution using my proven abilities with MAPPER Run Design, Microcomputers and Mainframes.

EXPERIENCE HIGHLIGHTS:

A COMPUTER PERIPHERAL MANUFACTURER, Denver, CO. 1988 - Present
DATA PROCESSING SUPERVISOR: Responsible for overseeing the work of seven full-time and three part-time employees. Coordinated, controlled, and directed the ordering, use, and maintenance of Unisys Equipment. Ensured accuracy and security with all Data Entry and output.

Accountable for the maintenance, operation, and performance of the UNIDATS Data Communications Network for Denver and all outside users. Responsible for the MAPPER site-coordinator and user community.

TECHNICAL PROGRAMMER: Responsible for the operation of DP Center. Extensive system programming in Assembler for the Univac 9300. Position required thorough knowledge of communications equipment.

EDUCATION:

UNIVERSITY OF SOUTH FLORIDA - St. Petersburg, Florida
B.A. Business Administration
Major: Management (with emphasis on programming languages)

AFFILIATIONS:

Member - Data Processing Management Association:

- 1992-93 Director
- 1991 Student Chapter Chairperson
- 1990 Program Chairperson.

PERSONAL ATTRIBUTES:

I am accustomed to accepting responsibility and delegating authority, and am capable of working with and through people at all levels. Am able to plan, organize, develop, implement, and supervise complex programs and special projects. Have a good sense of humor and a personal dedication to producing timely, cost-effective results.

Database Administrator

Jane Swift
9 Central Avenue
New York, NY 10021
(212) 555-1212

SUMMARY: Twelve years' data processing experience in a Mainframe/Transaction Database environment that includes eight years as Corporate Database Administrator.

HARDWARE & SOFTWARE:. Univac 1108, 1100/40, 60, 62, 80; IBM 33X, 43X ANSI COBOL, COBOL Database Manipulation Language, UNIX, LIUNIX, NT Server 4.0, 3.51, Windows 95, SQL Server, SQL Anywhere, Power Builder, Oracle, Visual Basic.

COURSES: COBOL Database Manipulation Language, Database Design Assembly Language Programming, Systems Support Programming, Transaction Processing Programming.

1988 to present   ***SULIKAN COPPER, Database Administrator***

- Database usage monitoring, database maintenance and sizing, database reorganizations. Also schema/subschema enhancements
- Designed and successfully implemented schema and subsystem flow for the Order Entry Subsystem
- Designed and successfully implemented Corporate Micro Computer Hardware and Software Standards, saving the company over $40,000 in 1992
- Maintained communications network for over 150 terminals
- Corporate Micro Computer Hardware/Software Support Manager for an installed base of 400 personal computers
- Developed and maintained COBOL/Transaction/Database applications programs

1986-1988   ***INCO INC. Database Administrator***

- Translated logical design through physical design into IMS control blocks
- Monitored and tuned IMS and CICS/IMS applications
- Forecasted capacity requirements for new IMS or CICS releases
- Assisted Applications by converting existing files to IMS Fastpath
- Designed and implemented numerous utilities which automated many DBA tasks

1982 to 1986   ***REDMARK RETAILERS, Programmer/Analyst***

Support of large online-batch purchasing system

References available on request.

Dietitian

Jane Swift
9 Central Avenue
Middleburg Heights, OH 44130
(216) 555-1212

JOB OBJECTIVE: To provide quality nutritional care to individuals through clinical or community responsibilities

EXPERIENCE:
August 1990-
Present

Dietary Director, Middleburg Community Hospital (Middleburg, OH)
Supervise in-depth nutritional assessment of patients on hyperalimentation, formulation of classes on weight reduction, diabetes, and geriatric nutrition. Chief of Staff describes the improvement in the quality of patient care and food served in the hospital as "nothing short of spectacular."

October 1990-
Present

Consultant Dietitian (part-time), Veterans Hospital (Cleveland, OH)
Developed standards for nutritional care, assisted the dietary director in preparation of the policy and procedure manual, conducted routine clinical duties.

April 1987-
August 1990

Clinical Dietitian/Assistant Director of Dietary, St. John's Hospital (Cleveland, OH)
Developed cost-effective nourishment center, produced videotaped modules on weight reduction, diabetic, and low-sodium diets. Established nutritional care standards for hepatic disease for use by local dietitians.

EDUCATION:

M.S. in Nutrition, Michigan State University
B.S. in Dietetics, Michigan State University
Dietetic Internship, Veterans Administration Hospital, Detroit, MI

REFERENCES: Available upon request

Director of Medical Records

JANE SWIFT
9 CENTRAL AVENUE
WATERBURY, VT 05676
(802) 555-1212

EMPLOYMENT HISTORY

SISTERS OF MERCY HOSPITAL. Waterbury, VT
Director, Medical Records   *1992-present*
Plan, organize, direct, and control the activities of two supervisors and fifteen employees in a
medical record department servicing a 320-bed non-profit teaching hospital with an annual
rate of 12,000 patient discharges, 17,388 emergency service visits, and 29,723 outpatient and
clinic visits.

Accomplishments:

- Reduced backlog of $1.2 million in suspended billing and a three-month backlog in
  coding within first three months of assumption of department in 1986.
- Eliminated a backlogged in-house transcription service with a direct-dial contract
  transcription service resulting in improved turnaround time, better-quality transcription.
  Reduced loss of transcription from 20% to negligible rate.

WATERBURY GENERAL HOSPITAL. Waterbury, VT   *1985-1992*
Assisted in planning, organizing, directing, and controlling the activities of five employees in a
medical record department servicing a 267-bed proprietary hospital with an annual rate of
8,000+ patient discharges.

Accomplishments:

- Opened the Medical Record Department in this new hospital, 1985.
- Planned departmental layout, staffing, policies, and procedures for new department.
- Prepared department for initial Medicare, state licensure, and JCAH surveys for Medical
  Record Services, Medical Audit Program, Utilization Review, and Library Services.

PROFESSIONAL ORGANIZATIONS
American Medical Record Association
Risk Management Association
DRG Management Association

EDUCATION
Vermont State University. Certification: Medical Record Administration
Connecticut State University: B.A. 1985

Electrical Design Engineer

Jane Swift
9 Central Avenue
Wilton, CT 21234
(203) 555-1212

CAREER
OBJECTIVE: Development and Design of Digital and Analog equipment.

SUMMARY: Experienced with TTL, ECL, GaAs, programmable arrays, and microprocessors. Familiar with RS-232, IEEE-488, and manchester code interfaces. Analog design included Op-Amps, D/A's, A/D's, multiplexers, and sample/holds. Secret clearance.

EXPERIENCE:
1994-Present   *ELECTRICAL ENGINEER (SIKORSKY, CT)*

Designed digital and analog equipment for Avionic Fuel Measurement and Management Systems. Prime flight hardware and support test equipment designs include:

> *Analog Signal Conditioner* - Unit to condition analog and digital signals provided to flight system computers. Design employed D/A converters, active filters, and digital logic.

> *Digital Display Indicator* - Indicator displayed fuel quantity information to ground crew. Design consisted of LCD displays, digital logic, and self-contained power supply. Dealt with small packaging requirements.

> *Analog Tester* - Designed support test equipment to perform Acceptance Tests on Analog Signal Conditioner.

> *Digital Tester* - Designed support test equipment to perform Acceptance Test on Digital Display Indicator.

1987-1993   *DESIGN ENGINEER (SIMMONDS PRECISION, VT)*

Member of circuit design group. Responsible for the design and debugging of various analog and digital circuits/systems. Responsibilities included:

> Video processing portion of a radar pulse processing system. Included work with video amplifiers, track/hold amplifiers, and the high-speed A/D convertors, as well as TTL (ALS, FAST, LS), and other high-speed logic.

> A servo-controller that used programmable array logic, TTL, Op-Amps, and D/A convertors.

> A spread spectrum radio that used high-speed TTL (FAST), programmable array logic, and a 16-bit microprocessor, with a custom interface and a RS-232 interface.

EDUCATION: Old Dominion University, Norfolk, VA
B.S.E.E., cum laude

Electrician

James Sharpe
9 Central Avenue
Metairie, LA 70002
(504) 555-1212

SUMMARY

Master Electrician (licensed in Louisiana A-15346). Experienced in all types of electrical work—residential, commercial, industrial, electrical construction, and estimating. Six years' management experience as a Foreman.

EXPERIENCE
1993 to present

Cajun Electric—Metairie, Master Electrician
Responsible for all sales, estimating, work scheduling, billing, ordering of parts and equipment, maintenance of inventories, and customer service. Projects have included complete wiring of a manufacturing business after relocation, new home construction, repair of equipment, building additions. Have worked as a contractor and subcontractor.

1993

Industrial Light—New Orleans. Journeyman Electrician
Foreman on medium-sized projects, with crews of 2 to 10. Scheduled the work, checked quality and productivity, provided layouts and supervision.

1991

Prudhomme & Sons—New Orleans. Journeyman Electrician
Crew member on construction of the New Orleans Sheraton.

1990

Bechte—Saudi Arabia. Journeyman Electrician
Worked on a nuclear power plant (heavy industrial project), where safety and reliability were extremely important.

1988 to 1989

Tujaques—New Orleans. Journeyman Electrician
A variety of commercial and industrial projects (hospital, high-rise condominiums, office-hotel complex).

TRAINING

Louisiana Technical College, New Orleans
Certificate in Completion of Apprenticeship program

PERSONAL

Willing to travel, relocate

References Available

Electronics Technician

JANE SWIFT
9 Central Avenue
Signal Hill, California 90806
(310) 555-1212

OBJECTIVE

To obtain a position as an **electronics technician**.

STRENGTHS

- 11 years of electrical/electronics experience.
- Skilled in blueprint reading and in a wide variety of electrical and electronic assembly methods.
- Proven ability to exercise good judgment and contribute to efficient operations.

EXPERIENCE

August 1994 to
Present

Douglas Aircraft Company, Long Beach, California
ELECTRICAL MECHANIC
Install and test electrical harness assemblies in aircraft applications. Repair & replace wiring systems, and assemble hook-ups with connectors, grounds, terminal boards and module blocks per blueprint specifications. Troubleshoot and repair damaged electrical parts on the MD-11 aircraft.

- Received 2 awards for money-saving suggestions which resulted in a total savings to the company of over $35,000.
- Awarded a "Certificate of Appreciation for Teamwork."

August 1993 to
August 1994

ELECTRONIC ASSEMBLER
Constructed electrical harnesses to blueprint specifications, and terminated 24-gage & 10-gage wires for the avionic racks, relay switch panel, overhead switch panel, center fuselage and bilge on the MD-11 aircraft.

June 1989 to
August 1993

Hughes Aircraft Company, Fullerton, California
ELECTRICAL MECHANIC
Fabricated radar cabs, soldered connections and built cards according to blueprint specifications.

July 1987 to
June 1989

American Magnetics, Carson, California
ELECTRONIC ASSEMBLER
Assembled PC boards for magnetic card readers, built cable & harness assemblies, and performed wire preparation and soldering.

EDUCATION

Santa Monica High School, Santa Monica, California
Diploma, 1985

Douglas Aircraft Company, Long Beach, California
Certificates in:

- Alodine Touch-up
- Solder Sleeve Splicing
- Power Cable Terminals

- Crimp Connections - New
- Lug Connections
- Lug Mil 24GA-10G

Engineering Secretary

Jane Swift
9 Central Avenue
Denver, CO 80223
(303) 555-1212

EXPERIENCE: <u>1990 - Present. MOUNTAIN BELL, DENVER. ENGINEERING SECRETARY</u>

Engineering Department Secretary, responsible to 11 managers: Typing, vouchers, conference/travel arrangements, supplies, office logs, and letter files, along with many other secretarial functions. Created and implemented office guidelines and procedures.

<u>1989 - 1991. MOUNTAIN BELL, DENVER. STENOGRAPHER</u>

Worked in the Downtown Business Office maintaining customer account logs for 28 Service Representatives. Answered customer calls and directed them appropriately.

<u>1987 - 1989. MOUNTAIN BELL, DENVER. SECRETARY</u>

In the Comptrollers Department. Handled heavy typing of Bell System Practices for 8 computer programmers.

<u>1985 - 1987. MOUNTAIN BELL, DENVER. PROCESSING CLERK</u>

Processed statistical paper work for 7 *Yellow Page* Sales Representatives.

EDUCATION: Currently attending Denver College - W.P. night classes.

TRAINING: Effective Writing - 1994. Vocabulary Study - 1992. Fortune Word-Fortune Electronic Mail - 1992. Effective Telephone/Communication Skills.

PERSONAL:

- Volunteer work with Mountain Bell Telephone Pioneers
- Typing 90 W.P.M.
- Administrative Skills (efficient, good organizer, able to handle work systematically)
- Communication and telephone skills
- Self Starter - work independently to handle a variety of assignments
- Quick ability to learn the functions of any word processor

Entrepreneurial

JANE SWIFT

9 Central Avenue   Yardley, Pennsylvania 19067   (H) (215) 555-1212   (O) (215) 555-1213

QUALIFICATIONS SUMMARY
Human Resource Management
Program Development, Recruitment, Training, Quality Process Management

EXPERIENCE

Philadelphia College of Textiles and Science, Philadelphia, Pennsylvania   1988 to Present

Director, Career Planning and Placement   1993 to Present
Liaison between college and industry, building international reputation through development of the following support and services:

- Direct professional staff of three, semi-professional staff of 10 and $175,000 operating budget in providing comprehensive placement service for 3,000 BS students, 250 MBA students, and alumni.
- Develop network of corporate and government employers within Business, High Tech, Creative, and Science areas.
- Annually achieve 90% placement of graduates, and hundreds of alumni at management level.
- Market on-campus recruiting program resulting in over 200 companies visiting each season.
- Host VIP campus visits and receptions.
- Extensive travel includes organizing and supervising trade shows, attending conferences, visiting industry.
- Provide input for academic program development through analysis of industry trends.
- Initiated seminar and workshop programs covering all aspects of career planning and search.
- Publish bi-monthly nationally circulated Job Opportunities Bulletin, Annual Placement and Salary Survey, Resume Book, and Student Handbook on Placement.
- Supervise internship and summer job programs for undergraduates.
- Directed software development and computerization of department, 1988.

Assistant Director, Placement Office   1988 to 1993

INVOLVEMENTS

- Selected for Task Force, Middle States evaluation for college accreditation, 1995.
- Visited/consulted with South African organizations on recruitment program development, 1994.
- Member, College Placement Council.
- Member, Middle Atlantic Placement Association.
- Past Chairman of Membership, Publicity and Office Training Committees.
- Published articles for trade journals, appear on media, conference speaker.
- Volunteer, Freedoms Foundation of America at Valley Forge.
- Member, Toastmasters International.
- Member, Colony Civic Organization, West Norriton, Pennsylvania.
- Accomplished Photographer, enjoy painting.

EDUCATION
PHILADELPHIA COLLEGE OF TEXTILES AND SCIENCE
Evening Division, 1988 to 1996, Marketing/Management
Numerous Technical and Business Seminars
Executive Management Program
Werner Management Cosultants, 1997

Executive Assistant

Jane Swift
9 Central Avenue
Chicago, IL 60625
(312) 555-1212

WORK EXPERIENCE
11/88 to Present   Custom Mouldings Inc., Chicago, IL
Office Coordinator/Assistant to V.P. of Operations

Responsibilities and duties include:

- Supervise and direct Secretary to Manufacturing Managers
- Compile and graph financial data and manufacturing information for weekly management meetings
- Process project support requests
- Maintain weekly project time sheets; summarize and initiate monthly intercompany and direct customer billings (data entry - IBM System/38)
- Graphics (presentations, forms, graphs, etc.)
- Typing and layout of bi-monthly company newsletter (Digital Word Processor)
- Routine secretarial functions: i.e., typing, assisting callers, maintaining confidentiality of salaries, proposed business plans, etc.
- Act as backup for Administrative Assistant to C.E.O.
- Employee Activities Committee member

7/83 to 11/87   Plastic Products Ltd., Chicago, IL
Secretary to the Controller and Financial Planning Manager

Duties included:

- Data Entry (financial reports, budgets)
- Typed monthly and quarterly financial statements
- Assisted auditors with year-end audit
- Performed all day-to-day secretarial functions

EDUCATION
1982   Leominster High School Graduate (Business Course)
1991   C.M.E.A. Course - Basic Personnel Administration
1994   Calligraphy Course - Mount Wachusett Community College
1995   Introduction to Graphics course - Worcester Art Museum

OFFICE SKILLS   IBM System/38 user; IBM PC (Lotus/Symphony Software); Digital Word Processor; Dimension Switchboard; Dictaphone; IBM Typewriters. Typing 80 WPM.

REFERENCES   Furnished upon request

Executive Manager

James Sharpe

9 Central Avenue • *Sterling Heights, Michigan 48310* • *Ph: (810) 555-1212*

Executive Summary

A resourceful and team-oriented senior executive with more than 12 years progressive experience, personally mentored by the principal, in the successful and rapid growth of a privately held multi-divisional organization. Recognized for exceptional ability to develop and manage new business units and companies, create and implement successful marketing strategies, and form synergistic business alliances thus protecting the investment of the organization and assuring the attainment of the target return. Uniquely effective in building organizations through open channels of communication and cooperative relationships between executive management and members of the Board of Directors.

- Start Up/Project Management
- Sales/Marketing Stratagems
- Financial/Operational Cost Control
- New Business Development
- Operations Management
- Profit Optimization
- Strategic Alliance
- Business Valuation
- P&L Responsibility

Selected Achievements

- *Developed and implemented operational, administrative, and financial management strategies resulting in the growth of a 7 member start-up into a 1,000 employee, multi-divisional concern with **annual revenues exceeding $100 million.** Due to its significant growth, this organization was named to the **INC. 500 for four consecutive years.***
- ***Built a new educational/training business unit** initially serving the **Big 3 auto companies** and the UAW through the creation and development of a variety of training programs. Starting from the ground up, this unit generated $7 million in operating income on revenues of $32 million in just 42 months.*
- *Identified and led the development of a **mutually profitable strategic alliance** that united the purchasing and distribution systems of a national organization with a privately owned financing consideration. This alliance resulted in a 300% increase in annual operating lease additions, from $25 million to $75 million.*
- *Effectively directed the downsizing of an overgrown entrepreneurial organization. Through strategic staff and business unit reductions, the company achieved a **58% increase in income** and a **27% increase in ROE** within just three years.*
- *Spearheaded the implementation of innovative tax strategies that effectively utilized a separate line of business resulting in the conversion of **$2.5 million in underutilized assets into income.***

Employment History

Director, Business Development   **Performance Medical, Troy, MI**

Orchestrated new business development for this imaging software start-up from the successful negotiation of a royalty arrangement with a natal manufacturer through the $500,000 private placement securing expansion funding.

President O/E Automation, Inc., Troy, MI

Mentored by the founder of Vlasic Foods, Bob Vlasic, successfully progressing with the company for 12 years holding positions including Treasurer, Vice President-Finance and ultimately becoming President. During my tenure with O/E, I served on the Board of Directors on 13 different O/E companies, encompassing a variety of industries, while annual revenues grew from $3 million to $108 million.

Education

BSA, *University of Michigan, 1986*
CPA Certificate

Executive Marketing/Sales

JAMES SHARPE

9 Central Avenue • *Venetia, Pennsylvania 15367* • *(412) 555-1212*

Executive Summary

A fast-track, highly motivated, team oriented executive with a successful background in **turnaround situations.** *More than 8 years progressive experience in all phases of* **HMO Market Development** *and* **Regional Sales Management.** *Recognized for exceptional ability to develop specialized marketing stratagems, sales methods, and training procedures. Effectively motivates others on all levels in the achievement of individual and organizational goals.*

- P & L Responsibility
- Sales Management
- Market Optimization
- Marketing/Advertising Strategy
- Training Module Development
- Benefits Program Development
- Operations Management
- Interpersonal Relations
- Provider Contracting

Selected Achievements

- *Orchestrated the turnaround of the Pittsburgh region through the creation and introduction of a prototype Medicare Risk Marketing Program which set the standard for all other* **US Healthcare** *Regions.*
- *Developed and implemented sales management and advertising/marketing strategies resulting in a 260% increase in sales, from $71 million to $185 million in 1995, thus tripling profitability.*
- *Facilitated successful negotiations with Key Providers & Hospitals increasing the Primary Physician Network from 225 to 700.*
- *In just one year boosted* **US Healthcare** *net membership from 40,000 to 80,000 and Medicare net membership from 2,200 to 17,000, achieving 100% and 775% increases, respectively.*
- *Developed and implemented competitive training modules ultimately utilized company-wide. Initiated the management team's supervision of all marketing and sales representatives thus assuring full compliance and a successful continuing educational process.*
- *Spearheaded new business development in Boston, a highly penetrated managed care market, and increased regional sales from $9 million to $90 million as well as net membership from 5,000 to 50,000.*

Employment History

Regional Vice President   *1995 to Present*

   US Healthcare, Pittsburgh, Pennsylvania

District New Business Sales Manager   *1990 to 1995*
   US Healthcare, Boston, Massachusetts

Account Executive   *1988 to 1990*
   US Healthcare, New York, New York

Education

Bachelor of Science, Education/Mathematics, 1986
Cortland State College, Cortland, New York

Field Sales Manager

JAMES SHARPE, 9 Central Avenue, Arlington, MA 02174. (617) 555-1212.

QUALIFICATIONS SUMMARY

Ten years of demonstrated sales experience drawing upon planning, persuasion, problem-solving, and administration skills.

SELECTED ACHIEVEMENTS AND RESULTS

Planning
- Created and composed promotional materials for use with product line. Resulted in free product promotion in local and national publications. Valued at $650,000.
- Presented, demonstrated, evaluated and published product information on a national basis. Resulted in increased expansion of distributor base and sales by 49%.

Persuasion
- Influenced company management to expand product size through generated market research data and demonstrated product mix. Resulted in a 25% increase of total volume in each product.
- Persuaded organization to reduce sales territory and add personnel to form a first-time specialty products group. Results in increased awareness of product organizationally and within the industry.

Problem-Solving
- Resolved formulating equipment/product mismatch by designing new packaging. Resulted in increased sales of $250K.
- Identified high-use market for product and generated data to expand product usage. Resulted in increased sales of 70%.

Administration
- Co-directed the efforts of the marketing department through active participation on the corporate marketing board. Resulted in new advertising, package, and product promotions.
- Synthesized intricate and diverse marketing training and product publication information. Resulted in increased market penetration.

WORK HISTORY

Regional Sales Representative, Phone Relays. Boston, MA	1993-Present
Sales Representative, Walsh Chemical. Worcester, MA	1993
Retail Store Manager, Clothing Supply. Arlington, MA	1990-1992
Assistant Dept. Manager, Penny's. Boston, MA	1989-1990

EDUCATION

BA - Marketing, Columbia Pacific University, 1988

Finance (Entry-Level)

JAMES SHARPE   9 Central Avenue, Fox Hills, CA 90230

                                                (310) 555-1212

OBJECTIVE: Seeking an Internship

QUALIFICATIONS:

- Computer literate; knowledge of WordPerfect 5.1, Lotus 1-2-3, & dBase.
- Ability to work well under pressure and handle multiple tasks.
- Excellent interpersonal relations skills; able to relate well with people from diverse backgrounds and cultures.
- Highly motivated; work well both independently and as part of a team.
- Fast learner; quickly absorb and utilize new methods.

EDUCATION: UNIVERSITY OF SOUTHERN CALIFORNIA, Los Angeles, CA
                    CANDIDATE FOR A B.A. DEGREE IN ECONOMICS (1998)
                    MINOR IN FINANCE

                    WEST LOS ANGELES COLLEGE, W. Los Angeles, CA
                    ECONOMICS

                    LOS ANGELES HIGH SCHOOL, Los Angeles, CA

EMPLOYMENT:
1996 to Present   UNIVERSITY OF SOUTHERN CALIFORNIA, Los Angeles, CA
                    Tutor
                    Assist students in sharpening their math skills.

1993 to 1995   STEVEN M. HOEFFLIN M.D., F.A.C.S., Santa Monica, CA
                    File Clerk
                    Filed medical records and insurance forms.

1992 to 1995   YOUNG MEN'S CHRISTIAN ASSOCIATION, Baldwin Hills, CA
                    Assistant Manager
                    Tutored and supervised children and assisted the Director. Also, assumed Director's duties in her absence.

1991 to 1992   SEARS CO., Los Angeles, CA
                    Sales Person
                    Assisted customers, handled complaints and problems.

REFERENCES: Available Upon Request

Financial Executive Secretary

Jane Swift
9 Central Avenue
Nashville, TN 37211
(615) 555-1212

Employment History:
10/94 - Present

Commerce Bank & Trust Company, Nashville, TN
Executive Secretary
Secretary to two Vice Presidents of Commercial Loan. Duties included preparation of loan documents, processing of new funds, completion of computer input sheet for loan transactions, typing shorthand, and screening calls. Coordination and hostessing of a monthly breakfast meeting sponsored by the bank for area businesses. This involved mailing of invitations, taking reservations, making arrangements with the restaurant, and hostessing the meeting.

Started as a Clerk/Typist in the Collection Department. After one year of employment was promoted to Secretary in Secured Lending Department. Held this position for 1 1/2 years, at which time was promoted to above position as Executive Secretary in Commercial Loan Department.

7/91 - 10/94

The Nashville Bank, N.A. Nashville, TN
Executive Secretary
Secretary to Vice President of Commercial Loan and Marketing. Duties include general secretarial (typing, shorthand, screening calls). Customer service for loan transactions and depository accounts. Responsible for advising all departments of new bank products and advertising of these products.

Education:

Nashville Community College
Secretarial Science (one semester)
Spencer Dynes High School
Business/Secretarial (graduated 1981 with honors)

References:

Furnished upon request.

Food and Beverage Service Director

Jane Swift
9 Central Avenue
Metairie, LA 70003
(504) 555-1212

A professional in the restaurant and resort business with a thorough background in the culinary service and accounting fields.

PRESENT: **METAIRIE TURF CLUB Metairie, Louisiana**
                  Food and Beverage Director

Directly responsible for start-up and management of all restaurant operations, group sales, central kitchen operations, and purchasing.

The project hired 14 managers and 400 employees for a total Food & Beverage staff of $11,000,000. Formed the entire concession company in 3 months, including: systems identification and implementation, hiring of staff, menus, table-top and uniform identification, training, product identification.

1983-92   **BRAUTIGANS Vail, Colorado**
                  Food and Beverage Manager

Hired as the Executive Chef and moved into the position of a Senior Food Services Manager overseeing 10 managers and over 150 employees in the area of conventions, commissary operations, and purchasing for 14 restaurants.

Work Achievements: Restaurants served 25,000 quality meals per day. Successfully reduced the cost of sales consistently to 26% for the past three years on $8,000,000 gross revenue. Designed and implemented a new purchasing computer program, including a recipe costing and inventory system.

1980-83   **KANCOLA CORPORATION Vail, Colorado**
                  Executive Chef

Executive Chef of the Cadillac Club and John Bull pub and restaurant

ACTIVITIES: Involved in the Chef de Cuisine Association. Taught several classes connected with the Chef de Cuisine intern program, including a recent NIFDA course on sanitation.

Worked on the development and implementation of a two- and six-week culinary seminar course with the National Culinary School.

EDUCATION: Culinary Institute of America

Food Product Manager

JANE SWIFT

9 CENTRAL AVENUE • AKRON, OH 44303 • (216) 555-1212

EXPERIENCE 1978-Present	**JUSTSO!, AKRON, OH** Manufacturer of cookies, crackers, and snacks for the retail, food service, and industrial markets.
1994-Present	**GOVERNMENT PROGRAMS MANAGER**, Food Service Division Responsible for all governmental programs, including Federal, State, and Local. Directly involved in USDA Commodity Processing, Department of Defense, schools, military, and elderly feeding programs. Administers and submits bids to government agencies, institutions, and military service operations to achieve maximum sales and profit objectives. Supervises staff of four, including government sales manager and customer service coordinators. Sales increase of 22%.
1992-1994	**SENIOR PRODUCT MANAGER**, Food Service Division Developed new products outside traditional cookie/cracker markets via co-pack agreements. New Products now account for 15% of sales. Responsibilities included market analysis, product development, co-packer search and development, manufacturing agreements, and product introduction.
1991-1992	**PRODUCT MANAGER**, Food Service Division Developed new products program, pricing, promotional and sales strategies. Introduced new vendor line of products, accounting for 8% of total division sales.
1989-1991	**AREA MANAGER**, Mid-West Food Service Division. Responsible for Chicago, Detroit, Columbus, Akron. Developed and maintained Regional level contacts with major national accounts. Implemented sales and marketing programs with staff of five territory managers and two sales representatives.
1986-1989	**DISTRICT MANAGER**, Food Service Division Responsible for the Philadelphia and South Jersey Marketing Area.
1984-1986	**DISTRICT MANAGER**, Retail Division Supervised eight direct salesmen and Assistant District Manager. Responsible for the Shop 'n Save, 7-11, and K-Mart chain accounts.
1982-1984	**SALES TRAINER**, Retail Division Responsible for training all new salesmen in the Mid-West Sales Zone.
1978-82	**SALESMAN**, Retail Division Responsible for sales to the Retail and Food Service Trade.
EDUCATION	B.A. Marketing 1978 (Ohio State University)

Food Service Salesperson

JAMES SHARPE
9 Central Avenue
Dayton, OH 45401
(513) 555-1212

OBJECTIVE To secure a full-time marketing/management position offering personal growth, challenge, and responsibility

EXPERIENCE
1994 to present

FOOD SERVICE AND BAKERY CORPORATION, Dayton, OH
Territory Manager

Responsibilities include administration of a territory encompassing all of Ohio and Michigan. Extensive contact with distributors selling premium brand and private label shortenings, oils, and margarines. Took on additional responsibility of the East Tennessee territory after one year. Responsibility for 55 million pounds of product with $1.2 million profit contribution.

1993 to 1994

FASTFOODS, Cincinnati, OH
Territory Manager

Responsibilities included administration of a specified territory through contact with foodservice wholesale warehouse management and through operator contact on the end-user level. Account growth was achieved through sampling of products to qualified buyers, stressing features and benefits for specific menu applications, new product introductions, and effective promotions. Cited for Specialty New Account Sales.

1990 to 1993

KOSHER FOODS CORPORATION, New York, NY
Foodservice Division

Account Representative (1990 - 1991)
Sales Representative (1990 - 1992)
Salesman of the Year 1993. Runner-up, 1992

EDUCATION **Columbia University, New York, NY.** B.B.A. - Marketing, 1990.

AFFILIATIONS American Marketing Association

Health Care Professional

Jane Swift
9 Central Avenue
Seattle, WA 98102
(206) 555-1212

OBJECTIVE

Management/Marketing position in Health Care setting.

SUMMARY

Experienced Health Care professional with working knowledge of home health, in-hospital-based, and free-standing agencies. In addition to promotion of retail sales of medical equipment and services.

EXPERIENCE

1996   *Home Care Inc.*, Seattle, WA
Responsible for development and implementation of a total scope, home IV therapy program. Includes home total parental nutrition in accordance with NITA standards. Performed budgetary control duties and ensured organizational proficiency and compliance with all State and Federal regulations.

Additional responsibilities include: Sales, marketing, and purchasing for eleven durable medical equipment outlets.

1992-96   *Seattle General Hospital*, Seattle, WA
Progressive positions in the Home Care Department reaching the position of Home Care Coordinator for the City Hospital District. As Department Head, held responsibility for scheduling, planning, and supervision of 15 professional and numerous non-professional workers.

Developed community awareness and doubled the amount of services provided to the community in the area of home health care.

EDUCATION

1991   Registered Nursing Degree, Columbia Basin College (Pasco, WA)

Health Care Sales Manager

JAMES SHARPE
9 Central Avenue
Indianapolis, IN 46206
(317) 555-1212

SUMMARY:	Extensive experience managing a sales function selling directly and through brokers. Strong background in implementing sales techniques through training, motivation, and effective sales meetings.

BUSINESS
EXPERIENCE:

A Pharmaceuticals Manufacturer. Consumer Healthcare Division. **District Sales Manager** (1988 to Present)

Responsible for sales and profit objectives. Responsible for broker test program, broker selection, and broker management.

Recruit, train, and direct five Key Account Representatives and three Merchandisers.

Accomplishments:

- During my tenure, nine new products have been introduced and sales volume has climbed from $2.1 million to $7.3 million.
- Converted strong business relationships with retail customers into new broker business.
- Attained 14-21% sales increase through broker management in two years.
- District Manager of the Year for five of the last eight years.
- Second-highest Unit manager in 1993, with attainment of +137% of budget.

Key Account Representative (1986 to 1988)

Responsible for the sales, distribution and promotion of health care products to all classes of trade in Midwest. My territory contributed 28% of the district's volume.

Successfully introduced three new products and attained a 37% increase in sales my last full year in the territory.

MEAD JOHNSON, **Sales Representative** (1981-1986)

Responsible for the sales, distribution and promotion of Carter products to all classes of trade in West Texas.

Increased territory volume 31% in two years. Successfully introduced five new products.

EDUCATION:	1980, Princeton University. Major: Marketing
SEMINARS:	Master Salesmanship Course - Clement Communications
	Various other salesmanship and managerial courses
AFFILIATION:	American Marketing Association
REFERENCES:	References will be furnished upon request.

Health Services Manager

James Sharpe

9 Central Avenue • Freehold, New Jersey 07728-4091 • Ph: (908) 555-1212

Professional Summary

A fast track, highly motivated, team oriented executive with a successful background in **start-up situations** and **organizational growth**. More than 15 years progressive experience in all phases of **healthcare market development** as well **as multi-unit expansion and management**. Recognized for exceptional ability to develop specialized marketing strategies, sales methods, and training procedures. Effectively motivates others on all levels in the achievement of individual and organizational goals.

Areas of Expertise

- P&L Responsibility
- Sales Management
- Market Optimization

- Start-Up & Project Management
- New Business Development
- Marketing/Advertising Strategy

- Business Valuation
- Team Building
- Concept Development

Career Highlights

- Facilitated successful negotiations with Bally's Total Fitness Centers securing the expansion of **220 additional locations**. Projected annual revenues from this **contract exceed $80 million.**
- Orchestrated the successful turnaround of an unprofitable IPO candidate. Over a nine-month period, through a complete restructuring, recruiting and training of the staff, **revenues increased 750%.**
- Spearheaded all facets of an **international start-up and expansion** of a healthcare management organization. Within 24 months revenues exceeded $2 million.
- Key member in the development of **4 public companies**. As a Consultant and assistant to **Beryl Wolk of Goodway Marketing** was privileged to work with individuals including **Jack Goken of MCI.**
- Created, developed, and implemented chiropractic screening booth that was aggressively marketed and sold to hundreds of chiropractors around the country.

Employment History

Vice President, Operations & Development
Complete Wellness Centers, Inc., *Washington, D.C.*
Marketing Consultant
Goodway Marketing, Inc., *Jenkintown, PA*
Vice President/President
United Health Corpration, Inc., *Melville, NH*
Owner, Developer & Entrepreneur
Roston Chiropractic Promotion's , *Eatontown, NJ*
Clinic Director
Roston's Chiropractic & Podiatry Center, *Eatontown, NJ*

Education

B.S. & D.C., Docor of Chiropractic
National College of Chiropractic, Lumbard, IL

B.A., Architectural Engineering, Human Biomechanics
Ohio University, Athens, OH

High-Tech Salesperson

Jane Swift
9 Central Avenue
Boston, MA 02127
(617) 555-1212

POSITION DESIRED
Professionally rewarding sales position that will offer an opportunity for professional growth and advancement based upon a demonstrated strength in opening new accounts.

EXPERIENCE
1996 to present

Marketing Representative. Major Computer Manufacturer.
Marketed large mainframe CPU, disk drives, and tape drives. Quota: $2.5M. Competition: IBM.
Accomplishments:

Sales: $2.6 million
Opened Chevron Account with CPU, July 1996
Opened Bell Southwestern Services account, October 1996

1993 to 1996   **Account Manager. Storage Technology Corporation.**
Marketed disk drives, tape drives, and memory for CPU's printers and professional service packages to the *Fortune* 500 companies.
Competition: IBM.
Accomplishments:

Sales: $4.5 million
Helped open Southwestern Bell
Earned Corporate Club in 1994 and 1995
National recognition for first firm order of new product

1989 to 1993   **Marketing Representative. Control Data.**
Marketed disk drives, tape drives, and printers.
Competition IBM. Responsible for four new accounts and three add-on orders with existing accounts. Quota: $1.7M.
Accomplishments:

Sales: $2.3 million
#1 salesman in nation in 1993, 1991
#2 salesman in nation in 1992

EDUCATION
George Washington University, BBA; 1987

SUMMARY
My experience in the data processing world has provided me with a knowledge of large, medium, and small computer systems, as well as general business application software packages. My track record proves my belief that every objection brings you closer to the sale.

Hospital Pharmacist

James Sharpe, 9 Central Avenue, Clifton, NJ 07013. (201) 555-1212

OBJECTIVES:

To use my pharmacy, communication, administrative, and organizational skills in a challenging position as a hospital pharmacist.

EXPERIENCE:

Resident Pharmacist. *Teaneck Community Hospital. May 1992 - Present*
Pharmacy administration, provision of drug information/poison control center services, clinical services, outpatient pharmacy services, and investigational drug services.

Duties included rotations throughout all areas of a progressive, computerized hospital pharmacy department. Including: Drug Information, Medical Information, Administration, Clinical Pharmacy, Outpatient Pharmacy, and Investigational Drug Services.

Staff Pharmacist, *Centralized and Decentralized Services. Mahwah Cottage Hospital. May 1989 - May 1992*
Inpatient unit dose drug distribution and IV admixture services; participation in daily hematology and GI patient rounds; discharge patient counseling. Provision of drug information to hospital staff; participation on aminoglyoside pharmacokinetic monitoring service; training and education of new pharmacists and pharmacy students.

Pharmacy Extern. *Mahwah Cottage Hospital. February 1989 - May 1989*
IV admixture preparation, unit dose drug distribution, maintenance of patient profiles, and quality assurance procedures.

Pharmacy Extern. *Apothecary. Mahwah Cottage Hospital. November 1988 - February 1989*
Participated in patient counseling, patient profile maintenance, extensive extemporaneous compounding service, and inventory control.

APPOINTMENTS:

American Hospital Formulary Service Reviewer

REGISTRATION:

State of New Jersey

AFFILIATIONS:

American Society of Hospital Pharmacists
American Pharmaceutical Association
American Society of Hospital Pharmacists

EDUCATION:

Bachelor of Science, Pharmacy, New Jersey Institute of Technology 1989

Interior Designer (Entry-Level)

Jane Swift

9 Central Avenue   Seattle, WA 98102   (206) 555-1212

OBJECTIVE	A challenging position in Interior Design where application and utilization of knowledge and skills may be applied.

EDUCATION

BFA - Interior Design	May 1998
Cornish College	Seattle, Washington
AAA - Fashion Merchandising	September 1991
Houston, Texas	Art Institute
High School for the Performing and Visual Arts	June 1988
Houston, Texas	Area of Study: Dance

CAREER PROFILE

Marshall Field   July 1994 - November 1991
Houston, Texas   Visual Merchandising Management Assistant
In charge of Women's Wear and Junior Apparel areas. Assisted Department Managers with floor layouts and fixturing. Set up promotions and prepared for Buyer visits. Developed and implemented props and graphics. Met with Buyers and Executives regularly. Generated ideas for "shop" concepts. Bookkeeping and inventory control.

Mad Hatter Agency   October 1991 - June 1991
Houston, Texas   Assistant to Barbara Rhyne, Fashion Director
Planned and organized workshops. Assisted with casting calls and runway auditions.

AB Productions   November 1991 - March 1991
Houston, Texas   Producer-Director-Choreographer
Marketed fashion show production to Agencies, Retailers, Nightclubs, and Hotels. Organized and held auditions. Designed promotional material. Managed over 25 people at one time.

Saks Fifth Avenue   February 1990 - November 1989
Houston, Texas   Display Associate
Assisted with installation and breakdown of holiday visuals.

Houston Grand Opera   Fall Season 1987 / Spring Season 1989
Houston, Texas   Dancer

WORKSHOPS & SEMINARS

Glassell School, Houston, Texas. Photography. March 1989 - January 1994
Retailer Seminar - Profit Program, Dallas, Texas. 10 hrs. May 1991

EXHIBITIONS & AWARDS

1997	Furniture and Light Show, Fisher Gallery Cornish
1996	ASID Award Recipient
1993	Black and White Photography Exhibition, The Museum School, Houston, Texas
1990	"Best Sales Promotion Presentation," Art Institute, Houston, Texas

REFERENCES AND PORTFOLIO AVAILABLE UPON REQUEST

Inventory Manager (Assets Manager)

James Sharpe

9 Central Avenue • Newark, Ohio 43055 • Phone: (614) 555-1212

Executive Summary

A highly innovative and seasoned Senior Executive with more than 15 years successful, progressive experience in all phases of Workouts and Liquidation management. Hands-on, pro-active manager recognized for exceptional ability to create and implement successful asset/receivable recovery strategies and to manage the dissolution of business units and portfolios. Uniquely effective in the development of asset liquidation techniques and the sale of capital equipment.

Areas of Effectiveness

- Capital & Operational Analysis
- Asset Valuation & Recovery
- Sales & Remarketing Strategies
- Business Valuation
- Arbitration/Litigation
- Liquidation management
- P & L Responsibility
- Project Management
- Contract Negotiation

Related Accomplishments

- Developed and implemented the company's first recovery unit (hired, trained and managed) with an exposure of **$50 million.** Over the first three years, this team successfully **held losses to 35 percent** of outstanding lease contracts.
- Aggressively restructured and worked out the sale of all capital equipment for two major sports facilities **recovering 100 percent of the $6 million debt.** Additionally, facilitated the sale of 5 distressed broadcasting organizations for $4.5 million, recouping **75 percent of the outstanding debt.**
- Directed the recovery and negotiated the resale of 9 airplanes, including **3 Boeing 727-100** aircraft. Total selling price exceeded **$11 million**, which limited losses to 10% book value.
- Orchestrated the **liquidation of a $30 million leased asset portfolio** including the consolidation of 16 regional offices into one central location. Over a 3 year period successfully recovered more than **$23 million, a 287 percent increase** over the original buyout offer of $8 million.
- Effectively managed a **$200 million asset portfolio** opening three new offices and increasing staff to 66. Responsibilities included: **asset management, collections, equipment sales and workout.**

Employment History

Principal   **1997 to Present**
E.B.O. Asset Management, Inc., Columbus, OH
  Personally purchased the remaining assets (accounts receivable & capital equipment) of Eden Air Freight, Inc. for $10,000. To date, total recovery exceeds $200,000.

Vice President, Lease Asset Liquidation   **1993 to 1997**
Aegon U.S.A., North American H.Q., Baltimore, MD

Asset/Receivable Manager   **1992 to 1993**
LeaseAmerica Corporation, Cedar Rapids, IA

Managing Partner   **1989 to 1992**
Wright-Holmes, Inc., d.b.a. Wright Holmes Law List
  Purchased majority interest of this firm, publishers of an annual directory of attorneys specializing in commercial collections, creditor rights, and bankruptcy. Increased sales and sold company in 1991.

Vice President, Regional Manager   **1983 to 1989**
Inter-Regional Financial Group (IFG) Leasing, Minneapolis, MN

Junior Accounting Clerk

James Sharpe
9 Central Avenue
Huntington Beach, CA 92649
(714) 555-1212

OBJECTIVE: A challenging position in the accounting profession

WORK EXPERIENCE:

June 1993 -   HUNTINGTON BEACH GAZETTE
January 1997   Huntington Beach, CA

Accounting Clerk for classified accounting. Duties included accounts receivable on Vax system, balancing, adjusting, and posting receivables. Heavy phone contact with customers for collections. Collections improved 7 percent.

March 1992 -   AIN ASSOCIATES
June 1992   Los Angeles, CA

General office work for temporary employment agency. Duties included clerk in Tax office, clerk in Health Insurance Company, and A/R for construction company.

August 1991 - CALA FOODS
March 1992   Los Angeles, CA

Cashier. Worked independently doing all cashier duties, some bookkeeping and inventory.

EDUCATION:
March 1992 -   CALIFORNIA SCHOOL OF ACCOUNTING
March 1993   Los Angeles, CA

Graduate in March of 1993 with a certificate as a Computer Accounting Assistant. Courses include Accounting, Business Math, Basic Programming, Integrated Accounting on IBM PC and Lotus. Plan on continuing with night courses for degree.

REFERENCES: Personal references available upon request.

Law Clerk

Jane Swift
9 Central Ave.
Downers Grove, IL 60515
(312) 555-1212

Objective: To obtain a position in which I can utilize my work experience and education.

EMPLOYMENT

1993 - Present   United States Court of Appeals. Second Circuit, Chicago, IL
INFORMATION CLERK

Answer procedural questions regarding local rules and Federal Rules of Appellate Procedures. Respond to inquiries from a wide range of sources including the media, attorneys, and litigants. Receive and review over-the-counter filings such as briefs, motions, appendices, and petitions for rehearing for format, time constraints, and proof of service.

1990 - 1993   United States District Court. Southern District, Chicago, IL
PRO SE WRIT CLERK

Answer procedural questions regarding local rules. Examine all complaints to determine if they are in proper form for filing. Ensure petitioners and complainants understand procedural requirements. Maintain liaison with State Attorney General's staff, state prison authorities, and other agencies concerning prisoner complaints and petitions. Prepare statistical reports and analyses of pending matters.

1987 - 1990   Department of Justice. U.S. Attorney's Office. Southern District of Chicago
LEGAL CLERK

Research of documents and inquiries for individual Assistant U.S. Attorneys. Issue warrants for arrest; process writs of habeas corpus, AD testificandum prosequendum; verify prison surrenders. Record keeping of criminal calendars, processing of legal documents, updating computer.

EDUCATION

City University of Chicago. B.A. 1986. Major: Business Management

References furnished upon request.

Law (Entry-Level)

JAMES SHARPE
9 Central Avenue, Apt 2
Brooklyn, NY 10017
(212) 555-1212

OBJECTIVE

Seeking a position with a Law Firm, where my interest in the law would be challenged, fostering a new curiosity and pointing toward my ultimate career path.

EDUCATION

FORDHAM UNIVERSITY, New York, New York
Bachelor of Science (anticipated date of graduation, January 1998)

Major: History—G.P.A.: 3.4
Courses included: European Medieval History, American History, Political Science, Politics as a Political Economy, International Law, Theology and Philosophy.
Topic of Research Papers: 14th Century Europe/Germany, Presidential Powers and American Intervention in Vietnam, and Thomas Aquinas.

Minor: Economics—G.P.A.: 3.0
Courses included: Financial Markets, New York Stock Exchange, American Stock Exchange, Marketing, Statistics and Math.

Extracurricular Activities: Member of the Greek Society

EMPLOYMENT
10/95 to Present

DR. ANDREAS COSMATOS, Astoria, New York
Assistant Office Manager/Sales Assistant
Dr. Cosmatos is a member and part owner of the Astoria Medical Center. Responsibilities include offering assistance with many key aspects of running the center. Utilizing the LY Tech Medical software program, competently manage all the medical billing. Handle credit and collections. Prepare the conference room for meetings of other Associates on routine basis.

Balance and enter daily totals of all money collected at the center. Utilize Quattro Pro with windows system. Keep accurate records and update Patient Ledgers; familiar with medical terminology (diagnosis, procedures, codes, etc.) Assist with the preparation of paperwork for incoming speakers from Pharmaceutical companies. Address gathering or patients for purposes of marketing Nicotrol Patches.

Function as a Receptionist. Take appointments, answer the phones, order supplies, and maintain the inventory of business supplies.

1995 (Summer)

HARRIMAN GROUP, Syosset, New York
Sales Assistant
Supported and actively participated with a Senior Partner of this Brokerage firm. As an auxiliary staff member retrieved daily quotes and disseminated information to clients based on their purchase and sale of stocks listed on the NYSE. Reconciled client's ledgers, recording all transactions. Word processed documents and handled outgoing mail.

REFERENCES

Available upon request.

Lawyer (Entry-Level)

JAMES SHARPE
9 Central Avenue, Chicago, IL 60606 (312) 555-1212

OBJECTIVE

A position as an Associate in a Law Firm…where I can expand my knowledge and gain experience and expertise in the area of Corporate and Transitional Law.

SOME SELECTED REFERENCES

- "…professional in manner, dress and approach…well-educated, articulate and well prepared…passionate, committed and focused on a goal-or goals…ethical and honest…will make a difference wherever (he) goes…," John Bryant, Chairman, Founder and CEO, OPERATION HOPE.
- "…outstanding young man, intelligent, capable and hard-working…well respected by his peers, a team member, a natural leader that I recommend for scholarship…," Marc Massout, Accounting Professor, Claremont McKenna College.

EDUCATION

UNIVERSITY OF CHICAGO LAW SCHOOL, Chicago, IL.

J.D. Degree, to be awarded June, 1998

- **Student Lawyer**, University of Chicago Mandel Legal Aid Clinic Member, Employment Discrimination Project, 1997 to Present
- **Member & Prospective Student Host Coordinator**, Student Admissions Committee, 1995 to 1996
- **Treasurer**, Black Law Students Association, 1996 to 1997

CLAREMONT McKENNA COLLEGE, Claremont, CA

- **B.A. Degree, Dual Major, Government & Economics/Accounting**
- **Graduated with Honors**, May 1995
- **Awarded "Claremont McKenna College Scholar"**
- **Appointed Member of Student Board,** Academic & Student Affairs Committee
- **Awarded 4-Year Merit Scholarship**
- **Senior Thesis:** "The Nature and Extent of Police Power in the United States" (Tracing Evolution from Plato, Socrates, Machiavelli to Current Community-Based Policing)

PROFESSIONAL EXPERIENCE

Legal Experience……

1996 to present   **UNIVERSITY OF CHICAGO MANDEL LEGAL AID CLINIC**, Chicago, IL
Student Lawyer. Member of Employment Discrimination Project. Appeared in Federal Court and State Administrative Court; co-authored a brief submitted to Illinois State Appellate Court. Certified to practice as a Senior Law Student under Illinois Supreme Court Rule 711. Research issues regarding handicapped discrimination, racial discrimination, and procedural issues. Develop legal theories; interview prospective clients; negotiate and opposing counsel; prepare briefs and argumentative memoranda.

1996   **KIRKLAND & ELLIS**, Law Firm, Los Angeles, CA
Summer Associate. Participated in Kirkland & Ellis Institute of Trial Advocacy. Researched and produced memos, gave oral presentations regarding a wide range of legal issues, i.e., real property, trade libel, procedural issues, employment law, environmental matters, white-collar crime.

Page 2 of Sharpe

PROFESSIONAL EXPERIENCE (Continued)

<u>Business Experience</u>......
1995   **OPERATION HOPE**, Los Angeles, CA
                <u>Summer Intern</u>. Selected to intern directly for the CEO of Organization. Created and reviewed
                proposals to the Department of Commerce.

                Drafted a general framework of proposal and created a condensed synopsis of a specific
                proposal to operate a Minority Business Development Center in Los Angeles. Contributed
                promotional ideas and support to launch of Operation Hope Banking Center.

1990 to present **"REAL MEN COOK" FOUNDATION**, Fund raising Organization, Marina Del Ray, CA
                <u>Board Member,</u> 1995 to present, <u>**Executive Administrative Assistant**</u>, Summers, 1990 to
                1993 in conjunction with major pharmaceutical company, key member of team to plan,
                promote, and implement annual fund-raisers for 600 to 800 guests. Funds raised have
                supported 4 minority medical schools and increased awareness and prevention measures for
                prostate cancer. Additionally, prepare in-house financial reports for the Program Director.

<u>Government Experience</u>......
1994   **U.S. DEPARTMENT OF COMMERCE** (California Task Force), Washington, DC
                <u>Summer Intern</u>, researched to assure acquisition of funds and grants allocated for California.
                Worked directly with Office of Management of Budget as well as HUD. Prepared and delivered
                oral reports directly to Task Force Director. Helped to evaluate the potential of grants to foster
                recovery and economic growth in California cities formerly engaged in the defense industry.

1993   **OFFICE OF CONGRESSMAN CRAIG WASHINGTON**, Washington, DC
                <u>Summer Intern</u>. Attended committee hearings, researched issues and bills, and
                corresponded with constituents regarding legislation.

ADDITIONAL REFERENCES AND RELATED DATA AVAILABLE UPON REQUEST

Legal Office Manager

James Sharpe
9 Central Avenue
Raleigh, NC 27612
(919) 555-1212

EXPERIENCE

9/91 to Present **Glick & Gregory, Raleigh, NC**

Office Manager for general-practice law firm. The firm has 40 attorneys and 50 support staff.

Achievements

- Provided direction and supervision for support staff. Recruited, interviewed, and hired support personnel. Conducted annual performance reviews and recommended salary and bonus increases for staff. Developed office manual with general policies and procedures for the firm.
- Evaluated and recommended word processing and data processing equipment. Created word processing center to best meet the demands of the firm. Participated in the conversion of manual accounting system to an in-house IBM-36 System.
- Planned and executed major installation of telephone equipment. Instituted long-distance discount service to reduce cost of long-distance calls. Established a central message center to alleviate demands on the main board.
- Established an alpha/numerical filing system that provided a standard format and resulted in a decrease in lost or misfiled files.
- Administered insurance benefits for the firm and its employees. Reviewed insurance policies to keep premiums within reason and insurance coverage at appropriate levels.

2/87 to 9/91 **Law Office of Richard Kiley Esq, Raleigh, NC**

Assistant Office Manager with responsibility for petty cash for office, filing, inventory, and ordering of supplies; bookkeeping for special clients; travel arrangements.

- Instituted automated W.P. for the firm

EDUCATION: Fordham University

REFERENCES: Available upon request.

Legal Secretary

Jane Swift
9 Central Avenue
Billings, MT 59104
(406) 555-1212

OBJECTIVE:
Seeking responsible position that will utilize my diversified experience.

WORK EXPERIENCE:
John Courtis & Partners - 1993-Present
Legal Secretary to Senior Managing Partner

Administrative responsibilities extending to preparation of highly confidential/sensitive legal documentation and correspondence; mergers and acquisitions, litigation, criminal. Interviewing/testing/hiring/training/supervision of non-management-level support staff.

Duveen, Eal & Gold - 1990 -1993
Office Administrator/Executive Assistant to Senior Managing Partner

Interviewing/hiring of non-management level support staff; monitored financial investment portfolio; preparation and production of correspondence and financial information for lending institutions and clients; heavy client contact and coordination of appointment calendar. Assisted in preparation of annual budget.

Capital Management Corporation - 1987-1990
Office Manager/Executive Assistant to CEO

Responsible for all phases of start-up operation; preliminary contract negotiations with electricians, carpenters, maintenance staff, telephone installers. Researched and evaluated all equipment requirements, purchased all office furniture and supplies. Extensive travel arrangements; year-end compilation of all tax-filing information; maintained corporate bank accounts up through bank reconciliation.

Bays Discount Stores - 1985-1987
Office Administrator/Executive Assistant to President

Developed and monitored an effective customer service program; instrumental in incorporation of same in overall training program; liaison for management staff and executive committee.

EDUCATION:
B.A., Psychology, Minor: economics - Fordham University
Further Graduate Studies - New York University
Notary Public for State of New York
Licensed Insurance Agent - State of New York

LPN

JANE SWIFT, LPN
9 Central Avenue
Nassau, NY 12345
(315) 555-1212

OBJECTIVE....
A position as a Licensed Practical Nurse in a Health Care Facility...utilize my Nursing Education and Training, interpersonal strengths gained through my Teaching career...realize my ultimate career goal by representing my employers professionally, providing my highest level of comfort and care to patients.

SUMMARY OF QUALIFICATIONS....
- Project attitude of commitment to patient well-being and comfort, sincerity of effort...encourage patient's recovery through a healthy therapeutic relationship.
- A dedicated listener and learner...accustomed to creating and implementing mutually beneficial approaches and solutions to all levels of challenge...employ bilingual ability where necessary.

LICENSURES....
Licensed Practical Nurse, New York State, 1998
Certified Residential Health Care Facility Nurse's Aide, 1998
Public School Teacher Certificate (Permanent), State of New York, 1979
Secondary School Teacher of Spanish, State of New Jersey, 1971

AWARDS & SELECTED REFERENCES....
VOCATIONAL EDUCATIONAL & EXTENSION BOARD, School of Practical Nursing, County of Nassau, NY
- "Outstanding Classroom & Clinical Performance Award"

- Graduated with #2 Standing in Class

- "...attained high achievement in academic work, interacts well with her peers and other staff members...caring and professional demeanor, will be an asset to any nursing situation..."
  Daphne Taylor-Pharmacology Instructor

- "...intelligent, compassionate with patients...showed a caring attitude and desire for professional growth...
  Kathleen Atkinson-Clinical Instructor

NURSING EDUCATION & TRAINING....
VOCATIONAL EDUCATION & EXTENSION BOARD
School of Practical Nursing, County of Nassau, NY
Certificate of Completion, Practical Nursing   August, 1998

Certificate of Completion Courses:
Cardiopulmonary Resuscitation, EKG Technology & Venipuncture, Universal Precautions & Fire Safety   August, 1998

JANE SWIFT   Page Two

NURSING EDUCATION & TRAINING.... (Continued)

 NEW YORK STATE DEPARTMENT OF HEALTH
 <u>Certified, Residential Health Care Facility Nursing Assistant</u>   April, 1998

 <u>Clinical Rotations, 1996 to 1998</u>
 NORTH SHORE UNIVERSITY, Manhasset, NY
  Advanced Medical Surgical Rotation, Pediatrics, Maternity: Labor & Delivery,
  Postpartum, Newborn Nursery, Psychiatric

 ST. JOHN'S EPISCOPAL HOSPITAL, Far Rockaway, NY
  Medical Surgical Clinical Rotation

 PARKER JEWISH GERIATRIC CENTER, NY
  Geriatrics

TEACHING EDUCATION & EXPERIENCE....
 More than 17 years as a Spanish Teacher—3 years in the Public School System, 4 years in the Catholic
 School System—teaching and assisting children ages 4 to 18.

 Concurrently, 3 years as a Librarian where, in addition to one-on-one interaction, I developed a formalized
 program of instruction to provide each grade level the opportunity to utilize resource material to support their
 academic study.

 Wherever appropriate and helpful, expanded contact with general and Hispanic community population to
 further support the educative process of my students.

 ST. MARTIN de PORRES REGIONAL CATHOLIC SCHOOL, Uniondale NY, 1994 to 1997
 OUR LADY OF LORETTO CATHOLIC SCHOOL, Hempstead, NY, 1993 to 1994
 WESTHAMPTON BEACH HIGH SCHOOL, Westhampton Beach, NY, 1985
 WHITEHALL JR. & SR. HIGH SCHOOL, Whitehall, NY, 1974 to 1984
 AUDUBON JR. & SR. HIGH SCHOOL, Audubon, NJ, 1971 to 1974

 RUTGERS STATE UNIVERSITY OF NEW JERSEY
 <u>B.A.Degree, Secondary Education & Spanish,</u> 1971

 ADDITIONAL REFERENCES & INFORMATION AVAILABLE UPON REQUEST.

Maintenance

JAMES SHARPE 9 Central Avenue	(303) 555-1212 Littleton, Colorado 80123

PROFESSIONAL OBJECTIVE

A **Maintenance** position with an apartment community utilizing excellent maintenance and public relations skills for the benefit of an employer.

OFFERING

SKILLS:

Plumbing and Pipe Fitting	Electrical
HVAC/Mastering & Rekeying	Linoleum and Tile Installation
Carpet Repair and Installation	Drywall Installation and Repair
Painting, Texturing	Lawn Care and Maintenance
Hot Tub, Pool and Jacuzzi	Snow Removal and Equipment Maintenance
Sprinkler System Installation	Make-readies, Apartment Inspections

EQUIPMENT:
Appliances
Mowers and Trimmers
Snow Plows
Own Tools and Van

PROFESSIONAL EXPERIENCE

ASSISTANT MAINTENANCE SUPERVISOR — Englewood, CO
THE MEADOWS APARTMENTS/LINCOLN PROPERTY MANAGEMENT — 1994 - Present

Assisted Supervisor with maintenance of 276-unit mid-rise apartment community, supervising staff of 2 and scheduling maintenance and personnel in his absence. Responsible for plumbing, electrical, HVAC, appliance repairs, painting, texturing, tile replacement and tub surrounds, make-readies, cleaning and inspections, and general maintenance.

PRINTER/GENERAL MAINTENANCE — Englewood, CO
GOOD DECAL — 1988 - 1989

Responsible for printing and quality checks on printed stickers and labels; cleaned, repaired, and maintained presses, printers, and workspace.

EQUIPMENT MAINTENANCE TECHNICIAN/CUSTOMER SERVICE — Littleton, CO
ADAMS RENTAL — 1993

Responsible for maintenance and customer service for an equipment rental company. Assembled and repaired equipment such as lawn mowers, weeders, trimmers, heaters, snow blowers, sump pumps, chain saws, trucks, etc. Explained operation to clients, diagnosed problems, effectively managed complaints, and controlled inventory.

STATEWIDE COURT INFORMATION REPORTER — Denver, CO
STATEWIDE INFORMATION SYSTEMS/CREDIT BUREAU, INC. — 1991 - 1993

Examined public files throughout the state of Colorado for credit information relating to court judgements. Demonstrated excellent public relations skills with court personnel and Attorneys in obtaining information.

REFERENCES AVAILABLE UPON REQUEST

Major Account Executive

James Sharpe, 9 Central Avenue, Glendale, CA 91209. (818) 555-1212

OBJECTIVE

Sales management position using expertise in motivating sales personnel, increasing sales and creation of effective programs contributing to higher organizational profits and market share.

WORK HISTORY

HEADQUARTERS ACCOUNT MANAGER
1992 - Present
National account management of a two-million-dollar account. Responsible for staff of fourteen, covering five states. Responsibilities include formulating profit structure, constructing and formulating all promotional activities, setting up all co-op advertising, feature pricing, establishing goals, organizing inventory control of spoils and damages.

- Doubled promotional activity, which has increased sales by 12% and profits by 5%.
- Reinstated extender and merchandising program, increasing sales by over twenty thousand dollars per month.

SALES REPRESENTATIVE
Grocery Products Division. May 1989 - October 1992
Serviced territory consisting of Northern and Southern California; concentration on independent and chain accounts. Complete control of service, sales and in-store promotional activity.

- Increased client base through prospecting by 28%, or eight new accounts, for a total of 1.9 million in increased sales.

SALES REPRESENTATIVE
Durkee, Inc., Institutional Sales Division. Cleveland, OH. December 1986 - May 1989
Responsible for horizontal and vertical sales growth of full line of food service products to accounts within a defined territory.

- Doubled sales volume and profit margin within first year. #2 salesperson in region.
- Voluntarily relinquished territory to establish new territory in unsold area. Within six months built sales to match original territory.

MANAGER
Cheers Restaurant, Boston MA. June 1984 - December 1986
Responsible for 20 employees. Duties included: bookkeeping, pricing, ordering, and product inventory control, as well as food planning and preparation and a daily schedule. Implemented time study for daily operations.

- Reduced expenses and overhead by 20%.
- Maintained a 40% net profit.
- Increased business by 33%.

EDUCATION

Georgetown University (Washington, DC). B.S. Degree: Planning and Administration

- Graduated with honors.

Management (Entry-Level)

JANE SWIFT   9 Central Avenue, Los Angeles, CA 90019

(213) 555-1212

OBJECTIVE: **Seeking a Management Trainee position**

QUALIFICATIONS:

- Computer knowledge; Windows '95, Lotus 1-2-3.
- Education in business management and finance.
- Hands on market research experience, including planning and conducting surveys.
- Superior interpersonal skills.
- Deadline oriented; able to handle pressure and a hectic environment.
- Work well independently and as a team member.
- Experience with accounts receivable, collections and billing procedures.
- Organized…Reliable…Enthusiastic…Intelligent

EDUCATION: MOUNT SAINT MARY'S COLLEGE, Chalon, Brentwood, CA
Bachelor of Arts - Business Management—1998

MOUNT SAINT MARY'S COLLEGE, Doheny, Los Angeles, CA
Associate Arts Degree—Business Management—1996

ACTIVITIES: BUSINESS LEADERSHIP ASSOCIATION
Vice President
Initiated and planned membership recruiting. Scheduled, planned and directed meetings. Set up trips with local companies to tour their firm.

MARKETING RESEARCH TEAM
Conducted surveys, made calls to marketing reps for information, and initiated research plans.

BEST MOTOR AUTO SALES
Intern
Performed clerical work, including answering phones, filing, sending collection notices, and collecting payments.

REFERENCES: Available Upon Request

Management Consultant

James Sharpe

9 Central Avenue • Centreville, Virginia 20121 • Phone: (703) 555-1212

Professional Profile

A seasoned, highly motivated senior executive with a successful track record in international operations and project management. Recognized for exceptional problem solving and motivational skills as well as the ability to **negotiate, deal, and close successfully across cultural barriers**. Extensive experience in management consulting in diverse industries, ranging from unit construction and mining/drilling operations to industrial equipment procurement, sales and distribution. **Bilingual with extensive international experience**, including Africa, the Middle East, South Asia, and Western Europe.

Areas of Impact

- International Conflict Resolution
- Operation and Project Management
- Global Emergency Planning
- Worldwide Corporate Security
- New Business Development
- International Public Relations
- Risk Assessment
- International Law
- Recruitment/Training

Career Highlights

- Successfully provided diplomatic, risk management, and crisis resolution services to a broad range of Fortune 100 companies, Ambassadors, Heads of State, cabinet ministers, and senior government officials, U.S. and foreign.
- Successfully negotiated, on behalf of Mobil Oil, with an east African government to resolve a cross-cultural crisis and avoid closure of a $1 billion distribution facility.
- Developed and implemented logistics and training programs involving several thousand U.S. and foreign personnel and a $40 million annual budget. Effectively achieved all objectives with a budget savings of 12%.
- Directed Pratt & Whitney, Mack Truck, and Caterpillar International in the successful negotiation of more than $15 million of capital equipment sales to a west African government.
- Conducted numerous feasibility studies and risk assessments, both political and economic forecasts, for a variety of projects including gold, platinum and diamond mining, nuclear energy development, port, railroad and packaging facilities.

Employment History

International Affairs Consultant

Professional Services Provided to: Air Express International, Bhatia International Property Development, British American Tobacco, Caterpillar International, International Grain Corporation, Julius Berger, Mack Truck, Mobil Oil, National Cash Register, Occidental Petroleum, Orion International Services, Pan American Airways, Pratt & Whitney, Quorum International, Ltd., SIE/Bulldog Technologies, Telecel Telecommunications, USATREX.

Central Intelligence Agency

Near East and Africa Referent…Chief of Station…Chief of Operations…Chief of Branch, Counterterrorism…Deputy/Chief of Station.

Education

Juris Doctorate, *International Law,* University of Denver, Denver, CO
Master of Arts, *History,* University of Denver, Denver, CO
Bachelor of Arts, *History,* New College, Sarasota, FL

Manufacturing Systems Engineer

James Sharpe
9 Central Avenue
Warren, MI 48090
(313) 555-1212

SUMMARY:

A seasoned Manufacturing Engineer with strong developmental skills and realtime experience. Extensive work with C, C++, FORTRAN, and Visual Basic. New development work with Burroughs B7900 and A10

WORK HISTORY:

1992 to Present: **MANUFACTURING SYSTEMS ENGINEER, AMC, DETROIT, MI**
Assignments include:

- Programming major enhancements to realtime systems
- System support of current and new systems through transition period
- Extensive system use of TPS an DMS technology
- Rewriting batch system for Receiving Inspection function
- Extensive customer interface and user training

1990 to 1992   **INVENTORY SYSTEM CLERK, State University of California at Davis**
Assignments included:

- Computer and word processing input
- Computer maintenance reports
- Updating computer inventories
- Racking of excess/surplus university equipment

EDUCATION & TRAINING:

Bachelor of Science in Business Administration - 5/90
State University of CA at Davis. Concentrations in Finance and Computer Systems

Professional Workshops:

EDS - System Engineer Development Program
DMS II
Burroughs Workflow Language

REFERENCES:

References will be forwarded upon request.

Marketing Analyst

JANE SMITH
9 Central Avenue
DEARBORN, MI 48126
(313) 555-1212

EXPERIENCE:

Daytons, Inc. (Detroit, MI)   July 1993 to Present
MARKETING ANALYST - Provide a broad-based flow of data for merchandisers, buyers, Catalog Distribution Center associates, and management to assure continuing high-level profitability of the company's catalog sales. Access all databases by CRT terminal using CRIMS, an on-line system interfacing with ISA, IDB, and MIDB. Computer Analyses focus on:

- Historical applications, such as impact of season, media ads, space, price, and color changes
- Reliable pre-season forecasts of catalog demand patterns and in-season revisions where necessary to maintain inventory control
- Study of inventory turnover in relation to buying estimates, commitments, and quality of merchandise
- Choice of models and development of new ones for item estimating
- Identification of systems problems in estimates above or below plan
- Establishment of recommendations for inventory surplus solutions
- Decision-marketing, planning, scheduling to meet data deadlines

Zachary & Front Advertising, Inc.   New York, NY Summer 1992
OFFICE MANAGER - Arranged for in-house weekly newsletter and biweekly policy memos for new agency. Developed billing system, dealt with clients, and managed clerical staffing.

Tisch Properties   New York, NY Winter 1992
ASSISTANT BOOKKEEPER - Worked with accounts receivable/payable, bank reconciliations

EDUCATION:

State University of Ohio
B.S., Business Administration, 1993
Concentration: Marketing and Management Information Systems

COMPUTER SKILLS:
Visaul Basic, C++, FCS-EPS, and SPSS software package

References Available Upon Request

Mechanical Engineer

James Sharpe
9 Central Avenue
Morristown, NJ 07869
(201) 555-1212

OBJECTIVE
Seek employment as a design or project engineer with the opportunity for continued professional growth.

WORK EXPERIENCE
1992 to Present—**Project Engineer.** Purdue Farms
Responsible for project management during construction of a 600-ton feed receiving, storage, blending, and load-out facility. Design implementation and testing of heating/ventilation system for poultry grow-out houses. System design and cost estimate on complete system for caged grow-out.

1989 to 1992—**Project Engineer.** R.T. French Co.
Responsibilities included design and installation of an electronically controlled in-plant bulk caustic distribution system. Major repairs to a large multi-cell cooling tower and two evaporators. Feasibility study and cost estimate for 70,000 square foot dock-high warehouse development for renovating 1/4 mile of rail spur.

1986 to 1989—**Production Engineer.** Reckitt & Coleman Co.
Responsible for machine and system design, production scheduling, procurement scheduling, and quality control for walnut processing. Redesign of conveyors and elevators reduced manufacturing labor, simplified maintenance, and improved quality. Instituted a system of material control to account for all materials used.

EDUCATION
University of California, Davis, CA. M.S. in Engineering/Agricultural Engineering—1986.
B.S. in Agricultural Engineering—1984.

PROFESSIONAL ORGANIZATION
American Society of Agricultural Engineers
American Welding Society

REFERENCES AVAILABLE UPON REQUEST

Medical Goods Sales Manager

JAMES SHARPE, 9 Central Avenue, Syracuse, NY 13217. (315) 555-1212

OBJECTIVE   To continue expansion of business acumen, experience, judgment, and responsibility. To be compensated on achievements and have opportunity to work in challenging environment.

WORK EXPERIENCE

Present   **SALES MANAGER, S.W. REGION, for Pharmaceutical Co.**
Provided training, leadership, and decision-making responsibilities to expand the marketing efforts of the S.W. Region.

Contributed $3.2 million in revenues on budgeted operating expenses of $8,555,000.

Directed a sales force of four and an operational support staff of 15 people. 1990-1994.

SENIOR SALES CONSULTANT/NATIONAL ACCOUNT COORDINATOR
Coordinated American Medical International Account, which contributed $1.2 million for 98 hospitals.

Managed a territory which generated $1.7 million in 1991.

Responsible for marketing revenues in Texas, Oklahoma, Louisiana, and Arkansas.

1988-1990   **SENIOR SALES REPRESENTATIVE, Mead Johnson, Chicago, IL**
Attained Sr. Sales Representative position, one of nine in corporate sales force of 133.

Managed territory which represented $1.3 million in total revenues for 1990.

Contributed $550,000 in new account revenues, by duration, for 1990.

1985-1988   **SALES REPRESENTATIVE, Whitehall Labs, Syracuse, NY**
Responsible for marketing coverage for three branch offices in two states, Texas and New Mexico, for all market types.

Attained New Sales Leader for S.W. Region in 1st, 2nd, and 4th quarters for 1987.

Provided Whitehall with excess of $300,000 in new account revenues for 1988.

Managed territory that represents $1.1 million in total revenues for 1988.

EDUCATION   **TEXAS A & M:** B.A., 1985. Major-Biology; Minor-Chemistry

Neonatal Support/Nurse

Jane Swift
9 Central Avenue
Chicago, IL 60654
(312) 555-1212

**PROFESSIONAL
GOALS**

Integrating care in a neonatal nursery as a Clinical Specialist involving the clinical support of infants and children.

EDUCATION

1997

Master of Science in Nursing from the University of Illinois. This degree is a Clinical Specialty in Pediatrics with a minor in Education. The pediatric focus is neonatology.

1994

Bachelor of Science in Nursing. Graduated with honors.

EXPERIENCE

Methodist Conference Center, Chicago (1997, Summer)
Position: Media Specialist

- Created and executed special media presentations for the National Senior High Youth Conferences.
- Coordinated all media utilized during the conference, working with other conference leadership.

The University of Illinois Medical School (August 1996-May 1997)
Position: Graduate Assistant

- Worked in association with graduate faculty in planning and designing research studies.
- Performed literature searches and review for research studies, presentations, and journal writings.
- Consolidated data for reports.
- Executed telephone interviews for data gathering.

Children's Hospital, Chicago (October 1994-December 1995)
Position: Staff nurse in the neonatal intensive care unit.

AFFILIATIONS

Illinois Nurses Association
National Association of Neonatal Nurses
Association of Critical-Care Nurses

REFERENCES

Available upon request.

Nurse

JANE SWIFT, R.N., C.

9 Central Avenue • Phoenix, AZ 85016 • (602) 555-1212

CAREER PROFILE

Dedicated medical professional with nine years practical experience in a fast-paced hospital setting. Resourceful problem-solver capable of initiating formative solutions to complex problems. Possess special sensitivity to meeting diverse needs in varied situations. *Key strengths include:*

- Remain calm and professional during times of critical need.
- Strong analytical skills, easily assess conditions and implement appropriate intervention.
- Ability to motivate, produce and coordinate instructions, organize assignments, and evaluate staffing requirements.
- Relate well to people from a variety of cultures and socioeconomic conditions.
- Readily develop rapport with patients, families, staff, physicians, and other health care professionals.
- Proven record of reliability and responsibility.

PROFESSIONAL EXPERIENCE AND ACCOMPLISHMENTS

1988 to Present   ARIZONA MEMORIAL HOSPITAL, Phoenix, AZ

Staff Nurse—Respiratory Care
Responsible for respiratory patient care in a highly technical and complex hospital environment.
Participate in unit Quality Assurance program and work cooperatively with physicians, medical professionals, patients, their family members, and other hospitals to provide quality patient care.

Specific responsibilities:

- Alternating charge nurse accountability as assigned by nurse manager.
  - Supervise 8 to 12 staff nurses.
  - Evaluate staffing requirements, floor assignments and organize unit activities.
  - Communicate physician orders to appropriate departments utilizing computerized data system.
- Implement total patient care (physical, psychological and cognitive aspects) for 7 to 9 patient assignment.
- Supervise Licensed Practical Nurses, non-licensed support staff and orient new staff members.
- Perform clinical skills according to hospital policies and standards of practice.
- Interact with applicable departments regarding patient care.
- Act as patient advocate; assess patient status and notify physicians of clinical changes.
- Educate patient/family members to health care needs, conditions, processes, agendas and options.
- Collaborate with case management regarding discharge needs.
- Served on Hospital Quality Assurance Committee and Task Force to develop a new care system.

Jane Swift   Page 2

1993 to 1996   **Instructor**
Developed lesson plans and curriculum for the Nurse Refresher Program and Adult Respiratory Education for group of up to 35.

1987 to 1989   ARIZONA HEALTH CENTER, Phoenix, AZ
Nursing Assistant

EDUCATION

ARIZONA GRADUATE CENTER, Scottsdale, AZ
Master of Science in *Health Care Management,* 1998

UNIVERSITY OF ARIZONA, Scottsdale, AZ
Bachelor of Science in *Nursing,* 1990

LICENSURE/CERTIFICATIONS

- **R.N. License,** Arizona
- **R.N. License,** New Mexico
- Nurse Preceptor
- **Medical/Surgical Nursing Certification**

Occupational Therapist

JAMES SHARPE
9 CENTRAL AVENUE
ATLANTA, GA 30305
(404) 555-1212

Employment

3/90-Present   Occupational Therapy Department
St. Joseph's Hospital, Atlanta, GA
Staff Occupational Therapist, Registered/Licensed

1/88-3/90   Occupational Therapy Department, Baylor Medical Center, Dallas, TX
Staff Occupational Therapist

1/85-1/88   Occupational Therapy Department, Kaiser Medical Center, San Francisco, CA
Occupational Therapy Assistant

Education

University of Georgia. Graduated 1985
Degree: Bachelor of Science in Occupational Therapy
Cumulative GPA: 3.8   Major GPA: 3.93

Special Projects

Private Practice: Pediatrics, Independent Study: Child Life Program; Play Therapy

Fieldworks

Physical Dysfunction. Psycho-Social. Pediatrics

Affiliations

American Occupational Therapy Association (AOTA)
Georgia Occupational Therapy Association (GOTA)

Personal

Excellent health, no physical limitations. Will relocate.

Reference List Available Upon Request

Office Administrator

James Sharpe
9 Central Avenue
Columbus, OH 43232
(614) 555-1212

OBJECTIVE   To obtain a responsible and challenging position in the business field where my educational and work experience would have valuable application.

EXPERIENCE   OHIO WHOLESALE DRUG CO., COLUMBUS, OH. OCTOBER 1990-PRESENT

- Manage correspondence and all travel arrangements and accommodations for Executives.
- Meeting Planner for annual Trade Show.
- Handle billing of special orders for entire chain, plus Coupon Redemption Program.
- Responsible for all personnel records and payroll, Workman's Compensation Forms, and insurance claims.

PLAINS STATE COMPANY, COLUMBUS, OH. 1987-1990
EXECUTIVE SECRETARY

- Responsible for outgoing and incoming mail, inventory control, correspondence for late notices and reminders to overdue accounts, collection of salesman monies, and also the posting and cash application to these accounts.
- Processed orders, correspondence of all office Executives.
- Handled payroll, including salesman commissions, ordering of all office supplies, extensive telephone contact.

EDUCATION   Columbus Community College. Graduated May 1987, Dean's List, major course of study and concentration in Medical Secretary Procedures.

SKILLS   Typing: 95 W.P.M.
Shorthand: 100 W.P.M.

REFERENCES   Furnished upon request

Operating Room Services Specialist

Jane Swift
9 Central Avenue
Madison, WI 53708
(608) 555-1212

OBJECTIVE: Management Position: An opportunity in management to demonstrate how my skills and experience can improve operations.

PROFESSIONAL
HISTORY: **St. Cecilia Hospital,** Madison, WI. 1994 to Present
Director of Operating Room Services. Includes Operating Room, Post-Anesthesia Care Unit, Anesthesia, and Ambulatory Surgery.

Management of 110 employees.

Develop departmental goals and objectives, and establish and maintain departmental budgets.

Significant Accomplishments:

- Planned and oversaw renovation of sixteen Operating Room Suites;
- Developed team concept and clinical ladder;
- Established operating room preceptorship;
- Instituted block scheduling;
- Developed quality assurance program for departments.

Sister of Charity, Sebastopol, CA. 1989-1994
Assistant Service Supervisor, General Surgery. Maintained efficient unit activities. Assisted in training and education of service personnel. Assisted with employee performance appraisals. Requisitioned supplies and equipment.

Operating Room Specialist, Cardiovascular. 1987-1989. Planned, implemented, and evaluated patient care intraoperatively. Selected and prepared supplies and equipment. Assumed roles of scrub and circulating nurse.

Operating Room Nurse Intern. 1986-1987. Learned to function in the roles of scrub and circulating nurse.

EDUCATION:

University of Alabama, Birmingham
1986, BSN

Supervisory Management Course: American Management Association

Operations and Executive Project Management

James Sharpe

9 Central Avenue • PO Box 503 • White Sulphur Springs MT 59645 • Ph. (406) 555-1212 • Fax (406) 555-1213

Executive Summary

A seasoned, team-oriented business executive with a highly successful track record with start-up and turnaround situations. More than 15 years progressive experience in all phases of **Operations and Project Management** *with particular strength in feasibility analysis. Recognized for exceptional organization building skills as well as the ability to motivate others on all levels in the achievement of individual and organizational goals.*

- *Business Process Re-engineering*
- *Feasibility Analysis/Projections*
- *Negotiation and Arbitration*
- *Project Management*
- *Crisis Resolution*
- *Start-up Management*
- *Business Valuation*
- *Liquidation Management*
- *P&L Responsibility*

Selected Achievements

- Successfully administered a portfolio of contracts with a value exceeding $10 million. The average income of each client **increased by 15%, a gain of more than $1.5 million.**
- Provided consulting services to more than 1,090 clients from numerous parts of the U.S. and Latin America as well as conducted numerous feasibility studies for projects valued at up to **$100,000,000.**
- Orchestrated a successful start-up company with responsibilities including site selection and acquisition through P&L accountability; **annual sales exceeded $50 million within ten years.**
- Aggressively negotiated, supervised, or advised in the negotiation of several contracts totaling in excess of $68 million, **savings clients at least $6.5 million.** Recent negotiations resulted in a verifiable return of **40% over current market value, a total gain of $520,000.**
- Pioneered state-of-the-art plant expansion that involved a capital investment of $500,000 and realized a **50% increase in plant capacity.**
- Successfully restarted an organization that had been shut down due to severe labor-management and production problems. Through various management techniques and styles that motivated the employees, **production increased by nearly 50% while operating costs stayed constant.**

Consulting Highlights

Hawkins & Associates, Inc., *White Sulphur Springs, MT*   *Since 1982*
  President

Representative List of Clients

Metropolitan Life Insurance Co.	*Plum Creek Timber Company*	*Tricon USA*
First Trust Company of Montana	*Louisiana-Pacific Corporation*	*Hall & Hall Real Estate*
Intermountain Research Station	*Homestake Mining Company*	*City of Bozeman*
A.C.Warnack Investments	*Omark Hydraulics*	*Heller Financial*

Education

Bachelor of Science, Business Administration
University of Montana, Missoula MT

Interim assignments and consulting projects preferred. Available for extensive travel in U.S. and abroad.
Undeterred by the most arduous conditions.

Order Processing Manager

James Sharpe
9 Central Avenue
Nashville, TN 37222
(615) 555-1212

EXPERIENCE:

5/90 - Present ORDER PROCESSING MANAGER
Marketing Masters, Nashville, TN

- Report to Director of Operations.
- Oversee all functions of the Network Mail Order Processing Department, including reservations, firm orders, cancellations, contract review, and category exclusivity.
- Act as Liaison between Account Executives and Layout Department in the supervision of program development.
- Apprise Senior Management of weekly business activity, including firm and canceled orders.
- Instituted new departmental procedures to more effectively meet business requirements.
- Directed Systems Manager in the development and implementation of a direct mail order processing computer system.

2/89-5/90 TV MARKETING RESEARCH ANALYST
Rothen Public Relations, Nashville, TN

- Assisted Account Executives in planning client presentations.
- Calculated marketing variables such as product sales, market shares, percent changes; category and brand development indices; month's supply; advertising expenditures.
- Acted as Liaison between Client Service and Production Offices.
- Investigated unusual data or trends.
- Maintained electronic data base.

11/84-2/89 JEWELRY SALES REPRESENTATIVE
Southern Belle Accessories, Memphis, TN

- Assisted wholesale clients in the selection of their gold and silver product lines.
- Acted as Marketing Coordinator for several trade shows, including the National Boutique Show (New York Coliseum, 1987).

EDUCATION: Manhattan College, Riverdale, New York
Bachelor of Science Degree (Business Administration) Cum Laude. 1984
Marketing Major - 4.0 GPA
Computer Information Systems Minor - 3.8 GPA

REFERENCES:
Available upon request.

Paralegal

James Sharpe, 9 Central Avenue, Cleveland, OH 44115 (216) 555-1212

EXPERIENCE:

Robert Schoenberg P.C. Cleveland, OH
Paralegal
Responsibility for various financial aspects of the partnership; organized the office work schedule. Answered the calendar calls in motion part, argued the motions and adjourned cases when necessary; conferenced cases in pre-trial procedure.

Drafted summons and complaints, subpoena duces tecum and judicial subpoena, answers to interrogatories, and all notices of discovery.

Reviewed experts' reports and evaluated their relevance in the case.

Prepared clients for examinations before trial and city hearings.

1990 - Present

Appellate Division Municipal Court of Hong Kong
Judicial Assistant
Participated in civil and criminal trials; took depositions. Drafted the court decisions.

1982 - 1988

EDUCATION:

Brooklyn Law School, Brooklyn, New York
Graduated with diploma in Foreign Trained Lawyers Program
February, 1990

Ohio State Bar Examination taken in July, 1993

Bernard Baruch College of the City University of New York
Paralegal Studies
Certified as a Paralegal in August, 1990

University of Hong Kong
Faculty of Law
Master of Arts - Specialty: Law, February, 1987

SKILLS:

Fluent in Japanese and several Chinese dialects
Freelance writer for Asian newspapers published in the United States
Translator from above languages into English and vise versa

Payroll/Accounts Payable Supervisor

James Sharpe
9 Central Avenue
Campbell, CA 95008
(408) 555-1212

PROFESSIONAL BACKGROUND

1990 to Present   WHOLEFOODS NC., Campbell, CA
Food Processing and Distributing

Payroll/Accounts Payable Supervisor (1995 to Present)
Supervised accounts payable personnel and reviewed their daily work...Utilized IBM/3, Model 15 computer system for various accounting functions...Managed, calculated, and maintained weekly payroll records for 400 employees (800-900 at height of business)...Prepared weekly Federal, FICA, and State withholding deposits...Prepared monthly health and welfare, and pension reports...Delegated monthly bank reconciliations and reviewed work...Prepared monthly account analysis (detailing and verifying the general ledger balance sheet accounts).

Accounts Payable Clerk (1992 to 1995)
Checked vendor invoices for accuracy...Matched the invoice with the receiver and purchase order...Prepared the accounts payable voucher and entered the information into the CRT...Recorded cash receipts and disbursements and prepared the monthly journal entry.

Accounts Receivable Clerk (1991 to 1992)
Processed and reviewed accounts receivable billing for one thousand customers...Applied customer payments and charges...Reconciled accounts on a monthly basis.

Cashier (1990 to 1991)
Reconciled and deposited cash from driver salespeople on a daily basis...Calculated product sales per each driver and sales account.

EDUCATIONAL BACKGROUND
COMMERCE HIGH SCHOOL, Campbell, CA
Graduate of Business Program.

PERSONAL INFORMATION
Willing to travel and/or relocate.

REFERENCES
Furnished upon request.

Personnel Administrator

James Sharpe
9 Central Avenue
Bridgeview, IL
(312) 555-1212

EXPERIENCE: Hughes Ovens & Hewitt, Bridgeview, IL
9/91 - Present   *Personnel Administrator*
Support Staff Management
Duties include:

- support staff recruiting
- supervision of secretarial assignments and group leaders
- coordination of work flow
- supervision of night secretarial staff
- coordination of freelance and temporary staff
- support staff orientation and training
- coordination of payroll process with accounting department
- analysis of personnel data for staffing and planning
- assistance with year-end evaluations and salary review

Legal Recruiter
Duties include:

- presentation of weekly status reports to Recruiting Committee
- coordination of interview schedules
- organization of orientation programs for incoming attorneys
- review and screening all incoming resumes
- processing all correspondence with law schools and individual applicants
- organization of social functions

Benefits Administration
Duties include:

- administration of health benefits including medical, life, and short- and long-term disability
- administration of general insurance, including personal and professional liability and workman's compensation

10/89 - 9/91   University of Chicago
Coordinator of Loans

- responsible for processing all accounts receivable for long-term student loans

EDUCATION: University of Chicago
B.A., June 1989
Majors: Economics and Political Science
Minor: Computer Science
Bilingual (Spanish/English)

REFERENCES: Will be furnished upon request.

Personnel Assistant

Jane Swift
9 Central Avenue
Wheaton, IL 60187
(312) 555-1212

PROFESSIONAL OBJECTIVE

A challenging position and active involvement in a progressive organization offering the opportunity to fully utilize proven and developing people-oriented skills in the area of Human-Resources.

SUMMARY OF SUPPORTIVE QUALIFICATIONS

A results-oriented self-starter with highly developed administrative, problem-solving, and decision-making skills, including: Wage administration, personnel policies, staffing, benefit plans, performance appraisals and EEO.

WORK HISTORY

Personnel Assistant - JENKINS CAPACITORS, Wheaton, IL

March 1991 to Present: Assist the Vice President/Personnel in the administration of all personnel functions. Duties include recruiting, interviewing, hiring, writing and evaluating job descriptions. Administering the health care plans and other employee benefits, developing and administering the Affirmative Action Plan and the Performance Appraisal Program. Handle employee problems and interface with personnel from other companies.

Wage Administration Specialist - BELUSHI Inc., Wheaton, IL

December 1979 to 1991. Audited and processed weekly changes in wages and job status, new hires, and transfers for all nonexempt employees. Maintained job and rate history, wrote and evaluated job descriptions, conducted studies on wages and benefits and administered the annual wage and benefit survey conducted by the company. Interfaced with personnel from other departments and in the absence of the supervisor, was responsible for the functions of the department.

EDUCATION

1989   Wheaton State College, Wheaton, IL. Computer Principles Assertiveness Training. Effective Listening. Multi-Mate Word Processing. Affirmative Action/EEO Seminar. Personnel Diagnostics. Interviewing Workshop. Basic Personnel Administration. Your Employees and the Law.

PROFESSIONAL AFFILIATIONS

Personnel Management Association

Pharmaceutical Sales Manager

JANE SWIFT
9 Central Avenue
Syracuse, NY 12345
(315) 555-1212

OBJECTIVE

Apply my strengths and skills in **Pharmaceutical Sales and promotion of medical products** and services…utilize ability to relate confidently and effectively with expert, demanding audiences…subsequently enroll and maintain a satisfied customer base. Represent company and its products in a professional and creative manner…continue to consistently exceed employer's goals, earn commensurate compensation.

SUMMARY OF QUALIFICATIONS

- **"Jane shows a great ability to communicate…a good listener…conscientious, committed…will do well in any sales position!"…Senior Territory Business Manager, Bristol-Myers Squibb.**
- **A "can-do," "will-do" sales professional…approach goals with the absolute expectation of meeting or exceeding them**…operate easily and effectively with a minimum of supervision and maximum responsibility.

PHARMACEUTICAL/MEDICAL SALES EXPERIENCE

Sales…   Detail a wide range of Bristol-Myers Squibb prescription products; i.e., Anti-infective, Cardiovascular, CNS, Women's Health Care to a territory consisting of as many as 350 Physicians and Health Care Professionals…operating in Private Practices, Group Practices and Medical Centers…specializing in such areas as General Practice, Internal Medicine, Cardiology, Obstetrics & Gynecology, Neurology and Pediatrics.

Plan and implement Promotional Sales Presentations with Group Practices, and meetings with diversified specialties within Medical Center settings. Generate a natural enthusiasm for the quality and efficacy of products represented…presentations gain the interest of Health Professionals, provide the opportunity to emphasize the superior quality, cost consciousness and competitive edge of the products.

Marketing…   Make full use of company-developed marketing verbiage and collateral material; personally design and implement well-received, unique marketing strategies and tools to support product presentation.

Administration…   Exceptionally organized, accustomed to detailed reports, and tight, well-thought-out schedules…always on time with reports and sample inventories…supply immediate and thorough follow-up to queries from the field to maintain company and personal credibility and rapport.

- Increased market share in each of 5 products by exceeding sales goals and projections!
- Increased…at times doubled…sales/physician specification by successfully rejuvenating interest in existing products!
- With Sales teammate, elevated District to #1 in nation in sales of a highly competitive product!

Pharmaceutical Sales Representative…Professional Detailing Network-for Bristol-Myers Squibb, 1998

JANE SWIFT   Page Two

RETAIL SALES & MERCHANDISING

Sales Representative, Audrelli Design Studio (Unique & Customized Jewelry), 1995 to 1997
Salesperson, Arlene Levitan, Inc. (High Fashion Clothing & Accessories), 1995
Buyer, Jack Braunstein Inc. (Design Sportswear and High Fashion Clothing), 1989 to 1993

- Established rapport and credibility in high-end product environments by meeting demographic needs and preferences; designed and developed compelling sales presentation. Purchased merchandise within budget; negotiated the best possible prices.

EDUCATION

SYRACUSE UNIVERSITY, Syracuse, NY
B.S. Degree, Retailing (Sales), 1988

REFERENCES, ADDITIONAL DATA AVAILABLE UPON REQUEST

Physical Therapy

James Sharpe
9 Central Avenue
Westerville, OH 43801
(614) 555-1212

OBJECTIVE

To acquire a clinical position in a Physical Therapy facility emphasizing Orthopaedics and Sports Medicine, while continuing to develop my interests in manual therapy.

EXPERIENCE

Cleveland General, 844-bed acute care facility, 6/93 to present.
Staff therapist with responsibilities for managing outpatient department, supervising aides. Clinical instructor for graduate and baccalaureate students. Worked closely with a neurosurgeon in developing an exercise regime for post-op back fusion patients.

Middleburg Hospital, 325-bed acute care facility 3/89-6/93.
Responsible for total in- and outpatient physical therapy care with participation in a Sports Medicine clinic, home care, and Cybex evaluations. In addition, handled burn and multiple-trauma patients.

EDUCATION

University of Ohio. Bachelor of Science in Physical Therapy, 1989

PROFESSIONAL ORGANIZATIONS

Member, American Physical Therapy Association
American Heart Association-Basic CPR certification

REFERENCES

Available upon request

Plastics Engineer

Jane Swift
9 Central Avenue
Beaumont, Texas 77705
(409) 555-1212

EXPERIENCE:
June 1989 to present - CONSUMER PACKAGING Inc., Beaumont, TX
Senior Research and Development Engineer (3/91 to present)

Responsible to three General Managers: (1) Plastic Development; (2) Technology Development; and (3) Business development for new and existing packaging. Development is centered on shelf-stable food packaging. High degree of customer interaction: Responsible for customer technology acceptance.

Major achievements include: Direct involvement in promoting and implementing Nabisco's "Picnic Gourmet" package and Campbell Soup's "Cooks Kitchen" retortable crocks. Meet with potential customers to discuss concepts and make proposals. Prepare proposals, including tooling costs, design time frame, package costs, and equipment costs.

Research Engineer (5/90 to 3/91)

Held development responsibilities for dual injection molding program. Project leader concerning polymers selection, testing, and tooling design. Responsible for taking concept into prototype and semi-production state.
Production Supervisor (6/89 to 5/90)

Directly responsible for plastic enclosure engineering development and production. Responsibilities included injection molding, polymer testing, and selection. Product tooling engineering and design, ancillary engineering and purchasing, and financial project planning. In-depth research of mold monitoring systems, heaters, pressure transducers, temperature controllers and process controls for state-of-the-art injection molding operations.

March 1988 to June 1989 - BELL INDUSTRIES - MOULDING DIVISION, San Francisco, CA

Process Engineer

Responsible to Production Manager for technical supervision of modern, state-of-the-art molding department, comprising a 200-employee manufacturing facility. Responsibilities included scheduling and instruction of personnel, preparing daily production reports, maintaining inventory, providing technical expertise, troubleshooting, and ordering and assisting in design of auxiliary equipment.

EDUCATION:
1987 - B.S. Industrial Plastics; Illinois State University

Minor: Business Administration

Product Development Engineer

Jane Swift
9 Central Avenue
Kansas City, MO 64108
(816) 555-1212

OBJECTIVE: A challenging opportunity as Senior Staff Engineer or Project Leader involved with new product development.

SOFTWARE: C, C++, FORTRAN, COBOL, LISP, UNIX System 5.2, 5.3; UNIX Kernal and UNIX Tools.

EXPERIENCE:
5/89 - Present. WORKHORSE/MONEYMAKER SOFTWARE. Staff Engineer
Responsibilities have entailed design through implementation of front-end modules for new product development. Specifically developed:

- A command interpreter, menu system, help facility, utilities, tools and library routines.
- A modified A terminal driver within the operating system. Work uses C language on the Motorola 68000 under UNIX.
- Researched and selected alternate peripheral devices including larger disks, a laser printer, and scanners as a member of the advanced Development Group.
- A data collection system using C under UNIX 5.2. Functioned as technical advisor, provided training and support to a group of eight software engineers.

1986 - 1988. UNIVERSITY OF VIRGINIA. Graduate Research Assistant

- Adapted the UNIX operating system to Prime equipment. Set up a restricted UNIX environment for a programming course. Taught C++ and worked as a Grader/Consultant for FORTRAN.

EDUCATION: University of Virginia
M.S., Computer Science '88
B.A., Cum Laude '84

Project Leader

James Sharpe
9 Central Avenue
Miami, FL 33161
(305) 555-1212

OBJECTIVE: To locate a challenge for a superior Senior Programmer/Analyst or Project Leader utilizing hands-on expertise in IDMS applications development.

SUMMARY: Six years progressive experience in programming financial and insurance applications using IDMS, COBOL, and structured programming and design techniques in both batch and on-line environments.

HARDWARE: IBM 3083, 43x, 370.

SOFTWARE: COBOL; CICS; TSO/SPF, IDMS, ADS-on line (ADSO), On-Line Mapping (OLM), CULPRIT, ACF, OS/VS2, MVS, IMS.

EXPERIENCE: *AIR FLORIDA*

1994 - Present   *Programmer/Analyst* - Participated in the development of two major on-line projects utilizing IDMS, ADSO, and OLM. These projects included time/cost estimates, system design, screen design, report layouts, functional and technical analysis and specifications, programming, testing, implementation and system documentation.

     Responsibilities included purchasing, tailoring, interfacing and implementing an IDMS General Ledger software package. Interfaced with user community and support personnel, and provided user training on a functional level. Extensive knowledge and experience with IDMS, ADSO, OLM, ACF, CULPRIT, and SPF.

1992 - 1994   *STATE FARM INSURANCE*

     Programmer/Analyst - Responsibilities included maintaining, enhancing, and supporting group insurance applications. Specifically, handled analysis, programming and testing using structured methodologies and data base systems. Worked closely with users to define and support their needs. Project supervision and training responsibilities for three junior programmers.

EDUCATION: B.S. (Computer Communications), 1992, City University of New York

REFERENCES: Available upon request.

Public Relations/Media Spokesperson

JANE SWIFT
9 Central Avenue
Phoenix, AZ 85016
(602) 555-1212

OBJECTIVE:

A position in Public Relations where I can utilize my skills as a media spokesperson and my ability to execute a variety of projects simultaneously.

EXPERIENCE:

Public Relations Associate/Media
ADRIENNE ARPEL. Phoenix, AZ. 1992 to Present

- Media spokesperson for 12 western states: Interviewed and trained personnel for TV, radio and print
- Established contacts with producers and editors
- Wrote press releases
- Developed media and promotional packages
- Booked interviews with press

District Sales Manager
ADRIENNE ARPEL. Phoenix, AZ. 1989 - 1992

- Supervised 169 representatives with a $500,000 sales volume

Account Executive/Radio Reporter
KTUV RADIO. Phoenix, AZ. 1986 - 1989

- Designed and sold advertising for KTUV Radio
- Developed a $9,000 account list in the Phoenix metro market
- Sports and news announcer (included in-studio as well as location)
- Traffic reporter

Assistant Editor
Daily Arqus Observer, Ontario, OR, Summers 1984/1985

- Feature writer, reporter, photographer, layouts and design

EDUCATION:

B.S., Speech Communications, University of Arizona, 1986

AWARDS:

1994 Arizona Business and Professional Women's "Young Careerist" Annual Award

OTHER FACTS:

Experience as a Public Relations Seminar Leader

References/Portfolio/Video and Cassette Tapes available upon request

Publishing/Marketing Professional

Jane Swift
9 Central Avenue
Seacliff, NY 11579
(516) 555-1212

PROFESSIONAL   *A New York Publisher of trade and scholarly books*
EXPERIENCE: **DIRECTOR OF ADVERTISING AND PROMOTION (March 1992-Present)**

Key responsibilities include: managing advertising/promotion department with staff of four; overseeing and actively engaging in all aspects of promotion, advertising, and publicity. I have established and am maintaining a 22-person national sales force and make seasonal visits to the nation's two largest bookstore chains.

Active in negotiating special sales and acquiring new titles, and as liaison with domestic and foreign rights agents. In 1992 I traveled to England, visited several publishers, bought and sold rights.

Frequently arrange author appearances on television and radio talk shows. As a company spokesperson, I have been interviewed numerous times by newspapers, magazines, syndicates, and radio stations.

ADVERTISING AND PROMOTION MANAGER (1990-1992)

Advertising and Direct Mail: Created, designed, and wrote copy for brochures, flyers, and display ads; created direct-mail campaigns; represented company at publisher's book exhibits.

Publicity: Wrote news releases, selected media, made follow-up calls, arranged author media appearances.

ASSISTANT EDITOR (1988-1990)

Responsibilities included reading authors' manuscripts, copy editing, proofreading; writing jacket copy, coordinating and writing copy for catalog. Some editing and proofreading was done on a freelance basis.

Compton Burnett (New York, NY) ADVERTISING COPYWRITER (1984-1988)

Responsible for designing and writing copy for bimonthly catalog and supplementary flyers. Created ads and brochures; wrote sales letters and edited and rewrote direct-mail pieces.

EDUCATION: State University of New York at Buffalo
                    Degree: B.A. in English, 1984
                    Minor: Social Sciences

SKILLS: Typing, word processing, working knowledge of typography, research proficiency.

REFERENCES: Will be provided on request.

Purchasing Manager (Manufacturing)

James Sharpe

9 Central Avenue • Valparaiso, Indiana 46383 • Phone: (219) 555-1212

PROFESSIONAL PROFILE

A hands-on, senior level professional with extensive experience in manufacturing and distribution with an emphasis in the primary metals industry. Recognized for exceptional perception and ability through progressive, challenging assignments in operations systems enhancements and implementation. Accustomed to P&L responsibility including corporate asset management and development. Significant and varied commercial experience throughout the Midwest markets to include Pittsburgh, Cleveland/Youngstown, Detroit/Toledo, and Chicago.

- P&L Responsibility
- Operations Management
- Profit Maximization
- Sales/Marketing Management
- Negotiation/Arbitration
- Team Building/Development
- Crisis Resolution
- Interpersonal Relation
- Foreign Service

SELECTED ACCOMPLISHMENTS

- **Restored profitability** to the $60 million Chicago division of a major steel service center by expanding commercial effort and production capabilities while decreasing the unit cost of operations. Unit sales **increased by more than 40%** over three years.
- Developed and implemented sales management and marketing strategies which generated **$9.2 million in new business and increased customer base by 21%** over a 12 month period.
- In just one year **increased unit labor productivity by 10.4%** through the development and implementation of cross-training programs, labor force combinations, and benchmarking.
- Spearheaded the implementation of an incentive bonus and gain-sharing program for all employees that was based on the increased profitability of the company.
- Facilitated the successful reorganization of a company under Chapter 11. Structured and implemented a new business and marketing plan **generating profitability in just 15 months.**

EMPLOYMENT HISTORY

Vice President/Division President   1992 to 1997
Kenwal Products Corp., Kenwal Steel Company, Detroit, MI

Vice President, Manufacturing Services & Material Control   1991 to 1992
Sharon Steel Company, Farrell, PA

Vice President, Purchasing   1988 to 1991
Alpha Tube Corporation, Toledo, OH

Director Purchasing & Production Planning   1985 to 1988
Thomas Steel Strip Corporation, Warren, OH

General Manager, Raw Materials & Engergy   1981 to 1985
Wheeling-Pittsburgh Steel Corporation, Pittsburhg, PA

Division Controller   1979 to 1981
Bethlehem Steel Corporation, Bethlehem, PA

EDUCATION

MBA, International Economics/Accounting
Lehigh University, Bethlehem, PA

BS, Business Adminstration
University of Richmond, VA

Bethlehem Management Training Program (Looper)
Bethlehem Steel Corporation, Bethlehem, PA

Quality Control Manager

James Sharpe
9 Central Avenue
Kenner, LA 70062
(504) 555-1212

Career Objective:

Quality Control Manager with a food industry leader

Employment Experience:

Firebird Kitchens/Athens, Kenner, LA

Quality Control Director: Supervise Quality Control Department. Responsible for Research & Development and interaction with USDA program. Products include chicken and dumplings, noodles with chicken, canned deboned chicken, and barbecued chicken. July 1991 to Present.

Green Valley Canning Company, Jackson, FL

Quality Control Supervisor: Manager Quality Control program and assist the Plant Manager in planning and monitoring the production of dry bean products (canned & packaged), fruit juice, tortilla chips, and canned whole-kernel corn. Responsible for product development and improvement of existing products. February 1989 to July 1991.

Stouffers, Inc. Cleveland, OH

Quality Control Technologist; Supervised the Quality Control at Possum Trot plant. Assigned to two seasonal plants in Kentucky during the summer. 1984 to 1988.

Laboratory Assistant: Performed laboratory procedures and supervised the Quality Control Technicians. 1982-1984.

Assembler and Machine Inspector. 1980 to August 1982.

Education & Vocational Skills:

University of Louisiana. Better Process Control School

Kenner Technical Institute. Major: Laboratory Technician and Management-Food Science

Food Chemistry, Communications, Nutrition, Quality Control, Food Microbiology, Technical Math, Supervision, First Aid, Food Preservation, Laboratory Procedures.

Willing to relocate. References available.

Radiation Therapist/Technologist

JANE SWIFT

9 Central Avenue, Brooklyn, NY 11432   (202) 555-1212

OBJECTIVE   A position as a Radiation Therapist/Technologist

EDUCATION   NASSAU COMMUNITY COLLEGE, Garden City, NY
                 A.A.S. Degree, Radiation Therapy Technology, 1993
                 • Dean's List

EXPERIENCE
Equipment...

                 Varian Clinac 18 Linear Accelerator
                 Siemens 67 Linear Accelerator
                 Siemens 77 Linear Accelerator
                 Siemens MD 2 Linear Accelerator
                 Eldorado 6 Cobalt 60
                 Theratron 780 Cobalt 60
                 Odelff Simulator
                 Siemens Simulator

Clinical Roation...
1998   **NASSAU RADIATION ONCOLOGY CENTER**, Garden City, NY
                 Siemens MD 2 Linear Accelerator
                 Theratron 780 Cobalt 60
                 Siemens Simulator

1997 to 1998   **LONG ISLAND JEWISH MEDICAL CENTER**, New Hyde Park, NY
                 Siemens Mevatron 67 Linear Accelerator
                 Siemens Mevatron 77 Linear Accelerator
                 Odelff Simulator
                 RMS Record and Verify

1996 to 1997   **WINTHROP UNIVERSITY HOSPITAL**, Mineola, NY
                 Varian Clinac 18 Linear Accelerator
                 Eldorado 6 Cobalt 60
                 Picker Zephyr SuperficialUnit

Employment...
1995 to 1996   **Dr. Jack Heda, MEADOWBROOK FOOTCARE**, East Meadow, NY

                 Medical Assistant for podiatrist. Prepared patients for treatment, set up equipment, assisted in
                 procedures as directed by physician.

                 REFERENCES, ADDITIONAL DATA AVAILABLE UPON REQUEST

Real Estate Professional

James Sharpe
9 Central Avenue
Anaheim, CA 92803
(714) 555-1212

EDUCATION

Law: CORNELL LAW SCHOOL,
                Juris Doctor. Conferred May 1993
                Cum Laude, Grade Point Average: 3.5
                Client Counseling Competition - Quarter-finalist
                Course Emphasis: Land Use/Environmental Law

Undergraduate: CORNELL UNIVERSITY
                B.A. 1991
                Concentrations: Environmental/Urban Policy

EMPLOYMENT

May 1993 to   *Gerould, Zanke and Chivers. Anaheim, CA*
Present   **Associate.** Commercial Real Estate and Lending. Draft and negotiate loan documents. Advise
                lenders on various hazardous waste and land use issues. Review opinions of borrower's
                counsel relating to perfection of security interests, zoning, and environmental and land use,
                corporate authority, and enforceability and secured transactions issues. Prepare and
                negotiate commercial purchase and sale agreements.

Spring 1993   *Attorney General of New York, Albany, NY*
                Legal intern with Public Protection Bureau. Significant participation in litigation and research.

Fall 1992   *Kettering, Channel & Bly, Carle Place, NY*
                Legal intern. Assisted attorneys. Research in environmental law. Significant contact with
                public agencies.

Summer 1991   *Cornell Law Journal*
                Researched and developed topics for publication.

Real Estate Sales Manager

JANE SWIFT
9 Central Avenue
Charlotte, NC 28210
(704) 555-1212

OBJECTIVE

A challenging sales/sales management opportunity, utilizing my ability to stimulate and motivate a productive sales force. An opportunity in which I can significantly contribute to an employer through increase in sales volume and profit.

EXPERIENCE

A Merrill Lynch Affiliate, Charlotte, NC
Largest, oldest real estate sales office, producing highest sales volume for the Charlotte area.

Manager, 1990 - present
Salesperson, 1982 - 1990
Direct and coordinate all activities of 8-person sales office. Train in effective telephone canvassing techniques, and methods to accurately evaluate homes. Develop ways to expedite and effect the closing of the sales.

Form sales teams within office, establish sales quotas for inter-office contests, motivate staff individually and in groups. Annual turnover reduced from 60% to 18%, while individual production increased 33%.

Consistently secure all saleable exclusive and multiple listings, follow up to establish company credibility and the rapport essential to retaining clients in a competitive marketplace. Exclusives increased 45% under my management.

Negotiate final sale price and date of possession, secure most appropriate lending institution for buyers. Deal personally with real estate attorneys, devising contracts for consummation of sale.

Evaluate homes as prospects for company purchase for speculative purposes. Personally responsible for decisions to buy, rendering of dollar offer, initiating activity for resale.

Develop copy and photographs of homes for major advertising publications.

TRAINING

Dale Carnegie Institute, 1983: Seminar series for sales, closing and negotiating. Various additional courses and seminars to instill, polish, and perfect skills in salesmanship.

Records Manager

Jane Swift
9 Central Avenue
Glenhead, NY 11579
(516) 555-1212

EMPLOYMENT OBJECTIVE:

Supervisor of filing and records management

EMPLOYMENT:

Getchell & Getchell, New York, NY

Assistant Supervisor - Maintaining a large number of client documents, utilizing an alphabetized system; assigning daily workload to clerks; light typing; responsible for processing audit letters to assist partners in regulating billing procedures: some experience in conducting cost analysis for supplies. July 1994 to Present

Hardy, Hardy, and Hardy, New York, NY

Assistant Supervisor - Duties consisted of filing and recording documents for United States Trust Company of New York and all other clients in such legal areas as corporate, trusts and estates, litigation, and general matters utilizing an alphanumeric system; responsible for setting up and coordinating new matters; culling out non-active files for delivery to storage; experience in the field of researching and use of law library in conjunction with attorney request; knowledgeable in the performance of light typing tasks. February 1991 to June 1994

EDUCATION

Adelphia University, Spring Semester, 1993
Generalist course of study of the Lawyer's Assistant program.

Notary Public - New York County

Member of ARMA (Association of Record Managers and Administrators)

REFERENCES:

Furnished upon request.

Research Scientist

Jane Swift, 9 Central Avenue, Fort Lauderdale, FL 33309. (305 555-1212)

EXPERIENCE:

1990 to present - OWN BRAND FOODS, FL. *Research Scientist*

Current responsibilities include: developing new products for the Fresh Meats division and supervising operational implementation. Specific duties include:

- Providing input for generation of product concept; bench-top formulation; pilot plant testing; sensory evaluation; coordination of package development; development of quality control programs.
- Supervision of quality control personnel and three lab technicians in the corporate research laboratory. Production scale-ups in plants, and trouble-shooting operational problems.
- Extensive experience in formulating foods specifically for microwave cooking.

ACCOMPLISHMENTS:

- Developed a square bacon product sold to Wendy's Restaurants.
- Developed five pre-cooked entrees sold to Stouffers.
- Developed several pre-packaged retail cuts, currently in test market.

1983 to 1988 - University of Nebraska. *Research Assistant*

Meat Science Research duties included planning, implementing, and analyzing data for a variety of meat research products. Teaching assistant for introductory and advanced meats classes. Assisted with various consumer-oriented programs.

EDUCATION:

1988 - University of Nebraska - Lincoln, PhD
1985 - University of Nebraska - Lincoln, MS
1983 - Auburn University, BS-Food Science

PROFESSIONAL MEMBERSHIPS:

American Meat Science Association
Institute of Food Technologists

Publication list and references available upon request.

Retail Management/Merchandising

Jane Swift

9 Central Avenue • Quincy, MA 02169 (617) 555-1212

CAPABILITIES:

- Operations Management
- Customer Relations
- Store Design/Setup
- Personnel Management/Training
- Budget Control/Cash Management
- Advertising/Selling Techniques
- Merchandising
- Forecasting
- Inventory Control

ADDITIONAL EXPERTISE:

- Comprehensive, broad-based knowledge of all aspects of business ownership and apparel store management encompassing *over 37 years* in the fashion industry.
- Development of on-going client relationships with individual attention to detail, creating loyal customer following.
- Planning and implementation of merchandise presentation.
- Natural fashion ability; easily recognize upcoming style expressions and profitable ideas/situations.

HIGHLIGHTS:

- Facilitated the successful completion of local fashion shows utilizing 100+ models and business participants.
- Seasonal attendance at high-profile New York, Hartford, and Boston market fashion and gift shows.
- Received *Prominent Business Recognition* from the Town of Quincy.

PROFESSIONAL EXPERIENCE:

PARADISE RESORT & CASINO • Quincy, MA

Sales Associate Jan. 1996 to Present

Assist customers with fashion, accessory and gift needs. Field questions pertaining to Native American merchandise.

JANE'S SEASIDE FASHIONS

Pleasant View Inn • Boston, MA

Owner/Operator July 1993 to Present

Seasonal resort business tailored to Inn guests. Recent annual sales volume in excess of $350,000. Supervise all aspects of store operations and merchandising activities which include:

- Working directly with patrons to coordinate fashions;
- Maintain and direct staff of 10+ employees.

JANE'S, INC. • Cambridge, MA

Owner/Operator Feb. 1979 to Feb. 1994

Developed and built business from ground floor level. Generated annual sales volume of over $750,000. Actively involved in all operations.

- Designed store layout and merchandising displays.
- Hired, trained and supervised staff of up to 16 full and part time employees.
- Purchasing and selling merchandise.
- Inventory control and store maintenance.
- Maintenance of all records, accounts payable/receivable, bank deposits and reconciliation of all receipts.

PRIOR POSITIONS included Executive Secretary at General Dynamics and Pratt & Whitney.

Exceptional References Available Upon Request

Retail/Sales Management

JANE SWIFT

9 Central Avenue
Phoenix, AZ 85016
(602) 555-1212

12 Green Street
Los Angeles, CA 90019
(213) 555-1212

TARGET: Management Position

BACKGROUND

Retail management, Sales and Purchasing background encompassing expertise in business ownership, development, strategic planning and marketing with interests in real estate acquisition and management.

SUMMARY OF
EXPERIENCE

Business Experience
- Recognize and understand all aspects of business and how they interrelate.
- Successfully managed $4 to $7.5 million volume selling areas utilizing successful planning, merchandising, data analysis and inventory purchase and control.
- Handled advertising budgets, consignment accounts and vendor relations.
- Provided forecasting, market analysis, budgetary and profit requirements, balancing and allocation of funds in retail and independent markets.
- Entrepreneurial skills from simultaneous ownership of 2 retail stores.

Management
- Oversaw and directed day-to-day activities of diverse retail operations.
- Capable of working effectively in a variety of arenas requiring creative, innovative thinking.
- Supervised staffs of up to 35 including a 23-person commissioned sales force.
- Developed and implemented progressive policy for employees which helped divert impending legal actions against major area employers.
- Hired, terminated and trained sales personnel; handled employee relations.
- Proven ability to relate to professionals, staff and co-workers at all levels.

Marketing/Sales
- Skilled at recognizing buying patterns and designing sales strategies.
- Initiated and facilitated new layout of 50,000 sf store through data and market analysis, sales techniques, regional demands, demographics, sales trends, customer requirements and implemented in-house promotions.
- Responsible for the successful planning, buying and inventory maintenance of 2 departments of a 200-store chain and $5+ million selling area including stock distribution, assortment selection, mark-up control, store allocation & inspection.
- As a business owner, generated a vital network of business and industry contacts.
- Reviewed product features and differentiations to enhance business potential.
- Designed and approved advertising and promotional materials.

Negotiating/Customer Service
- Skilled negotiator. Listen to and fully understand all aspects of any dilemma.
- Successfully handled difficult clients, vendor negotiations and complex situations to each party's satisfaction while maintaining company objectives.
- Extensive experience negotiating property leases and terms.

Jane Swift   Page 2

WORK HISTORY	1996 to present	**Manager**	Entertainment Place, Phoenix, AZ
	1994 to 1996	**Department Manager** *($7.5 million volume selling area)*	HiTech Co., Los Angeles, CA
	1992 to 1994	**Sales Manager** *($5.5 million volume selling area)*	Groves Department Store, Scottsdale, AZ
	1987 to 1992	**Owner**	A & B Speakers, Phoenix, AZ
	1984 to 1987	**Buyer**	Musictown, Phoenix, AZ
	1982 to 1984	**Assistant Buyer** *($5+ million volume selling area)*	Guitar King, Scottsdale, AZ
	1979 to 1982	**Independent Property Manager**	

EDUCATION   University of Phoenix, Phoenix, AZ
Bachelor of Arts, 1979
- Member, National Honor Society

Sales Manager

Jane Swift
9 Central Avenue
Ft. Lauderdale, FL 33309
(305) 555-1212

Seeking a retail management position that allows for career growth.

WORK EXPERIENCE

6/96-Present | *Sales Manager, Penney's. Ft. Lauderdale*
Manage eleven dress departments and five coat departments. Supervise and motivate thirteen associates. Maintain excellent customer service. Ensure proper merchandise presentation on selling floor.

Review and react to merchandise information reports, establishing trends and best-selling items. Communicate with central merchants, as well as store managers and selling personnel. Control individual department inventory. **Management evaluation, "Excellent."**

2/93-6/96 | *Assistant Buyer Sportswear, Macy's. Ft. Lauderdale*
Facilitate prompt flow of departmental merchandise. Ensure accuracy of paperwork and inventory control. Maintain efficient vendor and branch store communication. Review stock levels and merchandise assortment. Track departmental trends. **Supervisor evaluation: "Superior performance."**

5/89-2/93 | *Secretary, Bergdorf Goodman. Ft. Lauderdale*
Secretary to store executives, orientation of new employees. Exposed to operational management. Work closely with assistant store managers. Familiar with compensation and insurance plans, payroll procedures, employee reviews, and customer service, including customer complaints and billing. **Performance evaluation: "Outstanding."**

12/85-5/89 | *Sales, Maxim's. Ft. Lauderdale*
Worked closely with Fashion. Prepare layout and merchandise display. **Performance evaluation: "Excellent."**

Sales/Marketing

James Sharpe
9 Central Avenue
Pittsburgh, PA 15213
Phone: (412) 555-1212

Professional Profile

A self-motivated and goal-oriented sales and marketing professional with successful experience in developing new business through highly innovative prospecting methods and closely coordinated team efforts. Recognized for exceptional achievement and the ability to create trust and build lasting business relationships.

Skill Set

- New Business Development
- Market Optimization
- Product Expertise
- New Market Identification
- Consumer Awareness
- Leadership Ability
- Motivational Speaking
- Interpersonal Relations
- Closing Techniques

Career Highlights

- Generated an average of $400,000 in monthly sales, $4.8 million annually, in new business revenue by acquiring more than 134 new accounts.
- Created a "communication loop" which stimulated product awareness, resulting in a 500% increase in physician participation and generated annual revenues exceeding $2.4 million.
- As a key team member of the Pittsburgh Region, increased area membership by 240% in just two years.
- Voted "Rookie of the Year" in 1994 based on first year's performance and was invited to participate in the Annual Corporate Roundtable with the CEO and other Senior Officers.
- Led the entire sales group of 1995 finishing with 131% of yearly quota and reached 80% of the 1996 quota in just the first quarter.

Employment Progression

US Healthcare

Manager, Broker Department	3/96 to Present
Senior New Business Marketing Representative	6/95 to 3/96
New Business Marketing Representative	3/94 to 6/95
Sales Associate	7/93 to 3/94

The University of Pittsburgh Medical Center

Medical Records Correspondence Clerk	8/91 to 7/93

Education

Bachelor of Science, Business
University of Pittsburgh, Pittsburgh, Pennsylvania

Salesperson

Jane Swift
9 Central Avenue
Mount Vernon, NY 10550
(914) 555-1212

OBJECTIVE   To obtain a challenging position in Marketing or Sales, providing an opportunity to apply skills and interest in Sales, Promotions, Customer Service, and related ideas.

QUALIFICATIONS

Retail Sales and Customer Service, in consumer products and services; dealt on an individual basis to help customers meet their needs. Ultimately responsible for customer satisfaction. Served also in the hospitality business.

As Marketing Consultant to retail businesses, have conceived, developed, produced, and executed advertising campaigns and promotional activities. Created advertising themes, wrote copy, prepared designs and graphics, made media decisions, subcontracted art and production, and placed advertising. Successfully developed programs within budgets and deadlines.

Developed Promotions and promotional campaigns, including a contest to name a new business, promoting a recreational league, publicizing the activities of a professional organization, including publicity support for a continuing lecture program.

Other Responsibilities: organize, plan, and carry out programs (including recruitment, scheduling, and financing); communicate with and teach patients health care practices; serve in several offices of a professional organization, with responsibility for organizing and carrying out activities; perform volunteer work, teaching and training in schools and youth groups.

WORK HISTORY

Marketing Consultant - 1993 to present

Spanky's Casuals, White Plains, NY
Retail Sales, Customer Service, 1988 to 1992

Crazy Eddie Electronics, NY, NY
Retail Sales, Customer Service 1978 to 1987

EDUCATION   *New York Institute of Technology*
A.S., with additional courses in Business Law, and Computer Science.

Sales Support/Administration Specialist

Jane Swift
9 Central Avenue
Dallas, TX 75247
(214) 555-1212

OBJECTIVE: Management responsibility with an organization where demonstrated skills in Marketing, Administration, and Sales can be translated into improved growth and profitability.

BACKGROUND
SUMMARY: Twelve years' business experience with increasing responsibility in Marketing, Finance, Personnel, Data Processing, Sales Administration functions. A thorough knowledge of all office procedures, Board of Directors meeting administration, sales/revenue/financial analysis, brochure/catalog preparation, trade show/seminar coordination.

EXPERIENCE: *DEVON PHARMACEUTICALS INC. Dallas TX (12/88-Present)*
Sales Support Administrator
Act on behalf of the Director in his absence and direct all matters for proper resolution. "Special projects" and committee assignments comprise the major portion of this position, including:

- Coordination of company relocation to a new facility, with five concurrent annual company functions.
- Coordinate the conversion to a new archival system.
- Control activities with executive search firms and interview candidates while under reorganization.
- Develop and revise corporate policies and procedures; and participate in a variety of special acquisition proposals for the Board of Directors.
- Prepare, administer and assist in the analysis of the Annual Employee Salary Review Program.

THE CUBBISON COMPANY, Dallas, TX (6/85-4/88)
Market Development Analyst
Investigate and recommend new programs and channels of distribution to increase revenue. Recommend new products for resale.

Administrative Assistant to General Manager
Coordinate revenue vs. plan reports as well as Marketing staff programs for division's branch offices. Input intelligence on competitive activity. Formalized divisional level personnel policies and procedures.

EDUCATION: BS/BA, Marketing, 1984. Smith College (Northampton, MA)

Secretarial

JANE SWIFT

9 Central Avenue
Northport, New York 11768
(516) 555-1212

OBJECTIVE A responsible position providing **excellent secretarial skills and support** to a busy
executive.

SUMMARY OF QUALIFICATIONS
- A skilled communicator with an enthusiastic yet professional presentation.
- Handle projects responsibly, create executive correspondence as directed…due to high
  level of integrity, accustomed to being entrusted with confidential information.

EXPERIENCE

Secretary to the President
Coach Real Estate Associates, Inc., L.I., N.Y.
Front Desk Assistant for rapidly growing real estate group. In charge of complex paper flow
system, managed telephone response network for 21 salespersons…1994 to 1998

Secretary to Manager
Page Communications, Honolulu, HI.
Personal Secretary handling confidential files, working with a wide variety of government
agencies. Served as secretarial assistant to visiting engineers…1991 to 1993

Secretary to Partners in Law Firms in San Francisco and New York City, performing
extensive typing and stenography for corporate and litigation attorneys…1985 to 1991

Secretary to Sales Representatives and Electronic Engineer
Allied Control Company, Inc., N.Y.C., N.Y.
Typed government quotes, correspondence, kept sales files and personally handled sales
queries where possible…1979 to 1985

Additionally…

Skilled at:
Keyboarding, Word Processing, Various IBM PC Software, Complex record keeping,
Shorthand, Machine transcription, Conversational German.

Educated at:
Grumman Data Systems Institute, Bohemia, N.Y.
DeMars Legal Secretarial Institute, N.Y.C., N.Y.

REFERENCES, ADDITIONAL DATA AVAILABLE UPON REQUEST

Senior Executive Secretary

Jane Swift
9 Central Avenue
Austin, TX 78745
(512) 555-1212

SUMMARY:

Depth of experience: Business management, business systems analysis, and communications. Areas of expertise include typing, shorthand, accounting, and dealing with confidential material generated by Executive Officers.

KEY QUALIFICATIONS:

Self-motivated - experience in instituting and conducting all phases of office procedures, organizing and coordinating projects for maximum efficiency.

Progressive development of excellent interpersonal and communication skills. Demonstrated record of high performance standards, including attention to schedules, deadlines, budgets, and quality of work.

Ability to work independently and institute creative improvements that allow better management work flow.

CAREER HISTORY:

Minsky Management, Austin, TX. 1992 - Present. A Property Management Co.

Senior Executive Secretary. Duties include all daily administrative and secretarial work, accounts receivable, accounts payable, general ledgers, payroll, including monthly deposits and quarterly returns, and quarterly tax estimates. Responsible for maintaining records and reconciling monthly statements for 36 investment accounts, 20 checking accounts, and 24 savings accounts.

Manage all real estate for six shopping centers, including leases, rents, common-area maintenance charges, and mortgage payments, which include verification of interest and principal amounts. Interact and correspond with tenants.

Coordinate travel arrangements.

Responsible for special projects as assigned.

Mr. Gatti's Inc. Austin, TX. 1987 - 1992. Pizza Franchisor

Office Manager, Assistant Treasurer. Duties included all daily administrative and secretarial work, accounts receivable, accounts payable, accounting through trial balance, and payroll, including monthly deposits and quarterly returns. Handled all banking, including loans and trade acceptances. Interacted and corresponded with customers and vendors.

EDUCATION

Auburn High School - Honor Graduate
IBM Award - Outstanding Business Student
NASD License

Senior Systems Programmer

Jane Swift
9 Central Avenue
Salt Lake City, UT 84106
(801) 555-1212

SUMMARY:

With eight-plus years of data processing experience comprising both operations and systems programming background, Jane Swift is a thoroughly knowledgeable Systems Programmer.

HARDWARE/
SOFTWARE:

308X, 303X, 370, System 34, 8100, 3725, P.C., OS/MVS, ASSEMBLER, CICS, RJE, JES II, SNA, ACF, VTAM, NCP, NPM, NPDA, MSNF, VSAM, NCCF, DISOSS, SNI, CNM, EREP, GTF, TSO/ISPF, SMP

EXPERIENCE:

Current Employer. A Technology Conglomerate.   *10/90 to Present*
Systems Programmer

Responsibilities include the installation and maintenance of networking software products (NCP, Version 3 NPDA, NPM, NCCF, etc.), supporting SNI, managing VSAM for CNM products, etc.

INCO Corporation   *7/87 to 10/90*
Systems Programmer   *11/89 to 10/90*

Installed and maintained NCCF, NPDA, DISOSS and EREP. Responsible for NCP generations and VTAM modifications. Worked with Support Center on assorted problems and disk problem determination using GTC and NCP dumps.

Operations Analyst   *9/89 to 11/89*

Responsible for training computer operators in networking; wrote network operations procedure manual with trouble-shooting flowcharts.

Network Operator   *7/87 to 9/89*

Gained Hands-on experience with ACF/VTAM, NCP environment. Installed IBM terminals, modems and 3274 control units. Used modem tests and datascope to work with AT&T on communication problems.

EDUCATION: *C.W. Post College*
B.S. - Data Processing, 1990

Software Engineer

Jane Swift, 9 Central Avenue, Yonkers, NY 10701. (914) 555-1212

OBJECTIVE: Challenging opportunity as Software Engineer utilizing expertise in C/UNIX programming.

HARDWARE: M68000 Series; DEC VAX 11/750, PDP 11/34; IBM PC.

SOFTWARE: C, Intel 8086 Assembler; UNIX 5.3, 5.2, 4.2, VMS, MS/DOS, LISP, FORTRAN, Visual Basic, Macro-II.

EXPERIENCE: **A Computer Peripheral Co.** 11/92 - Present

Engineer - Responsibilities include design, development, and installation of a software product that polls virtually any type of remote computer on a scheduled basis. Function as primary interface with field personnel for support of this product.

Involved with porting UNIX utilities to the proprietary system and supporting these utilities. Developed a user interface embracing: Design and coding with C on M68000 under UNIX. Utilized the Courses Library to develop a windowing environment. All code has been designed and ported to the IBM PC-AT under MS/DOS.

Vector Vision Systems, Inc. 1/91 - 11/92

Software Engineer - Developed an I/O interface between Intel 8086 software and 8031 firmware and developed numerous system test utilities for use on a PC Board Inspection System. Also provided overall maintenance of a M68000 super-micro running under UNIX.

New York University. 6/88 - 1/91

Systems Programmer - Responsible for various projects related to system software development including debugging and implementing a file transfer package using C on DEC VAX 11/750. Also handled computer operations for two DEC PDP 11/34's and a DEC VAX 11/750 running under UNIX.

EDUCATION: B.A. degree in Computer Science. New York University, 1990

Staff Accountant/Real Estate

James Sharpe, 9 Central Avenue, Brooklyn, NY 11432 (212) 555-1212

OBJECTIVE: To obtain a responsible position in a company, where my experience, accomplishments, and proficiency will allow me the opportunity for growth.

STRENGTHS: Motivated, with highly concentrated learning curve. Astute technician, and personable. Stamina and know-how to undertake the most challenging situations.

EXPERIENCE:

1993 to present CUSHMAN & WAKEFIELD, INC., New York City, NY
Staff Accountant
Accounting, financial, and planning responsibilities for 25 office buildings consisting of 25 to 100 tenants each.

Developed and implemented cash management procedures governing receipt, custody, and disbursements of funds.

Reviewed and verified rental condition reports to ensure timely billing. Acted as liaison with property manager, building manager and owner's representative. Prepared budget forecast for all properties.

1988-1993 PEN PLAZA, INC., New York City, NY
Collections Administrator
Monitored accounts receivable/accounts payable, recommended credit policies, collections, internal control implementation and administration. Planned and entered all credit/collection data into computer system. Conducted weekly staff meetings with account executives. Identified and collected all delinquent accounts; established and proved timely payments plans.

1981-1988 THE IMPORT & EXPORT CO., New York City, NY
Accounting Clerk
Responsible for accounts receivable/accounts payable, general ledger, and processed payroll for 800 employees. Compiled and performed various bookkeeping functions for two subsidiary companies. Calculated and reported all state and federal taxes. Oversaw petty cash.

EDUCATION: Rutgers University, Newark, NJ
B.A. in Business Administration, 1980

REFERENCES: Available upon request.

Store Manager

James Sharpe
9 Central Avenue
Oldsmar, FL 33557
(813) 555-1212

WORK
EXPERIENCE

Manager, A National Kitchen Utensil Retailer. 1988-present.
Manage daily operations of a $2-million annual business. Staff of 12 people. Responsible for increasing sales and profitability and decreasing expenses.

Increased gross margin by 25% and net contribution by 105% on a 3% sales increase.

Senior Assistant Buyer, Stern's. 1984 to 1988.
Controlled open to buy purchase journal, profitability reports, weekly three month estimate of sales, stocks, and markdown dollars. Planned and negotiated sales promotions, advertising, and special purchases.

Coordinated training and teamwork with managers and merchants in the 22 stores.

Increased department sales 18% more than the Division's increase.

Assistant Buyer. Assisted selection and distribution of merchandise. Managed all buying office functions while learning to plan sales, control stocks, and markdown dollars. Created weekly, monthly, and seasonal financial plans.

Developed all systems to support the growth of the branch from a $1-million volume to a $4-million annual volume.

Buyer/Manager. Gulf Gifts, FL. 1981 to 1984.

Bought merchandise for two different gift stores. Directed daily store operations and sales. Directed merchandise presentation, inventory control, and customer service. Scheduled and supervised a 7-person staff.

Increased sales volume 22% more than corporate projection.

Manager, Willis & Geiger, New York, NY. 1978 to 1981.

Direct daily store operations. Analyzed trends in fashion, merchandise, and consumer needs. Planned effective marketing strategy, displays, advertising, and an employee sales program.

Increased annual net sales volume by 33%.

EDUCATION   Fashion Institute of Technology, New York, NY. B.A. Merchandising, 1977.

Systems Programmer

James Sharpe, 9 Central Avenue, Waterbury, VT 05676. (802) 555-1212

COMPUTER SYSTEMS

IBM 370/158, MVS
IBM 3081, MVS, TSO

NCR PC-4, PC-8,
PDP 11-70, UNIX
Compaq

COMPUTER LANGUAGES

Apple Assembler
NCR PC-8 Assembler
IBM-370 Assembler
APL
Visual Basic

C, C++, Visual C++
COBOL
Database; SQL Server
FORTRAN

EXPERIENCE

SOFTWARE ENGINEER, Major Computer Co. 1992 to present.

Designed and developed printer Basic Input/Output Service routines for Windows NT Server intelligent retail terminal. Used in-circuit emulator to debug software and software interface to hardware. Key challenges include re-entrancy, interrupt service routines, and power recovery.

Contributed to design of software interface to new multifunction printer. Met tight schedules for important product. Currently developing a printer driver in C for an 801888-based dumb retail terminal. *Key challenge* is providing application compatibility given new hardware. Project received quality awards.

SOFTWARE ENGINEER, Compaq, Houston, TX. 1991 - 1992.

Designed tests for single-user record operations and user interface for file manager on Compaq Personal Computer. Responsibility for directory and system generation utilities. Received Compaq employee appreciation award.

PROGRAMMER, Computer Consultants, Houston, TX. 1988 - 1991.

Thirty-five assignments, consisting of program changes, IBM JCL changes and creation, new program creation in NATURAL, IBM-370 assembler, and UNIX shell.

EDUCATION

B.S. COMPUTER SCIENCE, U.C./Berkeley. 1988

Systems Team Leader

James Sharpe
9 Central Avenue
Saginaw, MI 48090
(313) 555-1212

SUMMARY:
MIS specialist, experienced in both systems and applications areas. Major experience, strengths, and skills are: Technical Supervision, Mapper, Telcon/CMS, OS 1100.

EXPERIENCE:
1994-Present. Transmission Systems Inc. Troy, MI. Team Leader
Responsible for all aspects of the MIS group. Provided computer services for the company business applications.

- Total processing output increased 500% with very little increase in equipment cost.
- Produced a plan to purchase disk drives that would pay for themselves in less than five years by reducing maintenance costs.
- Designed and implemented an online stock system.

1991-1994. Warren Power and Light Co., Troy, MI. Senior Systems Programmer
Responsible for all aspects of the software communications group. Provided communication services to over 1,500 screens.

- Responsible for installation of communications when the company moved to multiple computer sites. This involved five high-speed UDLC lines.
- Responsible for the installation of three new Pentium Pro front-end processors and one line switch module.
- Upgraded the network software to handle 300% increase in the number of terminals.

1989-1991. Power Consulting Ltd., Detroit, MI. Senior Systems Analyst
Responsible for applications, system design and implementations.

- Reduced cost of a major distribution system from over $200,000 to $25,000.
- Held Mapper-run design classes.
- Designed, wrote and implemented cash flow analysis system for a multibillion-dollar company.
- Responsible for several Mapper installations.
- Involved in several hardware and software conversions.

EDUCATION: B.S. in Business, City University of New York. 1988

Teacher (Entry-Level)

James Sharpe
9 Central Avenue
Mill Valley, CA 94941
(415) 555-1212

OBJECTIVE   I seek a challenging position as an elementary school teacher where my drive and ambition will be rewarded.

EDUCATION   C.W. POST - Long Island University, Brookville, New York
Bachelor of Science in Elementary Education, expected date of graduation May 1998
Overall G.P.A.: 3.63   Last Semester's G.P.A.: 3.90
Dean's List 1996, 1997

Coursework included:

- Methods of Teaching Elementary Science, Math, and Social Studies
- Multicultural Education
- Educational Psychology
- Theory and Practice of Diagnosing Reading
- Basic Drawing

Extracurricular Activities: Founding brother of Delta Phi Epsilon - assisted with organizing and participating in sponsored events. As active member, helped with community service fund-raising campaigns. Member of Phi Eta Sigma (National Freshman Honor Fraternity).

STUDENT TEACHING

1/98 - Present   HILLSIDE GRADE SCHOOL
New Hyde Park/Garden City Park School District
Assist with assorted classroom duties (3rd and 6th graders). Draft lesson plans; organize planbook for review and approval; mark tests and record grades; average class size approximately thirty students; teach two to three lessons per day. Additionally responsible for dance program activities, including working with 6th graders twice a week for seven weeks.

9/96 - 12/96   WESTSIDE SCHOOL
Cold Spring Harbor School District
Participated in the daily activities, observation (six credits), of a first grade class once a week.

EMPLOYMENT EXPERIENCE

8/93 - 1/98   FAZIO DANCE CENTER
Howard Beach, New York
Dance Instructor. Taught youngsters ages 3 1/2 to 9 years old the art of tap dancing, jazz, and ballet. Average class size approximately twenty students. Assisted with all aspects of yearly recitals.

6/97 - 8/97   SUMMER FUN DAY CAMP
Ozone Park, New York
Supervised the daily camp activities of large groups of youngsters. Responsible for weekly trips to museums, Hall of Science, Westbury Music Fair, and beaches. Also organized indoor play.

EXAMINATIONS   Passed NTE part I, II (March 1997) and III (December 1997).

OUTSIDE INTERESTS

As a member of the C.J. Dance Company my activities include studying tap, jazz, and ballet. Participate in charity work and fund-raising events.

REFERENCES   Furnished upon request.

Technical Services Manager

James Sharpe
9 Central Avenue
Beaverton, OR 97005
(503) 555-1212

SUMMARY:

Over 14 years of experience in Data Processing including Operations Management, Systems Programming, and Systems Programming Management. Technical experience includes three years of both NCP/VTAM and CICS systems programming as well as one year plus of MVS background.

**HARDWARE/
SOFTWARE:**

IBM 4341, 4381, Q14, 3380, 3375, 3705, VM/XA SF, MVS/XA, DOS/VSE, CICS/CL/I, IMS, VTAM, NCP, MSHP, SMP-E, TSO/ISPF PDF, MSA AP, MSA PAYROLL, EASYTRIEVE, ASSEMBLER, FAVER, UCCI

EXPERIENCE:

TECTRONIX, Manager, Technical Services. 11/93 to Present.

Plan and participate in the development and implementation of operating systems, data base systems, and related software packages.

Guide, monitor, and review the work of systems programming and data base administration. Support of MVS/XA, VM/XA SF, utilizing SMP-E and related software maintenance utilities.

Responsible for the telecommunications environment supporting 350 terminal devices utilizing VTAM/NCP.

CHEMICAL BANK: Systems Programmer. 6/89 to 11/93.

Planned and executed the interstate move of the Corporate Data Center. Installation and testing of all new hardware and telecommunication lines in the new data center, as well as coordinating the movement of data between the two centers.

CICS and VTAM support.

Applications group support in the consolidation of four corporations, data processing operations onto a single set of business applications.

Project leader of MVS conversion project. Responsible for the planning and installation of MVS, CICS, IMS, and NCP utilizing CBIPO. Also for the planning and implementation of MVS and VM/XA SF software packages.

James Sharpe, 9 Central Avenue, Beaverton, OR 97005...Page 2 of 2

DISC DRIVES INC. Operations Manager/Systems Programmer, 3/83 to 6/89.

Directed a three-shift operation in a DOS/VSE environment on an IBM 4381. Areas of responsibility included Computer Operations, I/O Control and Distribution, managing the activities of 12 people on the staff. Directly responsible for all systems programming activities, including:

- The installation and support of DOS/VSE SIPO 1.4.2, as well as tuning and DASD space management.
- Installation of MSA Payroll and Human Resources System.
- Installation of an IBM System 36 and related software components, and linked it to the mainframe for both 3270 and RJE support, to service the payroll application.

Operations Supervisor

Directed the activities of three Computer Operators, a tape librarian, and three I/O control clerks in a three-shift operation. Developed logs and procedures to ensure completion of all scheduled work. Developed standardized, documented scheduling procedures. Responsible for training all new personnel.

Lead Computer Operator

Responsible for training new operators and distribution personnel. Reviewed all work produced and resolved all problems.

PROFESSIONAL ATTRIBUTES:

I am a person who knows Technical Services from the ground up. I understand its importance in keeping a growing company productive, and take pride in creating order in the chaos of Technology.

Telecommunications Analyst

James Sharpe
9 Central Avenue
Jericho, NY 11753
(516) 555-1212

OBJECTIVE:

Challenging opportunity as Telecommunications Analyst

SUMMARY:

Eleven years' progressive experience providing network analysis, system planning, and product evaluation and selection. Comprehensive and cost-effective installation, troubleshooting, and maintenance of voice and data communications systems.

COMMUNICATIONS KNOWLEDGE:

Bell System, PBX's, Modems, MUX's and Fiber Optics. Specifically, Northern Telecom SLI, NEC NEAX 2400, Dimension 200, Rolm CBS, Mitel SX200, Strombergh Carlson DBX 1200/5000, GTE PIC, PCM Fiber Optic System, Equinox Data Switch and T1, Functional understanding of Packet Switches, WAGNET and ETHERNET.

EXPERIENCE:

A MAJOR BROKERAGE/FINANCIAL CORPORATION: TELECOMMUNICATIONS ANALYST

Project manager for the planning and implementation of a nationwide voice and data communications network. Included development of a multi-side RFP to replace fourteen phone systems. Issued RFP's to vendors, conducted evaluations according to formats and configurations. Network design and traffic engineering using ETN networks. 1991 - Present.

VIACOM, MANHATTAN: TELECOMMUNICATIONS VOICE/DATA ANALYST

Responsibilities included planning and implementing telecommunications for headquarters and field offices. Included long-range requirements, new products and software releases, and recommending upgrades as required. Reviewed and evaluated proposals, selected systems, assisted in system software design, and supervised implementation. 1989 - 1991.

CHASE MANHATTAN: TELECOMMUNICATIONS ANALYST

Responsibilities included: Coordinating installation for international data communications networks in Europe and Africa. Reviewed company's product usage, and provided recommendations for effective use of data switches or data through PBX. Assisted in the selection and implementation of data switch (RS-232) for a CM subsidiary. 1987 - 1989.

EDUCATION: B.S. Telecommunications. (New York University), 1990.

REFERENCES: Available upon request.

Textile Designer/Stylist

JANE SWIFT, 9 Central Avenue, Phoenix, AZ 85020. (602) 555-1212

Textile designer / stylist with 17 years' experience in the apparel and home furnishing industries. I have developed management skills in the areas of creative development, merchandising, and manufacturing.

SUMMARY

MERCHANDISING   In Jack Winter Ltd., I utilized my skills as a textile designer in the apparel market by producing moderate-priced garments within a vertical structure. I organized a company to merchandise, produce, and distribute finished goods throughout the U.S. and Canada. Worked closely with department and specialty stores. Sales volume in three years grew from 0 to $1,500,000 a year.

DEVELOPMENT   As designer for Continental Textiles, worked closely with prominent textile printers in U.S. and Italy. Designed both the fabrics and the finished products for an untapped market. Organized a manufacturing and marketing force to produce and distribute products throughout the U.S. Commitments for the first season of business amount to $1,000,000.

MANUFACTURING   Experience working for manufacturers of both volume and limited distribution. Developed technical skills and knowledge of a wide range of production methods. I have done business with numerous printers as well as subcontractors throughout U.S.

WORK EXPERIENCE

JACK WINTER DESIGNS, INC.   **1992-Present**
Custom-designed printed and hand-painted fabrics for interiors. Worked with major decorations and displayed in Kips Bay Decorator Showhouse.

    Pierre Deux, Inc.
    Designed major collection of decorative fabrics and wall coverings. Most successful sales growth to date in its category.

CONTINENTAL TEXTILES, INC.   **1989-1992**
Textile designer / stylist for wholesale manufacturer of luxury home furnishing products and loungewear. Worked closely with mills in Kentucky and Italy.

JACK WINTER, LTD.   **1985-1989**
Designer, manufacturer of moderate-price printed fabric and fashion apparel. Wholesale distribution across the U.S. in major department and specialty stores.

    Smithsonian Museum, Philadelphia Art Museum, Minneapolis Art Institute
    Designed and manufactured fabricated products for catalogs and gift shops.

MODERN TEXTILES INC.   **1981-1985**
Textile designer / stylist. Worked closely with mills and apparel designers. Moderate-price sportswear.

References available upon request.

Traffic Control (Shipping and Receiving)

JANE SWIFT

9 Central Avenue • Greenwich, CT 06830 • (203) 555-1212

SUMMARY OF QUALIFICATIONS

- Extensive, large volume *Traffic Control, Shipping & Receiving* knowledge; strong leadership abilities.
- Solid record of promotions based on performance. Insightful commitment to positive communication.
- Willing to take on new challenges within demanding deadlines utilizing progressive, results-oriented performance style.
- Strong time management and interpersonal skills. Extremely organized.
- Self-motivated, adaptable, loyal team player. Impeccable work ethic.
- Competent blueprint reading capabilities. Computer literate—proficient with spreadsheets.

EXPERIENCE

ABC EXTRUSION, Division of General Corporation • Greenwich, CT   1990 to 1998
Manufacturer of machinery for the rubber & plastic industry. Company name changed several times due to new ownership. Retained as a valuable employee through each transfer.

- **Traffic Control Manager**—Facilitated all shipments of large machinery and spare parts. Coordinated all paperwork and documentation including Bill of Lading, Certificate of Origin and Customs documents. Entered applicable data into computer system.
- **Receiving Manager**—Handled all receiving and stockroom department responsibilities. Identified, tagged and located parts in stock area. Retrieved components and piece parts for assembly floor personnel. Skilled using Federal Express Powership & Pitney Bowes shipping equipment.
- **Receiving**—Supported all receiving department functions. Identified, verified and received parts optimizing the computerized database.
- **Stockroom**—Stocked parts; recorded and cataloged items in database. Assisted in retrieving parts for assembly floor work orders.
- **Shipping**—Prepared and arranged U.P.S. shipments and packing of parts. Operated U.P.S. equipment documenting size, weight and type of cargo. Types Bills of Lading and Customs forms. Recorded all shipping data.
- **Data Entry**—Logged all new parts and stockroom locations into database.
- **Expediter**—Identified, traced and accelerated parts in process to the next manufacturing operation. Directed finished parts to appropriate assembly areas. Tracked and updated shortage lists.
- **Licensed**—to operate overhead crane, forklift and overhead lifts.

HOMETOWN MARKET • Greenwich, CT   1973 to 1990
Produce Market

- **Owner/Manager**—Directed and oversaw daily store operations. Supervised up to ten employees. Facilitated operational performance of store, implemented all phases of management functions inclusive of inventory, presentations, display, advertising, customer and employee relations, all accounting/bookkeeping, payroll and receivables. Generated and maintained reports, spreadsheets and mailing lists of over 10,000 people.

CONTINUING EDUCATION

- Blueprint Reading Certification, ABC
- Forklift Operation, ABC
- Crane Operation, ABC
- Accounting I, II, Connecticut State University

References Available Upon Request

Ultrasound/Nuclear Medicine Technician

Jane Swift
9 Central Avenue
Bellevue, WA 98007
(206) 555-1212

JOB OBJECTIVE:

To utilize my knowledge and experience in non-invasive cardiology to provide the highest-quality examinations.

EMPLOYMENT:

Bellevue Medical Center, Bellevue, WA. 1991 - present.

Chief Nuclear Medicine.

Nuclear medicine procedures, including:

SPECT, gated heart studies, thallium, programming and operation of nuclear computing systems. Responsible for development of procedures and protocols. Perform ultrasound procedures, including abdominal, gynecological, and small parts.

Beaverton County Hospital, Beaverton, OR. 1988 - 1991.

Ultrasound/Nuclear Technician

Performed nuclear medicine and ultrasound procedures, instigation of the ultrasound department. Management of the two departments under the supervision of the chief technologist. Marketing new technology and procedures to staff physicians.

EDUCATION:

University of Tennessee of Memphis
B.S. Nuclear Medicine Technology
School of Medicine
Certificate in Ultrasonography

SOCIETIES:

Society of Diagnostic Medical Sonographers
Society of Nuclear Medicine

Veterinary Intern

Jane Swift
9 Central Avenue
Englewood, NJ 07631
(201) 555-1212

EDUCATION

DVM - New Jersey State University, 1986
BS - State University of New York, Southampton
Currently completing MS in Poultry Science of NJSU

EMPLOYMENT

School of Veterinary Medicine, NJSU. Avian Medicine Intern (1996 to present)
Involved in avian medicine research and field service areas of the NJSU School of Veterinary Medicine.

- Assist in the instruction of veterinary and undergraduate students.
- Diagnostic workup of avian cases at the Animal Disease Diagnostic Laboratory of the Department of Agriculture.
- Extensive co-op work with private poultry companies in New Jersey and other states.

School of Veterinary Medicine, NJSU. Research Technician (1993 to 1996)
Responsibilities included:

- Management of experimental sheep, swine, horses, and cattle.
- Collection of blood, urine, and feces for determination of clearance rates for a radioactively tagged anthelmintic.

Department of Poultry Science, NJSU. Farm Manager (1991 to 1993)
Responsibilities included:

- Weekend management of turkey research unit, including care and feeding of birds, egg collection and hatchery management.
- Collection and analysis of tissues and data, performance of various electrolyte and hormone assays.
- Assistance in endocrinology laboratory instruction.

VETERINARY SCHOOL ACTIVITIES

- Freshman Class President
- Student representative to the NJSU Outstanding Teacher Selection Committee
- Student representative to the Ethics in Veterinary Medical Education Symposium, Knoxville, TN

PROFESSIONAL ASSOCIATES

- American Veterinary Medical Association
- American Association of Avian Pathologist
- Association of Avian Veterinarians

Visual Merchandising Specialist

Jane Swift
9 Central Avenue
Manhasset, NY 11575
(516) 555-1212

With fifteen years' experience in Visual Merchandising Management, I have successfully:

- Coordinated all Visual Merchandising in Macy's third-most-profitable store.
- Supervised visual aspects of a successful $3 million store renovation with responsibility for new fixturing and merchandising.
- Conducted seminar in Visual Merchandising for all new department managers in Macy's eastern region.
- Utilized innovative image control techniques that contributed to a new high-fashion store's becoming the volume leader for its entire chain in one year.

RECENT ACCOMPLISHMENTS

Visual Merchandising Manager of a Macy's store with a $40 million sales volume, I coordinated fixturing, merchandising, and seasonal changes for all twelve departments, along with responsibility for overall store image.

- Analyzed stock levels to determine new fixture needs, prepared requirement reports, and coordinated on-time deliveries of all fixtures.
- Reporting directly to the Vice President for Corporate Visual Merchandising, I supervised five Visual Merchandising Managers brought in from other stores to assist in the project.
- Interfaced with both union and non-union construction personnel while directing movement of departments under construction.
- Guiding all Department Managers through renovation and construction, I familiarized them with new fixturing and applicable merchandising techniques.

EARLIER ACCOMPLISHMENTS

As District Display Director for Laura Ashley Inc., a 100-store specialty women's ready-to-wear chain, I developed fashion awareness, coordinated displays, and trained staff, including new District Display Directors throughout the country. Reporting directly to the Corporate Display Director, I was:

- Given responsibility for image control at the company's new flagship store on 57th St, where fashion image was crucial. My innovative merchandising and display techniques contributed to this store's becoming the number-one-volume store for the entire company by its first anniversary.
- Recognized for my planning, organizing, and coordinating abilities, I was involved in several new store openings throughout the U.S. and Canada.

As Display Coordinator/Visual Merchandising Manager with ESPRIT, Inc., I progressed to having a five-store responsibility. Developing my functional skills, I was promoted to Visual Display troubleshooter for a multi-state region.

JANE SWIFT (516) 555-12-12...PAGE 2 OF 2

EMPLOYMENT
MACY'S, 1987 - Present
LAURA ASHLEY, 1983 - 1987
ESPRIT DE CORPS, 1979 - 1983

EDUCATION
A graduate of Harper College, Palatine, Illinois, with a specialty in Fashion Design, I have also completed intensive course work in Architectural Technology which has significantly contributed to my expertise in store renovation and floor plan know-how. Course work in photography has rounded out my background.

PERSONAL
Interests include apparel design and construction, sketching, and free-hand drawing.

Wholesale Electrical Salesperson

JAMES SHARPE
9 Central Avenue
Rock Island, IL 61204
(309) 555-1212

Sales/Sales Management
Administration…Distribution…Advertising

Versatile, goal-oriented sales professional with wide experience in sales, marketing, and training. Expertise includes start-up/turn-around sales operations, increasing sales, and new product/market development. Heavy exposure to advertising, outlet management, pricing, distribution, merchandising, and sales analysis.

CAREER HIGHLIGHTS

SALES:
As inside sales and quotation specialist, I contributed $3,000,000 of the company's $30,000,000 annual sales.

MARKETING:
I improved by 25% a territory that was in the beginning stages of economic crisis in an oil-related economy.

COMMUNICATIONS: I created and developed the Chicago Chapter of the Illinois Electric League Man of the Year, 1988.

PROJECT MANAGEMENT:
Conceived and implemented systems and procedures to increase sales territory from $1,500,000 to $2,000,000.

NEGOTIATIONS:
As manager of the California branches of a multi-store electrical supply chain based in Mississippi, I negotiated purchases of special materials for promotion and sales effort. I also negotiated large-job material purchases up to $1,500,000.

PROMOTION:
I conceived and directed in-house "tent shows" and "open houses" and regional "trade shows" to promote our chain throughout Midwest. Chairman Greater Chicago Electric League Trade Show Attendance Committee.

COMPUTER:
Established systems for handling $600,000 in materials through stock each month, reducing overhead by 4.5%.

WORK HISTORY

Large Electrical Distributor   Chicago, IL 1991-Present
Lake Lighting & Supply   Sacramento, CA 1989-1991
Stern Electrical Sales   Brownsville, TX 1987-1989
Top Supply   Chicago, IL 1986-1987
Metro Electric Supply   Chicago, IL 1985-1986

ADDITIONAL PROFESSIONAL TRAINING

Dale Carnegie Sales course
Dale Carnegie Public Speaking and Leadership course

EDUCATION

Extensive credits from University of Michigan, University of San Jose, and Duke University.

Word Processing Specialist

JANE SWIFT
9 CENTRAL AVENUE
LEXINGTON, KY 40579
(606) 555-1212

EXPERIENCE:
January 1995 - present
Word Processor. General Motors, Detroit, Michigan.

Currently working in a program that involves editing, creating, and printing of corporate budgets, memos, and a variety of charts, letters, and telecommunications. I also assume all of the Supervisor's responsibilities in her absence.

January 1993 - January 1995
Data Librarian/Scheduler. Kentucky Turf Club, Lexington, KY.

Included the control, input and output of data tapes. Prepared a processing schedule and coordinated all input and output to meet objectives of schedule. Responsible for preparing a morning report to management, accounting for all variances from the prior day's processing schedule, and assisting in problem determination and resolution.

March 1988 - January 1993
Data Entry Operator/Senior Operator. Kentucky Turf Club.

Started with the company as a data entry operator and after six months was promoted to senior operator. In early 1984 the data entry staff was cut to only myself, which gave me full responsibility for all turnover of data entry and for maintaining a schedule on the priorities of the work.

September 1986 - March 1988
Data Entry/Senior Operator. Blue Mountain Telephone Co., Lexington, KY.

Trained with Blue Mountain Telephone Co. during a work study program in high school and went on to the following companies as a data entry operator and was soon promoted in each to Senior Operator: Lexington Glass, Manny Kerber PC, and Kentucky Auto Rating Bureau.

HARDWARE EXPERIENCE:

Windows
Windows95
Macintosh

EDUCATION:

Computer Associates - 1991; Tape / Disk Management
IBM-1981; 3741
Lexington Business School - 1986; Data Entry

References available upon request.

Word Processing Supervisor

Jane Swift
9 Central Avenue
Milwaukee, WI 53201
(414) 555-1212

EXPERIENCE:
6/93 - Present: **Richfield and Simon, Milwaukee, WI.** Word Processing Supervisor

- Prioritize and distribute workload for operators on several shifts in a forty-attorney law firm.
- Manage and supervise day, evening, and weekend word-processing center on OIS-140 system.
- Thorough knowledge of all word-processing advanced functions, utilities, glossaries, and telecommunications.
- Interview, hire, and evaluate word-processing operators.

10/82 - 6/93   **National Cardboard Company, Milwaukee, WI**
6/89 - 6/93   Supervisor/Coordinator - Word Processing Operations

- Supervised and maintained Wang OIS-140 systems for several departments. Duties included: Solving and correcting general equipment problems, and monitoring capacity, library usage, and loading software.
- Coordinated activities of word processing operators for three centers. Created glossaries to aid operators in formats and styles. Devised instruction and reference manuals with easy-to-understand language.
- Trained personnel in equipment operation and maintenance.
- Liaison with Wang Laboratories' Software and Customer Engineers.
- Consulted with and performed trouble-shooting and maintenance for operators in other departments in the company.

10/82 - 6/89   Administrative Assistant to the Director of Investor Relations

- Researched market and financial data, communicated daily with security analysts, and handled highly confidential information.

5/80 - 9/82   **1st National Bank, Milwaukee, WI**
Administrative Assistant/Systems Assistant Supervisor - Research Department

Assisted Security Analyst in compiling statistics and information for research reports. Assisted Systems Supervisor in supervision of IBM Mag Card operators and secretaries.

EDUCATION:
- Numerous development courses.
- Various training courses at Wang Laboratories.

REFERENCES: Will be furnished upon request.

Appendix

Resumes for Special Situations

These are resumes that performed above and beyond the call of duty for job seekers whose background didn't "fit the mold." They're invaluable guideposts in presenting your own experiences in the most flattering light.

Jane is changing careers.

Jane Swift
9 Central Avenue
Calabasas, California 91301
(818) 555-1212

OBJECTIVE

A responsible and challenging entry-level position that will utilize my education and background, expand my knowledge, and offer opportunities for personal and professional growth.

SUMMARY OF KNOWLEDGE AND EXPERIENCE

- CUSTOMER SERVICE
- INTERFACE WELL WITH THE PUBLIC
- EXCELLENT COMMUNICATION SKILLS
- SET, MEET DEADLINES/GOALS
- CASHIERING
- MARKETING
- INVENTORY CONTROL
- KNOWLEDGE OF WORDPERFECT

- HIGHLY ORGANIZED
- KNOWLEDGE OF SPANISH
- DETAIL/EFFICIENCY ORIENTED
- RECORD KEEPING
- TROUBLESHOOTING
- TUTORING
- COORDINATION
- PUBLIC RELATIONS

EDUCATIONAL HISTORY

California State University, Northridge
Los Angeles Valley College, Van Nuys

B.A. Psychology - 3.8 GPA - 1992
A.A. General Education

ACCOMPLISHMENTS AND ACHIEVEMENTS

- Awarded Recognition Certificate for achieving 100% on Shoppers Report Evaluation for food service performance, salesmanship, and hospitality at Marie Callender.
- PSYCHI - National Honor Society for Psychology
- Golden Key Honor Society - National Honor Society

EMPLOYMENT HISTORY

4/96 - Present	**WAITRESS**
	Marie Callender, Sherman Oaks, California
2/94 - 3/96	**CASHIER / WAITRESS**
	Denny's Restaurant, Northridge, California
9/91 - 12/93	**MARKET RESEARCHER**
	Suburban Associates, Sherman Oaks, California
9/90 - 6/92	**ASSISTANT TO TEACHER / ART DIRECTOR**
	Temple Beth Hillel

VOLUNTEER/COMMUNITY SERVICE

San Fernando Valley Child Guidance Clinic - Tutoring

REFERENCES FURNISHED UPON REQUEST

James is leaving the military for a position in sales/marketing.

James Sharpe
9 Central Avenue
Portland, OR 97232
(503) 555-1212

OBJECTIVE   A career position with a progressive organization in the field of Sales/Marketing where there are opportunities for growth and advancement.

PROFESSIONAL SUMMARY

U.S. Marine Corp/Sergeant…Aircraft Mechanic/Embarkation Operations—participated in Desert Storm operations -'90 -'91…Squad Leader…Petroleum products distribution…Recruiter.

MILITARY TRAINING SUMMARY

Successfully completed Communications course by Xerox including instructions in Speech Techniques, Presentations and Outlines, Speaking Formats…Professional Selling Skills III and Advanced Closing Techniques…Administrative Plans/Procedures and Programs…Physical Training Management…Inspections/Customs/Courtesies…Leadership…Techniques of Military Instruction, etc.

PROFESSIONAL EXPERIENCE

RECRUITER, Queens, New York (1995-1997)
Assisted with preliminary screening and administrative processing, scheduling physical examinations, completion of enlistment documents and maintaining accurate records. Involved with applicant processing, clientele search, i.e., phone, one-to-one contact, mailouts. Thoroughly familiar with all aspects of the enlistment process. Provided the community with publicity material and assisted with civic events, etc. Supervised six Lance Corporals and Corporals. Achievement: Recruiter of the quarter (1992) for Six-State Region of the First Marine Corp District.

AVIATION MECHANIC - Sergeant/Lance Corporal (1990-1995)
Camp Pendelton, California
Activities centered on testing hydraulic systems; familiar with basic theory of flight and aircraft nomenclature; basic aircraft systems; aircraft cleaning and handling; aviation fuels; oils and hydraulic fluids; aviation support equipment; mechanic of heat and gases and principle of hydraulics.

SUPPLY CLERK (1989-1990)
Duties and responsibilities included all aspects of inventory and stock control of large number of military supplies. All record keeping; issued supplies and spare parts for automotive/military vehicles.

CONSTRUCTION/PETROLEUM SUPPLY SPECIALIST (1987-1989)
Okinawa, Japan - Squad Leader/Corporal
Assisted with the distribution of petroleum products, i.e., gasoline and diesel fuel, for military vehicles and jets. Responsible for storage of products. Participated in hands-on construction of embarkation gear and mobilization equipment. As Squad Leader, involved with the direct supervision of team of twelve Lance Corporals to Privates.

James is an Electrician changing to a career in sales & promotion.

James Sharpe
9 Central Avenue
Ferndale, MI 48220
(313) 555-1212

CAREER OBJECTIVE

To support the growth and profitability or an organization that provides challenge, encourages advancement, and rewards achievement with the opportunity to utilize my substantial experience, skills, and proven abilities in a position involving Sales and Promotion within the Consumer Goods industry.

STRENGTHS

- Skilled in motivating and interacting with the public.
- Disciplined and well organized in work habits, with ability to function smoothly in pressure situations.
- Ability to identify problems and implement effective solutions.
- Possess a "pro" company attitude dedicated to the growth and profitability of the company.

EMPLOYMENT HISTORY

McMURRAY ELECTRIC, 22036 Woodward, Ferndale, MI 48220
Journeyman Electrician - April 1990 to Present
Responsible for the installation and servicing of commercial, residential, and industrial accounts. In my current position as Foreman Leader, I supervise the activities of four to five electricians/helpers and have been responsible for as many as thirteen employees.

- Ability to read and effectively implement blueprints, along with extensive layout skills.
- Because of vast knowledge of jobs performed for the company and ability to deal effectively with people, was selected by management to train new employees.

POWERS DISTRIBUTING COMPANY, INC., 2000 Pontiac Dr., Pontiac, MI 48053
On-Premise Promotions - August 1992 to Present
Responsible for representing Miller Brewing Company at promotional functions in on-premise accounts situated in Oakland and Macomb Counties.

- I possessed the energy, enthusiasm, and poise necessary for implementing successful brewery promotions, was selected for newly created position.
- Have acquired extensive knowledge of motivating/sales techniques, which has contributed substantially to increased sales at brewery promotions.
- Active in the development and coordination of brewery promotions.

EDUCATION

Associated Builders and Contractors, Inc. - Graduated June 1991
Course of Study: Electrical
Oakland Community College - Courses relating to Electronics Field (Attended 1982 and 1983)
Ferndale High School - Graduated June 1981

REFERENCES FURNISHED UPON REQUEST

Jane is changing careers after a period of self-employment.

Jane Swift
9 Central Avenue
Burlingame, CA 94010
(415) 555-1212

Objective   Sales representative or showroom position in the fashion industry

Summary of Qualifications

- Five years' experience in design and manufacture of Women's Wear
- Extensive production management and operations experience
- Fifteen years' sales experience in inside sales, showrooms, and tradeshows
- Expertise in conducting tradeshows, designing booths, and managing customers
- Capable and flexible self-starter who is able to travel for trade shows

Work Experience

1992 to 1998   **Owner/Designer**
Gene Sims Designs
Design and manufacture of Womens' Wear accessories, earrings, hair clips, purses, and pins. Extensive experience in buying, trade shows (Canada and Washington state), payroll, collections, billing. Hired 22 sales reps throughout the U.S. and Puerto Rico. Employed 12 people to make accessories.

1988 to 1992   **Outside Sales and Trainer**
West Coast Financial Services
Extensive selling experience cold-calling, canvassing, and prospecting to corporations for medical insurance plans. Organized and set up an entire department and trained department staff.

1982 to 1988   **Personnel and Collections Manager**
Physio-Control
Interviewed potential employees for several department heads. Managed credit and collections. Trained managers on how to interview and hire the right person.

1976 to 1982   **Office Manager/Executive Recruiter**
Betty White Employment Agency
Interviewed prospective employees for professional and clerical positions with corporations.

James has changed careers many times.

James Sharpe
9 Central Avenue
Aurora, CO 80014
(303) 555-1212

OBJECTIVE   A challenging position providing an opportunity to apply broad Management experience.

EDUCATION   University of Colorado
MBA program—presently enrolled
B.S. Public Administration, Colorado College

QUALIFICATIONS   Progressively responsible management background in a large medical facility, with successful experience in the following areas:

Staff Supervision—presently responsible for 30 skilled, semi-skilled, unskilled, and managerial employees. Hire, train, direct, and evaluate the staff. Responsible for their output and the quality of their work. Maintain morale, motivation, and positive employee relations. Solve problems, take corrective action, apply company policy.

Operations Management—direct staff and activities in several support departments, including maintenance, grounds and buildings, laundry, housekeeping. Manage a budget of nearly a half million dollars. Schedule all departments for the most effective use of manpower, equipment, and facilities.

Inventory Control/Purchasing—maintain an inventory control system for non-medical supplies and food.

Other—frequent involvement in customer and public relations, promoting the facility; work with other staff to prepare for licensing, compliance reviews; involved in Real Estate Management—buying, renovating, and maintaining rental properties; licensed in real estate sales.

As public administration Intern at both the state and federal levels, involved in labor relations activities, legislative actions, communications.

EMPLOYMENT
1990 to present   Aurora Rest Home, Aurora, CO
Supervisor—promoted from Assistant

1986 to 1990   Coors Brewery, Golden, CO
Construction Worker

1984 to 1986   Intern—federal and state

Jane is a handicapped worker who wants to change careers.

Jane Swift
9 Central Avenue
Monroe, WI 53566
(608) 555-1212

OBJECTIVE   Seeking a challenging position in Customer Service.

SUMMARY

- Possess a combined Customer Service and Financial background. Responsible for administering several aspects of pension plans. Significant customer service responsibilities as Office Manager and Credit Coordinator.

QUALIFICATION

- Present position requires accuracy and efficiency in creation of files, calculation of benefits and options, analysis of IRS qualification, preparation of tax forms, and other similar activities.
- Effective verbal and written negotiations with agents, attorneys, plan participants, accountants, and others. Good communications skills are necessary for confidential interdepartmental communications.
- Experience includes Credit and Office Management. My responsibilities in credit include taking applications, securing credit approvals, ordering products, and arranging for delivery. I also calculated salespeople's commissions. As Office Manager, I handled customer service duties, accepted and booked payments, maintained inventories, and performed other functions associated with keeping the office running smoothly.

EXPERIENCE
1980 to present   BC/BC
Pension Technical Specialist

Sears
Credit Coordinator—for major appliance

3M Products
Office Manager

Big Brothers/Big Sisters; United Cerebral Palsy Assoc.
(6 years, part-time)
Office Manager/Clerical

James is a blue-collar worker and wants a white-collar job.

James Sharpe
9 Central Avenue
Claremont, NC 28610
(704) 555-1212

OBJECTIVE An opportunity to apply technical skills and communications ability in a Sales or Customer Service position.

SKILLS SUMMARY Thoroughly familiar with the process of quoting and producing industrial products for a wide range of customer applications. Work with customers' specifications, ideas, or blueprints to produce parts on a special or stock basis. Call on accounts to assist with product development, to provide service in the event of discrepancies or quality questions. Duties require the ability to communicate effectively on technical problems, and to established rapport.

In a retail setting, have held major responsibility for staff supervision and customer service, managing several functions with high customer and employee contact.

As a supervisor, held responsibility for training, scheduling, directing, and evaluating the work of skilled machinists. Keep areas of responsibility supplied with tooling, materials, and equipment to ensure the most effective use of manpower and machinery.

Acted as buyer of industrial products: drills, reamers, slotting saws, collects, high-speed carbide steels, ceramics, lubricants, and NC screw machine programs, among others.

Operated and troubleshot sophisticated machine shop equipment, including Swiss screw machines, grinders, lathes, milling machines, drill presses. Able to program CNC equipment. Conversant with the full range of machine shop practices, as well as quality and production control procedures.

EXPERIENCE
1989 to present **Jig Tools, Claremont, NC**
Supervisor, Quality Control Inspector
Production Machinist

1985 to 1989 **Finest Foods, Raleigh, NC**
Front End Manager, supervising an evening shift.
Involved in cashiering, packing, credit voucher cashing.

1980 to 1985 **Atlas Moving Co., Raleigh, NC**
Truck Driver, Mechanic

PERSONAL References available upon request.

Jane has had multiple jobs and needs to combine her experience.

Jane Swift
9 Central Avenue
Kenner, LA 70062
(504) 555-1212

OBJECTIVE

A challenging Sales or Sales Management position, providing an opportunity to apply broad experience and a record of success in marketing a variety of products and services.

QUALIFICATIONS

Sales—Thoroughly familiar with techniques for generating new business in industrial, commercial, and consumer markets. Employed cold call, referral, and other prospecting techniques. Skilled at assessing client needs and making effective sales presentations, often involving technical product details.

Have regularly exceeded sales quotas.

Sales Management—Responsibilities included selecting, training, motivating, and supervising professionals in sales, service, and other operations.

Performed market research and promotions, forecasting, the development of distribution systems, and other marketing administration functions.

Developed marketing plans, arranged financing, helped establish distribution networks.

EMPLOYMENT

ADT Systems—Worcester, MA
Commercial Sales Representative   1995 to present

Patriot Marketing—Worcester, MA
Owner/Consultant   1993 to 1995

1980-1990

Maxxum Industries, Inc.
Self-Employed Restaurateur
Cherry Buick
Goodnick Miller
International Harvester

TRAINING

Studied Business Administration, Management, and Marketing at Louisiana Institute of Technology, the University of Texas, and Kenner Junior College. Have received technical product and sales training in numerous courses and seminars throughout my career.

PERSONAL

U.S. Navy—honorably discharged
References available upon request

Jane is changing careers to become a Human Resources Worker.

Jane Swift
9 Central Avenue
Rockville, MD 20852
(301) 555-1212

OBJECTIVE   Opportunity in Human Resources/Benefits/Compensation/Recruiting.

QUALIFICATIONS Extensive supervisory experience, managing administrative details of pension plans on behalf of corporate and individual clients. My responsibilities have required skills in several areas, including:

Financial/Analytical
Administrate details of pension plans ranging in size from 1 to 2,500 participants. Thorough knowledge of plan design, funding practices, benefits, taxation, and disclosure. Supervise the systems and people who gather detailed pension data, conduct analyses, and report on valuations, benefits, tax information, reporting requirements.

Communications
Successfully employ written and oral communications skills when dealing with clients, their accountants and attorneys, actuaries, in-house technical experts, field offices, and government agencies. Responsible for timely and accurate preparation of a wide array of reports and filings.

Supervision
Direct a small staff. Assisted in their selection. Responsible for training, supervision, evaluation, and motivation. Ensure that the flow of work is smooth and that all deadlines are successfully met. Responsible for problem solving, and handling difficult or unusual cases. Able to manage and coordinate multiple projects simultaneously.

EXPERIENCE
1988 to present   Maryland Life Assurance Company
                     Rockville, Maryland
                     Pension Specialist, Group Pension Services

EDUCATION   B.S. Education, 1987
                     Vassar

PERSONAL   Willing to travel, relocate

Jane is changing careers to become a Salesperson.

Jane Swift
9 Central Avenue
Utica, MI 48087
(313) 555-1212

OBJECTIVE   An opportunity to apply Medical Technological background in a challenging Sales or
Marketing position.

QUALIFICATIONS

- Over six years experience in Medical Technology in hospital laboratory and outpatient settings. Have worked successfully with physicians in a number of disciplines, including pathology, geriatrics, oncology, other areas; interact daily with laboratory staff (supervisory and technical), patients, and other people throughout the hospital.
- Thoroughly familiar with complex, sophisticated laboratory equipment, such as Coulter S plus IV, Coulter 550, MLA 700, Fibrometer. Provide technical training to other operators and to medical technology students. Accountable for the accurate calibration of equipment, basic troubleshooting, and maintenance.
- Maintenance of inventory, purchase of supplies, and quality control procedures in general.
- These duties require a person who is thoroughly knowledgeable about laboratory and highly technical equipment and associated procedures, is familiar with materials, and is precise in performance of duties.

EMPLOYMENT

1992 to present   Utica Family Hospital—Utica, Michigan
Special Hematology Laboratory Technologist, promoted from Laboratory Technologist

EDUCATION   B.S. Medical Technology, 1992
Detroit State College (Detroit, Michigan)

Registry eligible in Hematology

Additional training by laboratory equipment manufacturers

REFERENCES   Excellent professional references are available upon request.

James is only fourteen years old!

James Sharpe
9 Central Avenue
Dallas, TX 75231
(214) 555-1212

SUMMARY

Expert in bicycle freestyling. Starting in 1994 at the age of 10, I've developed my skills to the point where I'm a regular participant in demonstrations, parades and shows, as well as a winner in several competitions. I've been asked to appear on TV, in magazines, and in commercials.

Shows

Since June of 1995, I've been a member of the Stuntsters Trick Team (sponsored by Athlete's Foot). Both individually and with other team members, I've been in more than 20 shows throughout Texas. Some of these are paid appearances, some provide premiums, and others are done as a courtesy.

Competitions

In statewide meets, competing against others in my class and in higher classes, I've consistently placed in the top 5. My specialty is the Flatland event. I'm presently competing on a national level. In addition to competing, I've won awards for bicycle safety.

TV/Broadcast/Print

I've appeared in numerous TV news film clips, and in a *PM Magazine* feature. I was featured in a 30-second commercial spot for *BMX* bicycles, and recently completed filming a 30-second national TV spot for *Snapple*. *Rad Zone* magazine, a national newsletter for the sport, will be featuring me in an upcoming edition. I'm now under active consideration for a part in a soon-to-be produced feature film.

Other Activities

When not practicing freestyling (up to five hours a day), I like to ski and surf. During the summer I work as a golf caddy.

A complete portfolio is available for inspection.

Jane is a recently divorced homemaker reentering the work force.

Jane Swift
9 Central Avenue
Wichita, KS 67218
(316) 555-1212

OBJECTIVE

An entry position in Personnel or Human Resources Management, providing an opportunity to apply formal education in the field, and business experience.

EDUCATION

Anna Maria College—Paxton, Massachusetts
B.A. Psychology
Graduated *magna cum laude*

SUMMARY OF SKILLS

Studies have included courses in Industrial Psychology, Personnel Management, Marketing, Management, Accounting, other Psychology and Liberal Arts courses.

Experience in *Interviewing/Communications*, gained from extensive dealings with customers, clients, students, and peers in the organization. Capable of effective written and oral communication where the ability to gather precisely and act on it is critical.

Background in *Counseling*, with both adults and students in academic and professional settings. Assisted with *Career Counseling* and other forms of personal assistance.

Experience includes work as a *Telemarketing Representative* and as an Administrative Assistant. Have held leadership positions in volunteer organizations, including *Chairperson, Fundraiser, Advisory Board Member,* and *Counselor*. Duties have required the ability to organize, set up, and implement systems for getting tasks completed, as well as the ability to be persuasive and obtain cooperation.

EXPERIENCE

Wichita Employment Services
Telemarketing Representative. Working from research, leads, and cold calls, identifying target markets and make over 500 sales calls per month. Provide quotes, and refer results of research for further action. Set up relevant sales administration systems.

1988 to 1992

Kansas State University
Worked part and full time while attending college.
Assignments included:
Secretary in the Graduate Office, in the Development Office, and to the Director of the Nursing Program.

ACTIVITIES

Chairperson, Boy Scout Troop Committee; Member, Advisory Board; Fundraiser, Counselor, Navy Officers' Wives Association; Fundraiser, Library Committee.

PERSONAL

Health: excellent
Willing to travel/relocate

Off the Beaten Track

Following are some of the more impressive resumes in employment areas you don't come across every day. Some of these fields may not seem to require a resume—at first glance. The fact is, virtually any position is competitive, even the unusual ones. The authors of these samples thought twice, set themselves apart from the competition, and picked up the jobs they deserved.

Copywriter

Jane Swift, 9 Central Avenue, Chicago, IL 60611. (312) 555-1212

Call Me Top Gun.

A writer committed to excellence. A writer who wants to be the best, work with the best, learn from the best.

A Top Gun who's been around—especially around consumer and high-tech. Who's always reaching for breakthrough. And who's very, very fast.

I'm looking for an agency that's sincerely committed to outstanding creativity. One where my best work won't go through life as a comp.

What can I do for you? Write ads, radio, and TV spots that soar above the noise. Produce AV and videos that perform up to promise. And back you up, whatever it takes. If you need a Top Gun—a team player who knows tactics and reaches for the top—maybe we should talk. What we already share is a passion for excellence.

Let's schedule a check ride.

OBJECTIVE

To be the best, work with the best, learn from the best.
CURRENTLY
Senior Copywriter. Compton Burnett
Clients:
>Dynatech * Communications* Dennison * Augat Pylon * Avanti Communications * Corporation * AFI/Datatrol Telesis * Datel * Amperex * Advanced Technology * Xyplex

1994-95
Account Executive, Foote Cone Belding. Set up Midwest branch of International Agency.
Clients:
>Applicon * Itek Graphics Systems * BBN * plus introduction of the Ricoh line of personal computers

1993-94
Writer/producer. Creative Services Source. Chicago: Film, video, radio and TV.
Clients:
>Marathon Development * Saunders & Associates * The United Way * Colibri * Stanley Hardware * Fram * Key Microsystems * Fleet National Bank

1989-93
Copywriter, Pierce Brown Associates, Rochester, NY
Clients:
>Bausch & Lomb * Corning Glass Works * R.T. Company * Citibank * Telex * Xerox

EDUCATION

B.A. Duquesne University, 1989
Art direction, RISD. 1995

Mail Clerk

James Sharpe
9 Central Avenue
Houston, TX 77031
(713) 555-1212

EXPERIENCE

10/89-present   **Gordon, Roffe, Sinclair** (Houston, TX)

Position: Mail/File Clerk

Duties: Daily upkeep of alphanumerical, cross reference, domestic and international filing system; opening, organization and closeout of files; daily operation of Xerox machines; processing of daily incoming and outgoing mail, including operation of Pitney Bowes Postage Meter machines; inventory, ordering and stocking of supplies; general upkeep of file department.

11/84-3/89   **Boggs, Evans & Horn** (Houston, TX)

Position: Mail Clerk/Messenger

Duties: Processing of daily incoming and outgoing mail, including operation of Pitney Bowes Postage Meter machines; distributed interoffice material; operation of Xerox machines. Operation of the Kodak Ektaprint Copier Duplicator. Transmission of Telex & Telex copy messages.

EDUCATION

1894-1985   LaGuardia Community College, NY
Major: Accounting

References will be provided upon request.

Physician (Seeking Fellowship)

Jane Swift, 9 Central Avenue, Baltimore, MD 21201. (301) 555-1212

CAREER OBJECTIVE

To pursue a career in OB/GYN, with a sub-specialty in Fetal Maternal Health, with an opportunity to combine my interests in Surgery and Internal Medicine. I expect to seek board registry in both OB/GYN and in Internal Medicine.

EDUCATION

Carte School of Medicine—University of Maryland
Doctor of Medicine — 1994

University of Maryland
M.S. Pharmacology — 1992
B.A. Biology, cum laude — 1990

PROFESSIONAL

St. Joseph Medical Center—Baltimore, Maryland
Internal Medicine Residency Program (Level II) — 1996

TRAINING

Categorical Internship, Internal Medicine — 1995
The Memorial Hospital—Baltimore, Maryland

Internal Medicine Residency Program (Level III) — 1996
OB/GYN Elective

University of Maryland Medical Center—Baltimore
Gynecology Elective — 1997

HONORS AND AWARDS

National Honor Society 1984-86

Carter School of Medicine—Biomedical Research Symposium
First Prize, Medical Student Category — 1992
First Prize, Best Paper in Oncology — 1992

St. Joseph Medical Center
Award, Outstanding Intern of the Year — 1994-95

PRESENTATIONS/ PUBLICATIONS

Eastern Student Medical Research Forum—Presentation, — 1992

"Regulation of Mitogen Response and Erlich Acites Tumor Growth by Miconzone." (Abstract)

"Effect of Arachidonic Acid and Prostaglandin Hemolytic Plaque Formation." 1989. (Abstract)

ACTIVITIES

University of Maryland Pre-Med Society *Treasurer*
Eastern Student Medical Research Committee
Representative, University of Maryland
American Medical Association
St. Mary Medical Center Housestaff Association

Plant Breeder

James Sharpe
9 Central Avenue
Ft. Lauderdale, Fl 33339
(305) 555-1212

EXPERIENCE
4/90-present

SOUTHERN SEEDS—Ft. Lauderdale, FL
Research Director (1994-Present)—Responsible for citrus breeding activities in Florida and making product recommendations (canned, frozen, concentrates). Supervising one plant breeder, one technician, and up to 20 hourly workers.

ACCOMPLISHMENTS:

- Increased the size of breeding and testing program by 50%;
- Identified superior citrus products for a successful entry into the citrus market;
- Identified and developed superior citrus products to strengthen sales in all maturities;
- Provided product information to dealers and sales personnel in an understandable and concise form.

Plant Breeder (1990-1994)—Responsible for strengthening corn breeding and testing effort.

ACCOMPLISHMENTS:

- Improved mechanization of the citrus project;
- Initiated and developed to computerization of the citrus project;
- Increased size and scope of citrus breeding and testing by 100%, while introducing numerous frost-resistant strains.

FLORIDA STATE UNIVERSITY—Tallahassee, FL
3/4 Time Research Associate (1/88-2/90)

- Researched the heritability of citrus quality traits.
- Assisted in operation of citrus project, including planting, harvesting, and data collection.

1/2 Time Research Associate (1/86-1/88)

- Researched frost tolerance in citrus.
- Assisted in operation of citrus project including planting, harvesting, and data collection.

EDUCATION

1990   *PhD. Plant Breeding*—Florida State University
1987   *MS. Plant Breeding*—Florida State University
1984   *BS. Agronomy*—University of Minnesota

Respiratory Therapist

James Sharpe
9 Central Avenue
Warminster, PA 18974
(215) 555-1212

SKILL SUMMARY:

Respiratory Therapist familiar with Bennett, Sechrist, and Bear respirators (Adult and Infant), intubation, arterial blood gas sampling, transcutaneous monitoring, polysomnographic monitoring, transport techniques, and electrocardiography.

EXPERIENCE:

1991 to present   **Critical Care Respiratory Therapist**
Warminster Children's Hospital, Warminster, PA

Responsible for all aspects of infant critical respiratory care, plus routine respiratory patient care. Serve as an alternate shift supervisor, supervising four persons.

1984 to 1991   **Staff Therapist**
Veterans Memorial Hospital, Philadelphia, PA

Worked as a Staff Therapist beginning 1986; was responsible for intensive and general respiratory care hospital-wide.

EDUCATION:

Worked as a Therapist Assistant while in school, responsible for routine respiratory care in non-critical areas. Funded all educational costs.

1984   A.S. Respiratory Therapy, University of Oregon

1982   B.S. Biology, University of Oregon

CERTIFICATION:

Certified Respiratory Therapy Technician (CRRT) by NBRC
Registered Respiratory Therapist (RRT) by NBRC

REFERENCES:

Available upon request.

TV Installation Specialist

James Sharpe
9 Central Avenue, Apt. 45
New York, NY 10019
(212) 555-1212

OBJECTIVE

Seeking an opportunity to apply my skills and experience in Cable TV installation/construction.

QUALIFICATIONS

- Experienced in all phases of cable TV installation and construction. I've worked on residential and commercial installations in urban, suburban, and rural areas.
- Working individually or as crew chief, I've handled all kinds of installation projects, ranging from very simple to complex, both pre-finish and post-wire, in single or multi-family dwellings and high-rise buildings.
- My skills include blueprint and schematics reading, inside and outside wiring, finish plastering, painting and carpentry, drilling through concrete and flexcore, excavation, and cable testing.
- I serve as the company's troubleshooter, handling special projects as well as difficult or time-consuming installations, where technical skills, customer relations, and problem-solving ability are very important.
- In previous jobs, I've worked construction, remodeling, mechanical repair, and TV repair.

EXPERIENCE

1994 to present
Gotham Cable, New York
Siding and Roofing sub-contractor

1992 to 1994
Trump Construction, New York
Siding and Roofing sub-contractor

1992
Gray Construction, Brooklyn
Concrete Worker

1990 to 1992
Heavy Hauler Inc., Bronx
Diesel Mechanic, promoted to Bookkeeper.

PERSONAL

Health: excellent
Open to relocation

References and a portfolio with photos of the recent jobs are available.

Trades Supervisor (Electrician)

James Sharpe
9 Central Avenue
Campbell, CA 95008
(408) 555-1212

QUALIFICATIONS   Experienced Electrician with twelve years in job-site supervision (Foreman, General Foreman, Electrical Coordinator). Licensed in California and Arizona. Have studied electrical engineering and attended a number of electrical foreman seminars. Member, IBEW Local 356 since 1982.

Supervised the entire electrical operation for a major contractor on a variety of projects including: schools, fire stations, hospitals, colleges, restaurants, office building, housing for the elderly, municipal buildings, correctional facilities, and other similar jobs.

Responsibilities have included supervision and training of crews (electricians—apprentices and journeymen, as well as foreman). Coordinating electrical requirements of the job with all other subcontractors (fire protection, HVAC, plumbing, equipment installation). Ordering and expediting of materials: dealing with inspectors, general contractors, and other project officials.

Accountable for total control of all electrical aspects of the job, requiring day-to-day supervision, quality, safety, employee-labor relations.

Experienced on a wide variety of projects, from simple system updates to the most complex jobs, taking them from ground level to final completion.

Communicate effectively on a daily basis with architects, engineers, and others on interpretation of drawings, design modification, and problem solving.

Consistently bring in projects at or under budget.

EMPLOYMENT

1989 to present   Electrical Coordinator, General Foreman, Foreman Valley Electric—Burlingame, CA

1981 to 1989   Journeyman Electrician
M. Johns (Detroit), Barry and Jones (New York), Western Electrical (Flagstaff)

Woodcrafts Specialist

James Sharpe
9 Central Avenue
Memphis, TN 38137
(901) 555-1212

SUMMARY OF
BACKGROUND

- Qualified wood craftsman and artisan, with formal training in woodworking, sculpture, and photography.
- Business experience includes opening and operating a sawmill, creating and selling custom wood products, designing and producing furniture, home restoration, cabinetry, other similar work.
- Developing and producing woven products.

TRAINING

- U.T., Tennessee School of Fine Art
  Bachelor of Fine Arts, 1981.
- Studied Woodworking, Sculpture, and Photography in this jointly run program.
- Apprentice to Bernard Pennymaker (furniture designer) of Memphis for five years.

EXPERIENCE

1991 to present   Craftsman/Sawmill
Sole proprietor of a multi-faceted business: a sawmill, precision woodworking shop, supplier of specialty lumber to various industries, design and production of custom products, both on commission and for sale.

- Personally responsible for all creative and administrative aspects of this business.

1986 to 1991   Pennymaker Woodworking—Memphis
Sole Proprietor of this sawmill and woodworking shop.

- Quarter sawn lumber was the specialty. Projects included: custom-designed furniture, building of spiral stairways, cabinetry, sawmill operations.

PERSONAL   Health: excellent

REFERENCES

- Business, personal and customer references, as well as samples, photos and sketches are available, and will be gladly shown upon request.

Resources

HEALTH CARE

Publications

Hospital Phone Book
U.S. Directory Service, Miami, FL
Provides information on over 7,940
government and private hospitals in
the U.S.

*National Association of County Health
Officials Sustaining Membership
Directory*
National Association of County Health
Officials, Washington, DC
Lists national health officials for almost
every county in the U.S. Published
annually. $10. Call 202-783-5550 for
more information.

National Jobs in Dietetics
Jobs in Dietetics, Santa Monica, CA
Lists jobs nationwide in the field of
dietetics. Published monthly; an annual
subscription is $84. Call 310-453-5375
for more information.

U.S. Medical Directory
U.S. Directory Service, Miami, FL
Over one thousand pages of
information on doctors, hospitals,
nursing facilities, medical laboratories,
and medical libraries.

Associations

HEALTH CARE ADMINISTRATION

American Association of Medical
Assistants
20 North Wacker Drive, Suite 1575
Chicago, IL 60606-2903;
tel: 312-899-1500

American College of Healthcare
Executives
1 North Franklin, Suite 1700
Chicago, IL 60606-3491; tel: 312-424-2800

American Health Care Association
1201 L Street NW
Washington, DC 20005;
tel: 202-842-4444

American Health Information
Management Association
919 North Michigan Avenue
Chicago, IL 60611; tel: 312-787-2672

American Medical Technologists
710 Higgins Road
Park Ridge, IL 60068; tel: 708-823-5169

Healthcare Financial Management
Association
Two Westbrook Corporate Center,
Suite 700
Westchester, IL 60154;
tel: 708-531-9600

National Association of Emergency
Medical Technicians
102 West Leake Street
Clinton, MS 39056; tel: 601-924-7747

Nuclear Medicine Technology
Certification Board
2970 Clairmont Road, Suite 610
Atlanta, GA 30329-1634;
tel: 404-315-1739

NURSING

American Association of Nurse
Anesthetists
222 South Prospect Avenue
Park Ridge, IL 60068-4001;
tel: 708-692-7050

American Association of Occupational
Health Nurses
50 Lenox Pointe
Atlanta, GA 30324; tel: 404-262-1162
or 800-241-8014

American Hospital Association
1 North Franklin
Chicago, IL 60606; tel: 312-422-3000

American Nurses Association
600 Maryland Avenue SW, Suite 100 W
Washington, DC 20024-2571; tel: 202-651-7000

National Association for Home Care
519 C Street NE
Washington, DC 20002;
tel: 202-547-7424
(send SASE for general information)

National Association for Practical Nurse
Education and Service
1400 Spring Street, Suite 310
Silver Spring, MD 20910;
tel: 301-588-2491

National Association of Pediatric Nurse
Associates and Practitioners
1101 Kings Highway N, Suite 206
Cherry Hill, NJ 08034-1921;
tel: 609-667-1773

National Federation of Licensed
Practical Nurses
1418 Aversboro Road
Garner, NC 27529-4547;
tel: 919-779-0046

National League for Nursing
Communications Department
350 Hudson Street
New York, NY 10014;
tel: 212-989-9393

National Rehabilitation Association
633 South Washington Street
Alexandria, VA 22314;
tel: 703-836-0850

Medical Economics Publishing
5 Paragon Drive
Montvale, NJ 07645-1742;
tel: 201-358-7200

PHYSICAL HEALTH

Accreditation Council for Graduate
Medical Education
515 North State Street, Suite 2000
Chicago, IL 60610; tel: 312-464-4920

American Association for Respiratory
Care
11030 Ables Lane
Dallas, TX 75229-4593;
tel: 214-243-2272

American Association of Colleges of
Pediatric Medicine
1350 Piccard Drive, Suite 322
Rockville, MD 20850;
tel: 301-990-7400

American Board of Preventive Medicine
9950 West Lawrence Avenue, Suite 106
Schiller Park, IL 60176;
tel: 847-671-1750

American Medical Association
515 North State Street
Chicago, IL 60610; tel: 312-464-5000

American Occupational Therapy
Association
4720 Montgomery Lane, P.O. Box 31220
Bethesda, MD 20824-1220;
tel: 301-652-2682

American Physical Therapy Association
1111 North Fairfax Street
Alexandria, VA 22314;
tel: 703-684-2782 or 800-999-2782

American Podiatric Medical Association
9312 Old Georgetown Road
Bethesda, MD 20814-1621;
tel: 301-571-9200

American Society of Radiology
Technologists
15000 Central Avenue SE
Albuquerque, NM 87123-4605;
tel: 505-298-4500

Society of Diagnostic Medical
Sonographers
12770 Coit Road, Suite 508
Dallas, TX 75251; tel: 214-239-7367

DENTISTRY

American Association of Dental
Assistants
203 North LaSalle Street, Suite 132
Chicago, IL 60601-1225;
tel: 312-541-1550

American Association of Dental Schools
1625 Massachusetts Avenue NW
Washington, DC 20036;
tel: 202-667-9433

American Association of Orthodontists
401 North Lindbergh Blvd.
St. Louis, MO 63141-7816;
tel: 314-993-1700

American Dental Association
211 East Chicago Avenue
Chicago, IL 60611; tel: 312-440-2500
(for Commission on Dental
Accreditation, direct correspondence to
Suite 3400; for SELECT Program, direct
correspondence to Department of
Career Guidance, Suite 1804)

American Dental Hygienists Association
Division of Professional Development
444 North Michigan Avenue, Suite 3400
Chicago, IL 60611; tel: 312-440-8900

National Association of Dental
Laboratories
555 East Braddock Road
Alexandria, VA 22305;
tel: 703-683-5263

National Board for Certification in
Dental Technology
555 East Braddock Road
Alexandria, VA 22305;
tel: 703-683-5263

MENTAL HEALTH

American Association for Counseling
and Development
5999 Stevenson Avenue
Alexandria, VA 22304; tel: 703-823-9800

American Association for Marriage and
Family Therapy
11331 5th Street NW, Suite 300
Washington, DC 20005;
tel: 202-452-0109

American Association of Mental
Retardation
444 North Capitol Street, NW, Suite 846
Washington, DC 20001-1512;
tel: 202-387-1968 or 800-424-3688

American Psychiatric Association
1400 K Street NW
Washington, DC 20005;
tel: 202-682-6000

American Psychological Association
750 First Street NE
Washington, DC 20002;
tel: 202-336-5500

National Board for Certified Counselors
3 Terrace Way, Suite D
Greensboro, NC 27403-3660;
tel: 910-547-0607

BIOTECHNOLOGY AND ENVIRONMENTAL TECHNOLOGY

Publications

Corporate Technology Directory
CorpTech, Woburn, MA
Lists over 35,000 businesses and
110,000 executives. Describes
products and services in such fields as
automation, biotechnology, chemicals,
computers and software, defense,
energy, environment, manufacturing
equipment, advanced materials,
medical, pharmaceuticals, photonics,
subassemblies and components,
testing and measurements,
telecommunications, and
transportation and holding companies.
Published annually.

CorpTech Fast 5,000 Company Locator
CorpTech, Woburn, MA
Lists over five thousand of the fastest-
growing companies listed in the
Corporate Technology Directory, but
includes addresses and phone numbers,
number of employees, sales, and
industries by state. Published annually.

Directory of Environmental Information
Government Institutes, Rockville, MD
Lists federal and state government
resources, trade organizations, and
professional and scientific newsletters,
magazines, and databases. Published
every other year.

Environmental Telephone Directory
Governmental Institutes, Rockville, MD
Lists detailed information on
governmental agencies that deal with
the environment. The directory also
identifies the environmental aides of

U.S. Senators and Representatives. Published every other year.

Sales Guide to High-Tech Companies
CorpTech, Woburn, MA
Covers over three thousand company profiles and twelve thousand executive contacts. Includes specific details on each company's products and services. Published quarterly; a yearly subscription is $185. Call 617-932-3939 for more information.

Transportation Officials and Engineers Directory
American Road and Transportation Builders Association, Washington, DC
Lists over four thousand state transportation officials and engineers at local, state, and federal levels. Published annually.

Associations

Air and Waste Management Association
1 Gateway Center, 3rd Floor
Pittsburgh, PA 15222; tel: 412-232-3444

American Chemical Society
1155 16th Street NW
Washington, DC 20036;
tel: 202-872-4600 or 800-227-5558

American Institute of Biological Sciences
1444 Eye Street NW, Suite 200
Washington, DC 20005;
tel: 202-628-1500

American Institute of Chemists
501 Wythe Street
Alexandria, VA 22314-1917;
tel: 703-836-2090

American Institute of Physics
1 Physics Ellipse
College Park, MD 20740-3843;
tel: 301-209-3100

American Society for Biochemistry and Molecular Biology
9650 Rockville Pike
Bethesda, MD 20814-3996;
tel: 301-530-7145

American Society for Microbiology
1325 Massachusetts Avenue NW
Washington, DC 20005;
tel: 202-737-3600

American Society of Biological Chemists
9650 Rockville Pike
Bethesda, MD 20814-3996;
tel: 301-530-7145

American Zoo and Aquarium Association (AZA)
Office of Membership Service
Oglebay Park, Route 88
Wheeling, WV 26003;
tel: 304-242-2160

Association of American Geographers
1710 16th Street NW
Washington, DC 20009-3198;
tel: 202-234-1450

Botanical Society of America
1735 Nell Avenue
Columbus, OH 43210;
tel: 614-292-3519

Center for American Archeology
P.O. Box 366
Kampsville, IL 62053;
tel: 618-653-4316

Department of Energy Headquarters
Operations Division
1000 Independence Avenue SW, Room 4E-090
Washington, DC 20585;
tel: 202-586-4333
(hotline for job vacancies, updated every Friday)

Environmental Protection Agency Recruitment Center
401 Main Street SW, Room 3634
Washington, DC 20460;
tel: 202-260-2090/3308

Federation of American Societies for Experimental Biology
9650 Rockville Pike
Bethesda, MD 20814;
tel: 301-530-7000

Genetics Society of America
9650 Rockville Pike
Bethesda, MD 20814-3998;
tel: 301-571-1825

Geological Society of America
3300 Penrose Place, P.O. Box 9140
Boulder, CO 80301; tel: 303-447-2020

National Accrediting Agency for Clinical Laboratory Sciences
8410 West Bryn Mawr Avenue, Suite 670
Chicago, IL 60631; tel: 312-714-8880

National Solid Wastes Management Association
4301 Connecticut Avenue NW, Suite 300
Washington, DC 20008;
tel: 202-244-4700

Natural Resource Conservation Service, Personnel Division
P.O. Box 2980
Washington, DC 20013;
tel: 202-720-4264

ENGINEERING

Associations

American Association of Engineering Societies
1111 19th Street NW, Suite 608
Washington, DC 20034;
tel: 202-296-2237

American Chemical Society
1155 16th Street NW
Washington, DC 20036;
tel: 202-872-4600 or 800-227-5558

American Institute of Chemical Engineers
345 East 47th Street
New York, NY 10017;
tel: 212-705-7338 or 800-242-4363

American Society for Engineering Education
1818 N Street NW, Suite 600
Washington, DC 20036;
tel: 202-331-3500

American Society of Civil Engineers
1801 Alexander Bell Drive
Reston, VA 20191-4400;
tel: 800-548-ASCE

American Society of Mechanical Engineers (ASME)
345 East 47th Street
New York, NY 10017; tel: 212-705-7722

Institute of Electrical and Electronics
Engineers
345 East 47th Street
New York, NY 10017; tel: 212-705-7900

Institute of Industrial Engineers
25 Technology Park
Atlanta, GA 30092-0460;
tel: 770-449-0460

Society of Manufacturing Engineers
(SME)
1 SME Drive, P.O. Box 930
Dearborn, MI 48121; tel: 313-271-1500

INFORMATION TECHNOLOGY

Publications

Access
1900 West 47th Place, Suite 215
Shawnee Mission, KS 66205; tel: 800-
362-0681
(initial six-month nonmember listing,
$15; each additional three months,
$15; initial six-month listing for
members of the Data Processing
Management Association, $10)

AIIM Job Bank Bulletin
Association for Information and Image
Management
1100 Wayne Avenue, Suite 1100
Silver Spring, MD 20910;
tel: 301-587-8202
(four-month subscription: nonmember,
$100; member, $25; issued
semimonthly)

Associations

ASIS Jobline
American Society for Information
Science
8720 Georgia Avenue, Suite 501
Silver Spring, MD 20910-3602;
tel: 301-495-0900
(free; monthly)

Association for Computing Machinery
1515 Broadway
New York, NY 10036; tel: 212-869-7440

Association for Systems Management
1433 West Bagley Road, P.O. Box 38370
Cleveland, OH 44138; tel: 216-243-6900

COMPUTERS

Publications

ComputerWorld
500 Old Connecticut Path
Framingham, MA 01701-9171; tel:
508-879-0700 or 800-343-6474
(annual subscription: U.S., $39.95;
Canada, $110; issued weekly)

ComputerWorld, Campus Edition
500 Old Connecticut Path
Framingham, MA 01701-9171;
tel: 508-879-0700
(annual subscription, $5; free to
students; published each October)

High Technology Careers Magazine
4701 Patrick Henry Drive, Suite 1901
Santa Clara, CA 95054;
tel: 408-970-8800
(six issues per year, $29)

Technical Employment News
P.O. Box 1285
Cedar Park, TX 78613;
tel: 512-250-9023 or 800-678-9724
(weekly subscription, $55; annual
subscription, $88, U.S. and Canada)

Associations

IEEE Computer Society
1730 Massachusetts Avenue NW
Washington, DC 20036;
tel: 202-371-0101
(available to members only)

CU Career Connection
University of Colorado, Campus Box 133
Boulder, CO 80309-0133;
tel: 303-492-4727
(two-month fee for passcode to the job
hotline, $30)

Data Processing Management
Association
505 Busse Highway
Park Ridge, IL 60068; tel: 708-825-8124

Institute for Certification of Computing
Professionals
2200 East Devon Avenue, Suite 247
Des Plaines, IL 60018;
tel: 708-299-4227

Quality Assurance Institute
7575 Philips Boulevard, Suite 350
Orlando, Fl 32819; tel: 407-363-1111

Semiconductor Equipment and
Materials International
805 East Middlefield Road
Mountain View, CA 94043; tel: 415-
964-5111

BUSINESS AND PROFESSIONAL

Publications

The Almanac of American Employers
Corporate Jobs Outlook
Boeme, TX
Lists five hundred of the country's most
successful, large companies; profiles
salary ranges, benefits, financial stability,
and advancement opportunities.

America's Fastest Growing Employers
Adams Media Corporation, Holbrook, MA
A national career guide for those
seeking employment with the most
rapidly growing firms in the country.
Includes names, addresses, and vital
statistics for more than 275 companies
in today's economy. Each profile gives
key facts about the company's growth
and development.

Corporate Jobs Outlook
Corporate Jobs Outlook, Inc., Dallas, TX
Each issue reviews fifteen to twenty
major (five thousand employees or
more) firms. The report rates the firms
and provides information on salaries
and benefits, current and projected
development, where to apply for jobs,
potential layoffs, benefit plans, the
company's record for promoting
women or minorities to executive
positions, and college reimbursement
packages. Also includes personnel
contact information for each firm.
Published bimonthly; a yearly
subscription is $159.99. Call 210-755-
8810. Note: This resource is also
available online through NewsNet (800-
345-1301) or the Human Resources
Information Network (800-638-8094).
Call for more details.

Directory of Corporate Affiliations
Reed Reference Publishing Company,
New Providence, NJ
Lists key personnel in 4,700 parent
companies and forty thousand
divisions, subsidiaries, and affiliates.
Includes addresses and phone
numbers of key executives and
decision makers. Published once a
year, with quarterly updates. For more
information, call 800-323-6772.

Directory of Leading Private Companies
National Register Publishing Company,
Wilmette, IL
Profiles over seven thousand U.S.
private companies in the service,
manufacturing, distribution, retail, and
construction fields. Includes companies
in such areas as health care, high
technology, entertainment, fast-food
franchises, leasing, publishing, and
communications. Published annually.

Encyclopedia of Associations
Gale Research, Inc., Detroit, MI
Published in three volumes. Volume 1
lists national organizations in the U.S.
and includes over twenty-two thousand
associations, including hundreds for
government professions. Volume 2
provides geographic and executive
indexes. Volume 3 features full entries
on associations that are not listed in
Volume 1. Note: This resource is also
available online through Dialog
Information Services (800-334-2564).
Call for more information.

*International Directory of Corporate
Affiliations*
National Register Publishing Company,
Wilmette, IL
Lists over fourteen hundred major
foreign companies and their thirty
thousand U.S. and foreign holdings.
Published annually.

The JobBank Series
Adams Media Corporation, Holbrook, MA
A top-notch series of paperback local
employment guides. The 1997 editions
profile virtually every local company
with over fifty employees in a given
metro area. Company listings are
arranged by industry for easy use; also
included is a section on the region's

economic outlook and contact
information for local professional
associations, executive search firms,
and job placement agencies. The series
covers twenty-nine major metropolitan
areas, including Atlanta, Boston, the
Carolinas, Chicago, Dallas/Ft. Worth,
Denver, Detroit, Florida, Houston, Los
Angeles, Minneapolis/St. Paul, Missouri,
New York, Ohio, Philadelphia, Phoenix,
San Francisco, Seattle, Tennessee, and
Washington, DC. Many listings feature
contact names, common positions
hired for, educational backgrounds
sought, benefits, fax numbers,
internship information, staff size, and
more. Available at most bookstores.
Updated yearly.

The National JobBank
Adams Media Corporation, Holbrook, MA
The 1995 edition includes over sixteen
thousand company profiles. Many
listings feature contact names, common
positions hired for, educational
backgrounds sought, benefits, fax
numbers, internship information, staff
size, and more. Updated annually.

*National Trade and Professional
Associations of the United States*
Columbia Books, Washington, DC
Lists information on over sixty-five
hundred trade and professional
associations. Published annually.

Resume Bank
American Corporate Counsel Association
1225 Connecticut Avenue NW, Suite 302
Washington, DC 20036;
tel: 202-296-4522
(six-month registration: nonmembers,
$65; members, $25; complete job-
matching application, and five copies of
resume free)

FINANCIAL SERVICES

Associations

BANKING

American Bankers Association
1120 Connecticut Avenue NW
Washington, DC 20036;
tel: 202-663-5000

American Institute of Banking
1213 Bakers Way
Manhattan, KS 66502; tel: 913-537-4750

Association of Master of Business
Administration Executives
AMBA Center
South Summit Place
Branford, CT 06405; tel: 203-315-5221

Banking Federation of the European
Economic Community (BFEC)
Federation Bancaire de la Communaute
Europeenne (FBCE)
c/o Umberto Burani
10, rue Montoyer, B-1040
Brussels, Belgium; tel: 32-2-5083711;
fax: 32-2-5112328

Banking Law Institute (BLI)
22 West 21st Street
New York, NY 10010;
tel: 212-645-7880 or 800-332-1105;
fax: 212-675-4883

BANKPAC
(formerly: Bankers Political Action
Committee; Banking Profession Political
Action Committee)
c/o Meg Bonitt
American Bankers Association
1120 Connecticut Avenue NW
Washington, DC 20036;
tel: 202-663-5115/5076
or 202-663-7544 (fax)

Electronic Banking Economics Society
(EBES)
P.O. Box 2331
New York, NY 10036; tel: 203-295-9788

Savings and Community Bankers of
America Educational Services
Center for Financial Studies
900 19th Street NW, Suite 400
Washington, DC 20006;
tel: 202-857-3100

U.S. Council on International Banking
(USCIB)
1 World Trade Center, Suite 1963
New York, NY 10048;
tel: 212-466-3352; fax: 212-432-0544

Women in Banking and Finance
55 Bourne Vale
Bromley, Kent BR2 7NW, England;
tel: 44-181-4623276

Women's World Banking—USA
8 West 40th Street
New York, NY 10018;
tel: 212-768-8513; fax: 212-768-8519

SECURITIES

Association of Securities and
Exchange Commission Alumni
West Tower, Suite 812
1100 New York Avenue NW
Washington, DC 20005; tel: 202-408-
7600; fax: 202-408-7614

International Securities Market
Association—England
7 Limeharbour
London E14 9NQ, England;
tel: 44-171-538-5656;
fax: 44-171-538-4902

National Association of Securities
Dealers (NASD)
1735 K Street NW
Washington, DC 20006-1506;
tel: 202-728-8000; fax: 202-293-6260

National Association of Securities
Professionals (NASP)
700 13th Street NW, Suite 950
Washington, DC 20005;
tel: 202-434-4535; fax: 202-434-8916

North American Securities
Administrators Association (NASAA)
1 Massachusetts Avenue NW,
Suite 310
Washington, DC 20001;
tel: 202-737-0900;
fax: 202-783-3571

Securities and Futures Authority
Cottons Centre, Cottons Lane
London SE I 2QB, England;
tel: 44-171-378-9000;
tel: 44-171-403-7569

Securities Industry Association (SIA)
120 Broadway
New York, NY 10271; tel: 212-608-
1500; fax: 212-608-1604

Securities Transfer Association (STA)
55 Exchange Place
New York, NY 10260-0001;
tel: 212-748-8000

Western Pennsylvania Securities
Industry Agency
1 Oxford Centre, 40th Floor
Pittsburgh, PA 15219;
tel: 412-731-7185

ACCOUNTING

Academy of Accounting Historians
(AAH)
University of Arkansas, Department
of Accounting
Fayetteville, AR 72701; tel: 501-575-
6125; fax: 501-575-7687

Accounting Aid Society of Detroit
(AASD)
719 Griswold, Suite 2026
Detroit, MI 48226; tel: 313-961-
1840; fax: 313-961-6257
E-mail: itpass@igc.apc.org

Affiliation of Independent
Accountants
9200 South Dadeland Boulevard,
Suite 510
Miami, FL 33156; tel: 305-670-0580;
fax: 305-670-3818

American Accounting Association
5717 Bessie Drive
Sarasota, FL 34223;
tel: 941-921-7747

American Institute of Certified Public
Accountants (AICPA)
1211 Avenue of the Americas
New York, NY 10036-8775;
tel: 212-596-6200 or 800-862-4272
or 212-596-6213 (fax)

American Society of Tax
Professionals
P.O. Box 1024
Sioux Falls, SD 57101;
tel: 605-335-1185

American Society of Women
Accountants
1255 Lynnfield Road, Suite 257
Memphis, TN 38119;
tel: 901-680-0470

American Women's Society of
Certified Public Accountants
401 North Michigan Avenue,
Suite 2200
Chicago, IL 60611; tel: 312-644-6610

Associated Accounting Firms
International (AAFI)
(formerly: Association of Regional
CPA Firms)
1000 Connecticut Avenue, Suite 1006
Washington, DC 20036; tel: 202-463-
7900; fax: 202-296-0741

Associated Regional Accounting
Firms (ARAF)
3700 Crestwood Parkway, Suite 350
Duluth, GA 30136; tel: 770-279-
4560; fax: 770-279-4566 (fax)

Association for Accounting
Administration (AAA)
136 South Keowee Street
Dayton, OH 45402; tel: 513-222-
0030; fax: 513-2212-5794

Association of Accounting
Technicians (AAT)
154 Clerkenwell Road
London EC I R 5AD, England; tel: 44-
171-837-8600/814-6999;
fax: 44-171-837-6970
E-mail: aatuk@pipex.com

Association of Government
Accountants
2200 Mount Vernon Avenue
Alexandria, VA 22301;
tel: 703-684-6931

EDP Auditors Association
3701 Algonquin Road, Suite 1010
Rolling Meadows, IL 60008;
tel: 708-253-1545

European Accounting Association
(EAA)
European Institute for Advanced
Studies in Management
13 Rue d'Egmont, B-1050
Brussels, Belgium; tel: 32-2-511-
9116; fax: 32-2-512-1929
E-mail: vandyck@ciasm.be

Foundation for Accounting Education
(FAE)
530 Fifth Avenue, 5th Floor
New York, NY 10036; tel: 212-719-
8300 or 800-537-3635

Governmental Accounting Standards
Board (GASB)
401 Merrit 7, P.O. Box 5116
Norwalk, CT 06856-5116; tel: 203-847-
0700; fax: 203-849-9714

Information Systems Audit and Control
Association
3701 Algonquin Road, Suite 1010
Rolling Meadows, IL 60008;
tel: 708-253-1545

Institute of Certified Management
Accountants (ICMA)
10 Paragon Drive
Montvale, NJ 07645; tel: 201-573-9000
or 800-638-4427; fax: 201-573-8438

Institute of Internal Auditors
249 Maitland Avenue
Altamonte Springs, FL 32701-4201;
tel: 407-830-7600

Institute of Management Accountants
10 Paragon Drive
Montvale, NJ 07645; tel: 201-573-
9000; fax: 201-573-9000

InterAmerican Accounting Association
(IAA)
(formerly: InterAmerican Accounting
Conference)
275 Fontainebleau Boulevard, Suite 245
Miami, Fl 33172; tel: 305-225-1991;
fax: 305-225-2011

National Association of State Boards of
Accountancy
545 Fifth Avenue
New York, NY 10168-0002;
tel: 212-490-3868

National Society for Public Accountants
1010 North Fairfax Street
Alexandria, VA 22314; tel: 703-549-
6400

INSURANCE

Publications

Insurance Field Directories
Insurance Field Company
P.O. Box 948
Northbrook, IL 60065; tel: 708-498-4010
($55; published each September)

Insurance Phone Book and Directory
US Directory Service
121 Chanlon Road
New Providence, NJ 07074;
tel: 908-464-6800
($67.95, plus $4.75 shipping)

Associations

ACFE Job Bank
Association of Certified Fraud
Examiners
716 West Avenue
Austin, TX 78701; tel: 512-478-9070 or
800-245-3321
(membership fee $75; send two copies
of resume and cover letter indicating
salary requirements and where you are
willing to relocate)

Actual Training Program Directory
Society of Actuaries
475 North Martingale Road, Suite 800
Schaumburg, IL 60173-2226;
tel: 708-706-3500
(free; published each January)

American Academy of Actuaries
1100 17th Street NW, 7th Floor
Washington, DC 20036;
tel: 202-223-8196

American Agents & Brokers
330 North 4th Street
St. Louis, MO 63012;
tel: 314-421-5445

Best's Insurance Reports,
Property/Casualty Edition
A.M. Best Company
Ambest Road
Oldwick, NJ 08858-9988;
tel: 908-439-2200
(annual fee $70)

Independent Insurance Agents of
America
127 South Peyton
Alexandria, VA 22314;
tel: 703-683-4422 or 800-962-7950

Insurance Information Institute
110 William Street
New York, NY 10038;
tel: 212-669-9200

Insurance Institute of America
720 Providence Road
Malvern, PA 19355; tel: 610-644-2100

Life Insurance Marketing and Research
Association
P.O. Box 208
Hartford, CT 16141-0208;
tel: 203-777-7000

National Association of Life
Underwriters
1922 F Street NW
Washington, DC 20006;
tel: 202-332-6000

National Association of Professional
Insurance Agents
400 North Washington Street
Alexandria, VA 22314; tel: 703-836-9340

Professional Insurance Agents
400 North Washington Street
Alexandria, VA 22314; tel: 703-836-9340

Society of Actuaries
475 North Martingale Road, Suite 800
Schaumburg, IL 60173-2226;
tel: 708-706-3500

FINANCIAL MANAGEMENT

Associations

American Education Finance
Association (AEFA)
5249 Cape Leyte Drive
Sarasota, FL 34242; tel: 941-349-7580;
fax: 941-349-7580
E-mail: gbabigianc@aol.com

American Finance Association (AFA)
Stern, 44 West 4th Street, Suite 9-190
New York, NY 10012; tel: 212-998-0370

Association of Commercial Finance Attorneys (ACFA)
1 Corporate Center, 18th Floor MSN 712
Hartford, CT 06103; tel: 203-520-7094; fax: 203-240-5077

Commercial Finance Association (CFA)
225 West 34th Street
New York, NY 10122; tel: 212-594-3490 or 212-564-6053

Financial Analysts Federation
P.O. Box 3726
Charlottesville, VA 22903;
tel: 804-977-8977

Financial Management Association International
College of Business Administration
University of South Florida
Tampa, FL 33620-5500

Financial Management Service
Department of the Treasury
401 14th Street SW
Washington, DC 20227;
tel: 202-874-6750

Financial Managers Society
8 South Michigan Avenue, Suite 500
Chicago, IL 60603; tel: 312-578-1300

Government Finance Officers Association of United States and Canada
ISO North Michigan Avenue, Suite 800
Chicago, IL 60601; tel: 312-977-9700; fax: 312-977-4806

Institute of Certified Financial Planners
3801 East Florida Avenue, Suite 708
Denver, CO 80210; tel: 303-751-7600; fax: 303-759-0749

Institute of Chartered Financial Analysts
P.O. Box 3668
Charlottesville, VA 22903;
tel: 804-977-6600

Institute of International Finance (IIF)
2000 Pennsylvania Avenue NW, Suite 8500
Washington, DC 20006-1812; tel: 202-857-3600; fax: 202-775-1430

International Association for Financial Planning
2 Concourse Parkway, Suite 800
Atlanta, GA 30328; tel: 404-395-1605

National Association of County Treasurers and Finance Officers
c/o National Association of Counties
440 First Street NW, 8th Floor
Washington, DC 20001;
tel: 202-393-6226

National Society for Real Estate Finance (NSREF)
2300 M Street NW, Suite 800
Washington, DC 20037;
tel: 202-973-2801

New York State Consumer Finance Association (NYSCFA)
90 South Swan Street
Albany, NY 12210; tel: 518-449-7514; fax: 518-426-0566

New York State Government Finance Officers Association
119 Washington Avenue
Albany, NY 12210-2204;
tel: 518-465-1512; fax: 518-434-4640

North American Economics and Finance Association (NAEFA)
Department of Finance
Syracuse University
Syracuse, NY 13244-2130;
tel: 315-443-2963; fax: 315-443-5389

Securities Industry Association
120 Broadway
New York, NY 10271;
tel: 212-608-1500

HUMAN RESOURCES

Publications

HR Magazine
606 North Washington Street
Alexandria, VA 22314; tel: 703-548-3440

Associations

American Society for Training and Development
1640 King Street, Box 1443
Alexandria, VA 22313; tel: 703-683-8100

Employment Management Association
4101 Lake Boone Trail, Suite 201
Raleigh, NC 27607; tel: 919-787-6010

Institute of Management Consultants
521 Fifth Avenue, 35th Floor
New York, NY 10175; tel: 212-697-8262

International Personnel Management Association
1617 Duke Street
Alexandria, VA 22314; tel: 703-549-7100

National Training Laboratory
1240 North Pitt Street
Alexandria, VA 22314; tel: 703-548-1500

Society for Human Resource Management
606 North Washington Street
Alexandria, VA 22314; tel: 703-548-3440

LAW

Publications

ALA Management Connections
Association of Legal Administrators
175 E. Hawthorn Parkway, Suite 325
Vernon Hills, IL 60061-1428;
tel: 708-816-1212
(free; updated weekly)

Federal Careers for Attorneys
Federal Reports, Inc., Washington, DC
A guide to legal careers with over three hundred U.S. government general counsel and other legal offices in the U.S. Explains where to apply, the types of legal work common to each field, and information on special recruitment programs.

Judicial Staff Directory
Staff Directories, Ltd., Mt. Vernon, VA
Lists over eleven thousand individuals employed in the 207 federal courts, as well as thirteen thousand cities and their courts. The book also has information on court administration, U.S. marshals, U.S. attorneys, and the U.S. Department of Justice. Includes eighteen hundred biographies.

NDAA Membership Directory
National District Attorneys Association,
Alexandria, VA
Lists all district attorneys' offices across
the U.S.
$15 for nonmembers, $10 for
members. Call 703-549-9222 for more
information.

Paralegal's Guide to Government Jobs
Federal Reports, Inc., Washington, DC
Explains federal hiring procedures for
both entry-level and experienced
paralegals. The volume describes
seventy law-related careers for which
paralegals qualify and lists over one
thousand federal agency personnel
offices that hire the most paralegal
talent. Also profiles special hiring
programs.

Associations

American Association for Paralegal
Education
P.O. Box 40244
Overland Park, KS 66204;
tel: 913-381-4458

American Bar Association Information
Services
750 North Lake Shore Drive
Chicago, IL 60611; tel: 312-988-5000
or 800-621-6159

Internships for College Students
Interested in Law, Medicine, and Politics
Graduate Group
86 Norwood Road
West Hartford, CT 06117;
tel: 203-236-5570 or 203-232-3100
($27.50, published annually)

National Association for Law Placement
1666 Connecticut Avenue, Suite 328
Washington, DC 20009;
tel: 202-667-1666

National Association of Legal Assistants
1516 South Boston Avenue, Suite 200
Tulsa, OK 74119; tel: 918-587-6828

National Federation of Paralegal
Associations
P.O. Box 33108
Kansas City, MO 64114;
tel: 816-941-4000

National Paralegal Association
Box 406
Solebury, PA 18963; tel: 215-297-8333

NCRA Employment Referral Service
National Court Reporters Association
8224 Old Courthouse Road
Vienna, VA 22182; tel: 703-556-6272
(six-month registration: nonmembers,
$20; free to members)

Paralegal Placement Network Inc.
P.O. Box 406
Solebury, PA 18963; tel: 215-297-8333
(regular fee, $10; Nat. Paralegal
Association members, $15)

MEDIA/COMMUNICATION/
PUBLIC RELATIONS

Publications

P.R. Reporter
P.O. Box 6000
Exeter, NH 03833

Public Relations Consultants Directory
American Business Directories Inc.
5711 East 86th Circle
Omaha, NE 68127; tel: 402-331-7169

*SMPS Employment Referral Society for
Marketing Professional Services*
99 Canal Plaza, Suite 250
Alexandria, VA 22314;
tel: 703-549-6117 or 800-292-7677
(nonmembers, $100; members, $50;
five copies resume and SMPS
application—on file for three months)

Associations

American Society for Health Care
Marketing and Public Relations
American Hospital Association
1 North Franklin
Chicago, IL 60606; tel: 312-422-3737

American Society of Journalists and
Authors
1501 Broadway, Suite 302
New York, NY 10036; tel: 212-997-0947

Council of Sales Promotion Agencies
750 Summer Street
Stamford, CT 06901; tel: 203-325-3911

Dow Jones Newspaper Fund
P.O. Box 300
Princeton, NJ 08543-0300;
tel: 609-452-2820

Editorial Freelancers Association
71 West 23rd Street, Suite 1504
New York, NY 10010; tel: 212-929-5400

Institute for Public Relations Research
and Education (IPRRE)
University of Florida
P.O. Box 118400
Gainesville, FL 32611-8400;
tel: 904-392-0280

International Advertising Association
521 Fifth Avenue, Suite 1807
New York, NY 10175; tel: 212-557-1133

Investigative Reporters & Editors
University of Missouri
26A Walter Williams Hall
Columbia, MO 65211; tel: 314-882-2042

League of Advertising Agencies
Directory
2 South End Avenue #4C
New York, NY 10280; tel: 212-945-4314

National School Public Relations
Association (NSPRA)
1501 Lee Highway, Suite 201
Arlington, VA 22209; tel: 703-528-5840

PR Newswire Job Bank
865 South Figueroa, Suite 2310
Los Angeles, CA 90017;
tel: 213-626-5500 or 800-321-8169
(send resume and cover letter)

Promotion Marketing Association of
America, Inc.
Executive Headquarters
257 Park Avenue South, 11th Floor
New York, NY 10001; tel: 212-420-1100

Public Relations Society of America
33 Irving Place, 3rd Floor
New York, NY 10003; tel: 212-995-2230

Public Relations Student Society of
America (PRSSA)
33 Irving Place, 3rd Floor
New York, NY 10003; tel: 212-460-1474

Society for Technical Communication
901 North Stuart Street, Suite 904
Arlington, VA 22203; tel: 703-522-4114

Writers Guild of America
555 West 57th Street
New York, NY 10019; tel: 212-767-7800

SALES AND MARKETING

Associations

TRAVEL

Adventure Travel Society
6551 South Revere Parkway, Suite 160
Englewood, CO 80111;
tel: 303-649-9016; fax: 303-649-9017

Airline Employees Association, Intl.
Job Opportunity Program
5600 South Central Avenue
Chicago, IL 60638-3797

Air Transport Association of America
1301 Pennsylvania Avenue NW,
Suite 1100
Washington, DC 20004-7017;
tel: 202-626-4000

American Travel Inns (ATI)
(formerly: American Travel Association)
36 South State Street, Suite 1200
Salt Lake City, UT 84111-1416;
tel: 801-521-0732; fax: 801-521-0732

Association of Flight Attendants
1625 Massachusetts Avenue NW
Washington, DC 20036;
tel: 202-328-5400

Association of Retail Travel Agents
(ARTA)
845 Sir Thomas Court, Suite 3
Harrisburg, PA 17109;
tel: 717-545-9548 or 800-969-6069;
fax: 717-545-9613

American Society of Travel Agents
(ASTA)
1101 King Street, Suite 200
Alexandria, VA 22314;
tel: 703-739-2782; fax: 703-684-8319

Cruise Lines International Association
500 Fifth Avenue, Suite 1407
New York, NY 10110; tel: 212-921-0066

Freighter Travel Club of America
3524 Harts Lake Road
Roy, WA 98580; tel: 360-458-4178

Future Aviation Professionals of
America
4959 Massachusetts Boulevard
Atlanta, GA 30337; tel: 404-997-8097
or 800-JET-JOBS

Greater Independent Association of
National Travel Services (GIANTS)
2 Park Avenue, Suite 2205
New York, NY 10016;
tel: 212-545-7460 or 800-442-6871;
fax: 212-545-7428

Independent Travel Agencies of
America Association (ITAA)
5353 North Federal Highway, Suite 300
Fort Lauderdale, Fl 33308;
tel: 305-772-4660 or 800-950-5440;
fax: 305-772-5797

Institute of Certified Travel Agents (ICTA)
148 Linden Street, P.O. Box 812059
Wellesley, MA 02181-0012;
tel: 617-237-0280 or 800-542-4282;
fax: 617-237-3860

International Association for Air Travel
Couriers
P.O. Box 1349
Lake Worth, FL 33460;
tel: 407-582-8320; fax: 407-582-1581

International Association of Travel
Exhibitors (IATE)
P.O. Box 2309
Gulf Shores, AL 36547;
tel: 205-948-6690; fax: 205-948-6690

International Association of Travel
Journalists (IATJ)
P.O. Box D
Hurleyville, NY 12747; tel: 914-434-1529

International Federation of Women's
Travel Organizations (IFWTO)
13901 North 73rd Street, #210B
Scottsdale, AZ 85260-3125; tel: 602-
596-6640; fax: 602-596-6638

Travel Industry Association of America
1100 New York Avenue NW, Suite 450
Washington, DC 20005-3934;
tel: 202-408-8422

U.S. Travel Data Center
(affiliate of the Travel Industry
Association of America)
2 Lafayette Center
1100 New York Avenue NW, Suite 450
Washington, DC 20005;
tel: 202-408-1832

Yours in Travel Personnel Agency
12 West 37th Street
New York, NY 10018; tel: 212-697-7855

MARKETING/ADVERTISING

American Advertising Federation
Education Services Department
1101 Vermont Avenue NW, Suite 500
Washington, DC 20005;
tel: 202-898-0089

American Marketing Association
250 South Wacker Drive, Suite 200
Chicago, IL 60606-5819;
tel: 312-648-0536

The Convention Liaison Council
1575 Eye Street NW, Suite 1190
Washington, DC 20005;
tel: 202-626-2764

Direct Marketing Association
1120 Avenue of the Americas
New York, NY 10036-6700;
tel: 212-768-7277

Meeting Planners International
Informant Building, Suite 5018
1950 Stemmons Freeway
Dallas, TX 75207; tel: 214-712-7700

Retail Advertising and Marketing
Association
500 North Michigan Avenue, Suite 600
Chicago, IL 60611; tel: 312-251-7262

Sales and Marketing Executives
International
977 Statler Office Tower
Cleveland, OH 44115; tel: 216-771-
6650

Sales and Marketing Management
355 Park Avenue South
New York, NY 10010; tel: 212-592-6300

FOOD SERVICES

Associations

Alaska Culinary Association
P.O. Box 140396
Anchorage, AK 99514;
tel: 907-265-7116

American Culinary Federation
10 San Bartola Road, P.O. Box 3466
St. Augustine, FL 32085-3466;
tel: 904-824-4468

Berks Lehigh Chef's Association
2012 Redwood Avenue
Wyomissing, PA 19610;
tel: 610-678-1217

National Food Broker Association
2100 Reston Parkway, Suite 400
Reston, VA 22091; tel: 703-758-7790

National Restaurant Association
1200 17th Street NW
Washington, DC 20036;
el: 202-331-5900

SUPPORT SERVICES

Associations

American Society of Corporate
Secretaries
521 Fifth Avenue
New York, NY 10175-0003;
tel: 212-681-2000

California Federation of Legal
Secretaries
2250 East 73rd Street, Suite 550
Tulsa, OK 74136; tel: 918-493-3540

National Association of Executive
Secretaries
900 S. Washington Street, No. G-13
Falls Church, VA 22046;
tel: 703-237-8616

PUBLIC SERVICES/SOCIAL SERVICES

Publications

*Directory of Legal Aid and Defender
Offices in the U.S. and Territories*
National Legal Aid and Defender
Association, Washington, DC
Lists legal aid and public defender offices
across the U.S. Published annually.

Associations

ACTION International
120 Beacon Street
Somerville, MA 02143;
tel: 617-492-4930

American Counseling Association
5999 Stevenson Avenue
Alexandria, VA 22304;
tel: 703-823-9800 or 800-347-6647

American Friends Service Committee
1501 Cherry Street
Philadelphia, PA 19102;
tel: 215-241-7000

American School Counselor Association
801 North Fairfax Street, Suite 301
Alexandria, VA 22314;
tel: 703-683-2722

American Vocational Association
1410 King Street
Alexandria, VA 22314;
tel: 703-683-3111 or 800-892-2274

Child Welfare League of America
440 First Street NW, Suite 310
Washington, DC 20001;
tel: 201-638-2952

Council for Standards in Human Service
Education
Northern Essex Community College
Haverhill, MA 01830;
tel: 508-374-5889

Council on Social Work Education
1600 Duke Street, Suite 300
Alexandria, VA 22314-3421;
tel: 703-683-8080
(send $10 for Directory of Accredited
BSW and MSW Programs)

Educators for Social Responsibility
23 Garden Street
Cambridge, MA 02138;
tel: 617-492-1764

Human Service Council
3191 Maguire Boulevard, Suite 1150
Orlando, FL 32803; tel: 407-897-6465

National Association of Social Workers
750 First Street NE, Suite 700
Washington, DC 20002-4241;
tel: 202-408-8600

National Center for Charitable Statistics
1828 L Street NW, Suite 1200B
Washington, DC 20036;
tel: 202-223-8100

National Civic League
1445 Market Street, Suite 300
Denver, CO 80202-1728;
tel: 303-571-4343

National Exchange Club Foundation for
the Prevention of Child Abuse
3050 Central Avenue
Toledo, OH 43606; tel: 419-535-3232
or 800-760-3413

National Network for Social Work
Managers
1316 New Hampshire Avenue NW,
Suite 602
Washington, DC 20036;
tel: 202-785-2814

National Organization for Human
Service Education
Fitchburg State College, Box 6257
160 Pearl Street
Fitchburg, MA 01420; tel: 508-345-2151

Save the Children Federation
54 Wilton Road
Westport, CT 06880; tel: 203-221-4000

Social Service Association
6 Station Plaza
Ridgewood, NJ 07450;
tel: 201-444-2980

EDUCATION

Publications

Who's Who in Special Libraries and Information Centers
Gale Research Inc., Detroit, MI
Lists special libraries alphabetically and geographically. Published annually.

Associations

Academy for Educational Development (AED)
1875 Connecticut Avenue NW
Washington, DC 20009;
tel: 202-884-8000; fax: 202-884-8400
admind@aed-org (E-mail)

American Association of School Administrators
1801 N Moore Street
Arlington, VA 22209-9988;
tel: 703-528-0700

American Association of School Librarians
50 E. Huron Street
Chicago, IL 60611; tel: 312-944-6780

American Association of University Administrators
1012 14th Street NW, Suite 500
Washington, DC 20005;
tel: 202-737-5900

American Association of University Professors
1012 14th Street NW, Suite 500
Washington, DC 20005;
tel: 202-737-5900

American Educational Studies Association (AESA)
University of Cincinnati
Graduate Studies and Research
Cincinnati, OH 45221; tel: 513-556-2256

American Federation of Teachers
555 New Jersey Avenue NW
Washington, DC 20001;
tel: 202-879-4400

American Library Association
50 East Huron Street
Chicago, IL 60611; tel: 312-944-6780

Association for Community Based Education (ACBE)
1805 Florida Avenue NW
Washington, DC 20009;
tel: 202-462-6333 or 202-232-8044

Association for Educational Communications and Technology (AECT)
1025 Vermont Avenue NW, Suite 820
Washington, DC 20005;
tel: 202-347-7834; fax: 202-347-7839

Center for Adult Learning and Educational Credentials (CALEC)
1 Dupont Circle NW
Washington, DC 20036;
tel: 202-939-9475; fax: 202-775-8574

College and University Personnel Association
1233 20th Street NW, Suite 301
Washington, DC 20036-1250;
tel: 202-429-0311

Council on International Educational Exchange (CIEE)
205 East 42nd Street
New York, NY 10017;
tel: 212-661-1414; fax: 212-972-3231

Earthwatch
(formerly: Educational Expeditions International)
680 Mount Auburn Street, Box 403
Watertown, MA 02272;
tel: 617-926-8200 or 800-776-0188;
fax: 617-926-8532
E-mail: info@earthwatch.org

Educational Research Service (ERS)
2000 Clarendon Blvd.
Arlington, VA 22201; tel: 703-243-2100; fax: 703-243-1985

Federal Librarians Round Table
American Library Association,
Washington Office
1301 Pennsylvania Avenue NW, No. 403
Washington, DC 20004;
tel: 202-608-8410

High/Scope Educational Research Foundation
600 North River Street
Ypsilanti, MI 48198-2898;
tel: 313-485-2000 or 800-40-PRESS;
fax: 313-485-0704

Independent Educational Services (IES)
(formerly: Cooperative Bureau for Teachers)
353 Nassau Street
Princeton, NJ 08540; tel: 609-921-6195 or 800-257-5102; fax: 609-921-0155

Institute for Educational Leadership (IEL)
1001 Connecticut Avenue NW, Suite 310
Washington, DC 20036;
tel: 202-822-8405; fax: 202-872-4050

Intercultural Development Research Association (IDRA)
5835 Callaghan Road, Suite 350
San Antonio, TX 78228;
tel: 210-684-8180; fax: 210-684-5389

International Association for Educational Assessment (IAEA)
P.O. Box 6665
Princeton, NJ 08541; tel: 609-921-9000;
fax: 609-520-1093

Madison Center for Educational Affairs (MCEA)
455 15th Street NW, Suite 712
Washington, DC 20005;
tel: 202-833-1801; fax: 202-467-0006

National Association of Educational Office Professionals (NAEOP)
P.O. Box 12619
Wichita, KS 67277; tel: 316-942-4822;
fax: 316-942-7100

National Association of Secondary School Principals
1904 Association Drive
Reston, VA 22091; tel: 703-860-0200

National Association of Student Personnel Administrators
1875 Connecticut Avenue NW, Suite 418
Washington, DC 20009;
tel: 202-265-7500

National Council for Accreditation of Teacher Education
2010 Massachusetts Avenue NW, Suite 500
Washington, DC 20036;
tel: 202-466-7496

National Council of Educational Opportunity Associations (NCEOA)
1025 Vermont Avenue NW, Suite 1201
Washington, DC 20005;
tel: 202-347-7430

National Council on the Evaluation of Foreign Educational Credentials
c/o AACRAO
1 Dupont Circle NW, Suite 330
Washington, DC 20036;
tel: 202-293-9161 or 202-872-8857
E-mail: aacrao@umdd

National Education Association
1201 16th Street NW
Washington, DC 20036;
tel: 202-833-4000

National Rural Education Association (NREA)
Colorado State University
230 Education Building
Fort Collins, CO 80523-1588;
tel: 970-491-7022; fax: 970-491-1317

Special Libraries Association
1700 18th Street NW
Washington, DC 20009-2508;
tel: 202-234-4700; fax: 202-265-9317

University Council for Educational Administration (UCEA)
Pennsylvania State University
212 Rackley Bldg.
University Park, PA 16802-3200;
tel: 814-863-7916/7917 or
fax: 814-863-7918

GOVERNMENT

Publications

The Capitol Source
National Journal, Inc., Washington, DC
Includes names, addresses, and phone numbers for key figures in the District of Columbia; also features information about corporations, interest groups, think tanks, labor unions, real estate organizations, financial institutions, trade and professional groups, law firms, political consultants, advertising and public relations firms, private clubs, and the media. Published twice a year.

Congressional Yellow Book
Monitor Publishing Co., New York, NY
Gives detailed information on congressional staff positions, committees and subcommittees, and top staff in congressional support agencies. Published annually.

COSLA Directory
The Council of State Governments, Lexington, KY
Provides information on state library agencies, consultant and administrative staff, plus ALANER numbers, electronic mail letters, and fax numbers. Published annually. *American Federation of State, County, and Municipal Employees*
1625 L Street NW
Washington, DC 20036;
tel: 202-429-1000

Directory of Federal Libraries
Includes library's administrator and selected staff for three thousand special and general, presidential and national libraries, as well as library facilities in technical centers, hospitals, and penal institutions.

Federal Executive Directory
Carroll Publishing Co., Washington, DC
Profiles a broad range of agencies, both executive and legislative, including cabinet departments, federal administrative agencies, and congressional committee members and staff. The directory also outlines areas of responsibility for legal and administrative assistants. Published six times a year; an annual subscription is $178. Call 202-333-8620 for more information.

Federal Organization Service: Military
Carroll Publishing Co., Washington, DC
Lists direct-dial phone numbers for 11,500 key individuals in fifteen hundred military departments and offices. Updated every six weeks; an annual subscription is $625. Call 202-333-8620 for more information.

Washington Information Directory
Congressional Quarterly Inc., Washington, DC
Provides important information on the federal government as a whole, and on each federal department and agency. The volume also provides details on regional federal information sources, nongovernmental organizations in the Washington area, and congressional committees and subcommittees. Published annually.

Washington '92
Columbia Books, New York, NY
Contains addresses, phone numbers, and profiles of key institutions in the city. Includes chapters on the federal government, the media, business, national associations, labor unions, law firms, medicine and health, foundations and philanthropic organizations, science and policy research groups, and educational, religious, and cultural institutions. Published annually.

Associations

American Planning Association
122 South Michigan Avenue, Suite 1600
Chicago, IL 60603; tel: 312-431-9100

Civil Service Employees Association
P.O. Box 7125
Capitol State
Albany, NY 12210; tel: 518-434-0191
or 800-342-4146

Council of State Governments
P.O. Box 11910
3560 Iron Works Pike
Lexington, KY 40578; tel: 606-244-8000

International Association of Fire Fighters
1750 New York Avenue NW
Washington, DC 21006;
tel: 202-737-8484

International City/County Management Association
777 North Capitol Street NE, Suite 500
Washington, DC 20002;
tel: 202-289-4262

National Association of Counties (NACO)
440 First Street NW, 8th Floor
Washington, DC 20001;
tel: 202-393-6226

National Association of Government
Communicators
669 South Washington Street
Alexandria, VA 22314;
tel: 703-519-3902

National Planning Association
1424 16th Street NW, Suite 700
Washington, DC 20036;
tel: 202-265-7685

New York State Professional Firefighters
Association
111 Washington Avenue, Suite 207
Albany, NY 12210; tel: 518-436-8827

State Services Organization (SSO)
444 North Capitol Street NW
Washington, DC 20001;
tel: 202-624-5470

DISABILITIES

ADA Regional Disabled and Business Assistance Centers

Connecticut, Maine, Massachusetts, Rhode Island, and Vermont:
New England Disability and Business
Technical Assistance Center
145 Newbury Street
Portland, ME 04101; tel: 207-874-6535
(voice/TDD)

New Jersey, New York, Puerto Rico, and Virgin Islands:
Northeast Disability and Business
Technical Assistance Center
354 South Broad Street
Trenton, NJ 08608; tel: 609-392-4004
(voice), 609-392-7044 (TDD)

Delaware, District of Columbia, Maryland, Pennsylvania, Virginia, and West Virginia:
Mid-Atlantic Disability and Business
Technical Assistance Center
2111 Wilson Boulevard, Suite 400
Arlington, VA 22201; tel: 703-525-3268
(voice/TDD)

Alabama, Florida, Georgia, Kentucky, Mississippi, North Carolina, South Carolina, and Tennessee:
Southeast Disability and Business
Technical Assistance Center
1776 Peachtree Street, Suite 310 North
Atlanta, GA 30309; tel: 404-888-0022
(voice/TDD)

Illinois, Indiana, Michigan, Minnesota, Ohio, and Wisconsin:
Great Lakes Disability and Business
Technical Assistance Center
1640 West Roosevelt Road (M/C 627)
Chicago, IL 60608; tel: 312-413-1407
(voice/TDD)

Arkansas, Louisiana, New Mexico, Oklahoma, and Texas:
Southwest Disability and Business
Technical Assistance Center
2323 South Shepherd Boulevard,
Suite 1000
Houston, TX 77019; tel: 713-520-0232
(voice), 713-520-5136 (TDD)

Iowa, Kansas, Nebraska, and Missouri:
Great Plains Disability and Business
Technical Assistance Center
4816 Santana Drive
Columbia, MO 65203;
tel: 314-882-3600 (voice/TDD)

Colorado, Montana, North Dakota, South Dakota, Utah, and Wyoming:
Rocky Mountain Disability and Business
Technical Assistance Center
3630 Sinton Road, Suite 103
Colorado Springs, CO 80907-5072;
tel: 719-444-0252 (voice/TDD)

Arizona, California, Hawaii, and Nevada:
Pacific Coast Disability and Business
Technical Assistance Center
440 Grand Avenue, Suite 500
Oakland, CA 94610; tel: 510-465-7884
(voice), 510-465-3167 (TDD)

Job Accommodation Network
P.O. Box 6123
809 Allen Hall
Morgantown, WV 26505-6123;
tel: 800-526-7234 (voice/TDD)

The President's Committee on
Employment of People with Disabilities
1331 F Street NW
Washington, DC 20004;
tel: 202-376-6200 (voice),
202-376-6205 (TDD)

U.S. Department of Justice, Civil Rights
Division
Office of the Americans with Disabilities
Act
P.O. Box 66118
Washington, DC 20035-6118; tel: 800-
514-0301 (voice), 800-514-0383 (TDD)

Sample Questionnaire

This sample questionnaire was filled out by a fellow professional using the questionnaire guidelines on pages 33–39. Actual resume examples based on the following information—chronological, functional, and combination formats—can be found on pages 102–105.

1. Current or Last Employer:
   This includes part-time or voluntary employment if you are a recent graduate or about to reenter the work force after an absence. That does not mean you should ignore this section: Try looking at your school as an employer and see what new information you reveal about yourself.

   BRANCH MANAGER
Starting Date	*11/88*
Starting Salary	*$13,000*
Leaving Date	*8/90*
Leaving Salary	*$26,000*

   AREA MANAGER
Starting Date	*8/90*
Starting Salary	*$31,200*
Leaving Date	*11/93*
Leaving Salary	*$41,600*

   DIVISION MANAGER
Starting Date	*11/93*
Starting Salary	*$62,400*
Leaving Date	*3/95*
Leaving Salary	*$62,400*

2. Write one sentence that describes the products your company made or the services it performed.

   BRANCH MANAGER through DIVISION MANAGER: MICRO/TEMPS sold software consulting services to the computer-user industry.

3. List your starting job title (the one given to you when you first signed on with the company). Then write a one- or two-sentence description of your responsibilities in that position.

BRANCH MANAGER
Started a new division of the Technical Aid Corporation called MICRO/TEMPS. Was responsible for developing a client and applicant database, while showing a profit for the division.

AREA MANAGER
Opened an additional office in the Washington area. Was accountable for the profitability of both the Boston and Washington offices.

DIVISION MANAGER
Responsible for market studies for future branches to be opened. Directly involved in choosing new locations, opening office, training staff and having the office profitable in less than one year's time.

4. What were your three major duties in this position?

BRANCH MANAGER
A) Selling software services to clients.
B) Interviewing applicants and selling them on consulting.
C) Setting up interviews for applicants and clients to meet.

AREA MANAGER
A) Training sales and recruiting staff.
B) Developing and implementing goals from forecasts.
C) Interfacing with other divisions in order to develop a working relationship between different divisions.

DIVISION MANAGER
A) Hired and trained Branch Managers for all new offices.
B) Developed P & L forecasts for the B.O.D.
C) Developed and implemented division policies.

5. Now, for each of the above three duties, answer the following questions:

What special skills or knowledge did you need to perform this task satisfactorily?

BRANCH MANAGER
A) Knowledge of the computer industry.
B) Key contacts in the Massachusetts computer industry.

AREA MANAGER
A) Knowledge and experience developing a branch.
B) Experience training sales and recruiting staff.

DIVISION MANAGER
A) Knowledge and understanding of developing a profitable division.
B) Knowledge and experience hiring and training branch managers.

What has been your biggest achievement in this area? (Try to think about money saved or made, or time saved for the employer. Don't worry if your contributions haven't been acknowledged in writing and signed in triplicate, so long as you know them to be true without exaggeration.)

BRANCH MANAGER
Successfully developed a new division of the Technical Aid Corporation. Now generating $18,000,000 in revenues.

AREA MANAGER
Successfully opened new branches for the division and hired and trained the staff.

DIVISION MANAGER
Built division to $20 million in annual sales.

What verbal or written comments were made about your contributions in this area, by peers or managers?

BRANCH MANAGER
Hard-working, stay-at-it attitude.

AREA MANAGER
Hires good people and knows how to get the best out of them.

DIVISION MANAGER
Her division always makes the largest gross profit out of any of the divisions.

What different levels of people did you have to interact with to get this particular duty done? How did you get the best out of each of them?

BRANCH MANAGER
A) Superiors—Listened to their ideas and then tried to show them I could implement them.
B) Co-workers—Shared experiences and company goals—set up some competition.
C) Subordinates—Acknowledged their responsibilities as very important for the team.

AREA MANAGER
A) Superiors—Explained situations clearly and made them understand our options.
B) Co-workers—Challenged to reach goals.
C) Subordinates—Complimented when and where it was necessary.

DIVISION MANAGER
A) Superiors—Asked for their experience and advice in difficult situations.
B) Co-workers—Set up and accepted contest between managers.
C) Subordinates—Made them feel they were extremely important as a member of the team.

What aspects of your personality were brought into play when executing this duty?

PERSONALITY: BRANCH MANAGER TO DIVISION MANAGER
strong willpower
stick-to-it attitude
high achiever
aggressive
high goal setter

6. If you asked for a promotion or a raise while in this position, what arguments did you use to back up your request?

BRANCH MANAGER—Increase in sales.
AREA MANAGER—Increase in responsibility.
DIVISION MANAGER—Increase in gross profit and responsibilities.

7. Write down your current (or last) job title. Then write a one- or two-sentence description of your responsibilities in that position, and repeat steps 3 through 6.

   Current title—Personnel Manager

   Step 3: Description of responsibilities. Hiring all internal staff of technical managers and sales people, additionally responsible for hiring all external consultants.

   Step 4: Three major duties:
   A) Hiring of all internal and external consultants
   B) Setting up wage and salary guidelines
   C) Establishing the Boston office so it could become profitable quickly

   Step 5: Skills or knowledge needed:
   A) Ability to source qualified candidates
   B) Experience in start-up situation
   C) Knowledge of the Boston marketplace

   Biggest achievement: Helped in making the branch profitable in nine months.

   Verbal or written comments: A no-nonsense kind of person, aggressive and hard-working; good at getting the best out of people.

   Superiors: Was up front with any problems and clearly and concisely laid out all the alternatives.

   Co-workers: Set up good networking of communications to have information flow quickly and easily.

   Subordinates: Made them aware that we all had a lot to do, but that we were all important.

   Step 6: Raise or promotion.
   Increase in sales figures and was responsible for hiring more consultants than we had originally discussed.

8. Make some general observations about work with this employer.
   Looking back over your time with this employer, what was the biggest work-related problem that you had to face?

They wanted to grow rapidly, but didn't want to invest the money it took to recruit and attract good consultant talent.

What solution did you find?

Got consultants through Boston Computer Society and other related organizations, and set up a very aggressive referral program.

What was the result of the solution when implemented?

We started to attract quality consultants, and our name was beginning to circulate.

What was the value to the employer in terms of money earned or saved and improved efficiency?

Company did not spend a lot of money on recruiting efforts and was able to attract quality people.

What was the area of your greatest personal improvement in this job?

Made many key contacts in some excellent organizations.

What was the greatest contribution you made as a team player?

Brought internal staff members closer together as a working team.

Who are the references you would hope to use from this employer, and what do you think they would say about you?

Ken Shelly—He was one of our first external consultants hired. He would probably say that I identified some key consultants for this project at Sheraton, and that he could always rely on me to help him no matter what.

Dave Johnson—He was our technical manager. He would say that I did my job extremely well considering the little resources I had, and that I identified many quality applicants. He would also say that I knew how to find even difficult people.

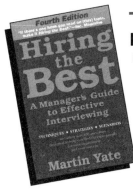